A geek in

JAPAN

by HÉCTOR GARCÍA (Kirai)

T0160474

TUTTLE Publishing

Tokyo │ Rutland, Vermont │ Singapore

CONTENTS

THE JAPAN FEW PEOPLE SEE

For centuries, Japanese culture has fascinated the world as something mysterious and remote. In classifications made by anthropologists, Japan's culture and that of other Asian countries are usually perceived as distinct: the Land of the Rising Sun has its own personality. Japan is also completely different from the West. It's like living in an alien country, and adjusting to life here is no easy matter. Even the smallest detail can be strange and fascinating at the same time. Japan's people have been able to preserve their past while adapting to new times and have turned their country into a worldwide financial and cultural leader. I am one of those people who feel passionate about Japan, so I set off for it with loads of questions, seeking answers. Living, studying, and working in this archipelago helped me gradually to understand the country, its people, its companies, its technology, its culture, its way of thinking, and so forth. I decided to write about it on the Internet, so I could share my experience of discovery and new understanding step by step, as I lived it every day. With this aim, I created a blog, www.ageekinjapan.com, "A Geek in Japan," where I continue to post as I learn and discover new things.

My blog became something of a phenomenon thanks to the enormous interest elicited by the unknown, for Japan has hardly any presence in Western media, despite being for decades the second largest economy in the world. Why doesn't it appear in the news very often? We'll begin to appreciate why through our journey in this book. We'll see that the Japanese are naturally reserved and don't like standing out. How many Japanese public figures can you name? But if we rarely see Japan in the media, it's always present in our daily lives. Every electronic device you use, your computers, phones, cars, trains, airplanes—Japanese technology is inside them. Japan is inside them! How have they managed to spread their creations all over the world in such a discreet, harmonious way, with us barely noticing? In this book, I try to sort out the keys to Japanese culture, the way of life of its inhabitants, the business culture of its companies, and its influence on the rest of the world. We'll find out what the Japanese are like, how they think, how we should relate to them. We'll learn about the origins of *manga*, *anime*, martial arts, Zen meditation, and other elements of Japanese culture that have reached the West, sparking great interest and passion.

You can read this book in two ways: by skipping around and reading those chapters that interest you most, or sequentially. I would recommend reading straight through, since some points are supported by concepts explained in earlier chapters and can't be fully grasped without them. But above all, enjoy the book. I hope it will help you better understand Japan and its people's way of being. Of course, the ideal ending for this book would be a trip to Japan. So I encourage all of you to come here and enter a world completely different from the West. It's an experience you'll never forget.

GEEK

Normally used to refer to enthusiasts who want to know as much as they can about the latest in technology. However, a broader definition might be: a person fascinated by learning and discovering new things. "A geek in Japan" would then be something like: a person fascinated by Japan and with learning and discovering all about its culture and traditions.

Héctor García Puigcerver

(Top) *Delivering food by bicycle in the Gion district of Kyoto.*

(Above) *The graceful way past and future merge is one of the beauties of Japan.*

(Left) *Ramen restaurants are among the best places to restore your energy. Cheap and good!*

WHY IS JAPAN DIFFERENT?

History and geography have been enormously important in defining the different cultures that coexist in the world. As far as Japan is concerned, the fact that it is an archipelago is fundamental. The history of Japan and the shaping of its present-day culture might be summarized briefly in three points that you should bear in mind as you read this book:

1. The great influence of China, source of the character system used in the Japanese language, its religions, and, historically, its system of governance.

2. Japan was closed to the outside world for centuries by dint of a law forbidding foreigners to enter and Japanese to leave. This period of isolation, known as the Edo Period (1603–1868), was fertile for the creation of indigenous Japanese traditions, such as *kabuki*, *geisha*, and *ukiyo-e*.

3. After the Edo Period, Japan became an imperialist power that came to a dramatic end with the country's defeat in World War II. When it recovered, it rapidly became the world's second largest economy.

Besides history, another essential element in defining a people's culture and their way of thinking is language. Japanese is a language with three alphabets, different levels of formality, and connotations that make it quite different from Western languages. Many words that are part of their way of life and value system are said to be "impossible to translate." Over the course of this book, we will try to explain many of these key words. Once we have grasped them, we will have a good general view of how the Japanese "think" and how we ourselves should behave in their world.

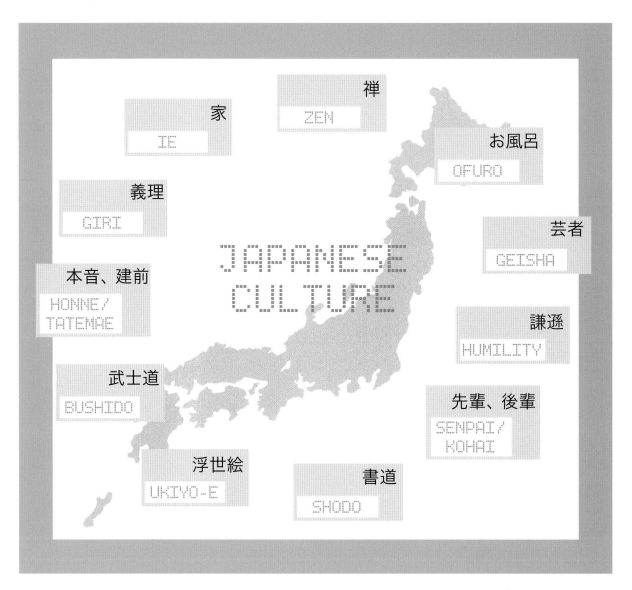

THE INITIAL CULTURE SHOCK

When I boarded the plane for Tokyo, I could already feel how things were starting to shift. Obviously, the plane was full of Japanese people, who besides being different from us physically are also very distinct in their manner. Silence reigned, and in the quiet I noticed the first small details of a certain Japanese style. For example, most of them removed their shoes as soon as they sat down.

Japanese flight attendants also behave differently. They provide our first experience of how the Japanese treat their customers. You feel extremely well cared for, as if you were a king or a god. For the Japanese, customers are very important, they are addressed in highly formal language, attention is paid to them at all times, and they are greeted and seen off with bows. In the plane, we have the opportunity to taste Japanese food and practice with chopsticks. And we can look at printed Japanese in the newspapers that are offered to us. Though we may not understand the language, we can see how different or similar the newspapers are to our own. For example, the sports section shows how much they like baseball, a sport that became popular in Japan due to the influence of the United States. Horse racing is another sport that fascinates the Japanese and is well covered in the media. Finally, a detail that caught my eye was that, instead of having a crossword puzzle or chess problem in the puzzles section, Japanese newspapers have *go*—a game with many enthusiasts in both Japan and China that is starting to spread throughout the world.

At Narita, Tokyo's international airport, we are welcomed with signs showing famous *manga* and *anime* characters, and it is now that we Western *otaku* really start to feel the thrill of our arrival in Japan. After taking a small, futuristic-looking elevated monorail from one side of the huge airport to the other, and after collecting your luggage, you board a Japanese train for the first time. What is so special about Japanese trains? Well, trains in Japan are a phenomenon. There are trains everywhere, there are a thousand different kinds, there are train enthusiasts, magazines and books about trains, and I've even seen stores that specialize in selling *only* train-related products. One of the things I like most about Japanese trains is that they are incredibly punctual, and when I say "incredibly" I mean it. Whereas in Europe or the United States a 10-minute delay is hardly considered a delay, a two-minute delay here can be disastrous. For instance, the average delay for Shinkansen trains over the last 20 years is only 54 seconds. Amazing!

It takes about an hour and a half to reach the center of Tokyo. Trains here are quite fast, but you soon realize that Tokyo is huge and also rather vague in concept. From now on, whenever I talk about Tokyo, I'll be referring to the whole metropolitan area, which includes close to 40 million people. It's almost like the entire population of my native Spain in one urban area.

Narita airport is in Chiba prefecture, east of Tokyo, and if you arrive during the day you'll be able to see how radically the landscape changes. You'll see small rice paddies and notice the style of the little Japanese houses, how almost all the cars are either black or white, the roads are narrow, and there are many elevated highways. You'll see posters and illuminated advertisements everywhere near train stops, though you may not "get" them. You'll also see the Japanese using their mobile phones like crazy to send emails and connect to the Internet, while others read *manga*, and most of them supplement their scarce hours of sleep with an improvised nap of a few minutes. In short, you'll begin to feel you are in a different world. Welcome to the world of Japan. How did this country and its people come to be like this? Let's study the causes, starting with their origins, with the birth of Japan.

"For the Japanese, customers are very important. They are addressed in highly formal language, attention is paid to them at all times, and they are greeted and seen off with bows."

Matsuri celebrations draw thousands of people, all dancing, eating, drinking, and asking the gods for good fortune.

CHAPTER 1
THE ORIGINS OF JAPANESE CULTURE

祈願

Ieyasu Tokugawa was one of the most influential shoguns in the history of Japan. You can visit his grave among the temples at Nikko.

Edo, currently known as Tokyo, 400 years ago, depicted in a woodblock print.

AN EXTREMELY BRIEF HISTORY OF JAPAN

Legend tells that Japan was born of the love between two deities, Izanagi and Izanami. These two deities had a daughter, Amaterasu, and the long dynasty of Japanese emperors descends from her. Even today, a large part of the Japanese population considers their emperor a living god.

The first settlers whose archeological remains have been found belong to the Jomon Period, more than 8,000 years ago. But not until the eighth century CE was there a real Japanese state, with its first capital being Nara. Nara was modeled after Chinese cities, and for a long time the emperor's residence was located there. During the early years of the Japanese state, however, wars and conflict between clans and sects were rampant, and the emperor eventually moved his court to Kyoto, which became the new capital for the following thousand years.

Wars and the struggle for power between families continued. Finally, the leader of the Minamoto clan was named *shogun*, or military leader of all Japan. He established his headquarters in Kamakura, near present-day Tokyo. The *shogun* controlled the country for centuries, and even though the emperor still existed as head of state, very often he was only a symbol, with no decision-making power. Thus, a new period began, characterized by a militaristic ideology and the introduction of Zen Buddhism from China. A new caste appeared, the *samurai*, who imposed their rule over the land. Between the fourteenth and sixteenth centuries, Japan was run as a system of fiefs, or local powers subordinate to the *shogun*, that were always fighting one another. The capital remained Kyoto, and the shogun "controlled" the whole country from there.

THE BATTLE OF SEKIGAHARA

Toward the end of the sixteenth century, under the government of *shogun* Toyotomi Hideyoshi, there reigned relative peace and calm. Everything changed in the year 1600, when one of the most important events in the history of Japan took place, the battle of Sekigahara. The Hideyoshi clan's defeat in this battle meant a new family became paramount, the Tokugawas, who would rule Japan until 1868. The first Tokugawa *shogun* was Ieyasu, who decided to govern from his castle in Edo, present-day Tokyo. The period under Tokugawa rule would become known as the Edo Period (1603–1868).

THE NEW EDO

Until then, Edo had been a small village of no significance, but from the seventeenth century on it was the capital of Japan, as it is today. Commercial routes between Kyoto and Edo quickly emerged, and *samurai*, merchants, and others gradually settled the island's new center. For the more than two centuries that the Tokugawa family ruled Japan, they were extremely conservative, to the point of barring any foreign influence. In other words, foreigners were prohibited from entering the country, and the Japanese were forbidden to leave. If a foreigner was found there, he or she was automatically condemned to death. Many Spanish and Portuguese explorers died upon their arrival on Japanese shores.

The Tokugawa forces at the battle of Sekigahara.

EXTREME PROTECTIONISM

Japan was completely cut off from the outside world until the year 1868. Think of the consequences this could have for any country and its people. During this period, the Japanese developed an almost neurotic love for their country. They believed it was the center of the world and they sweated blood laboring for it, while a great nationalist sentiment took hold. At the same time, this seclusion resulted in a great flourishing of native Japanese arts and traditions, with the appearance of new forms of theater, the *geisha*, and the Japanese printmaking technique known as *ukiyo-e*.

PERRY'S FLEET BREAKS THROUGH THE PROTECTIONISM

Around the middle of the nineteenth century, when the industrial revolution was already in full swing in Europe and the United States, Japan was still a feudal country run by military leaders and *samurai*, who held the power of life and death over the rest of society. In July 1853, an American squadron of warships led by Commodore Matthew Perry entered Tokyo Bay. Perry proposed a treaty with the Japanese government, authorizing the United States to trade with the archipelago.

Unsure what to do in the face of American cannons, the *shogun*, for the first time in six centuries of military power, consulted the emperor about a course of action. Without hesitation, the emperor replied that they must drive the Americans away. Unfortunately, the *shogun* didn't have the military might to expel the Americans, and he was forced to sign the agreement. After disobeying the emperor, considered a living god by all the Japanese, the last of the Tokugawa *shoguns* lost the people's trust. He had to resign, allowing the triumphal restoration of power to the imperial house. Mutsushito, better known by the name of Emperor Meiji, found himself leading the country at the young age of 15. The first thing he did was change the capital's name from Edo to Tokyo, meaning "Eastern Capital." Paradoxically, with the return to power of the emperor, Japan fully entered the modern world.

In 1868, we in the West already had trains and other technologies that didn't exist in Japan, where they still used horses and donkeys. How were they able to develop in only 72 years the means to challenge the United States in World War II? How could they then, once defeated, re-emerge after only a few years and become one of the world's great powers and leaders in technology? In what follows, we will try to discover the keys that enabled Japan to achieve such a position of prominence after rising from the ashes.

"The first settlers whose archeological remains have been found belong to the Jomon Period, more than 8,000 years ago. But not until the eighth century CE was there a real Japanese state, with its first capital being Nara."

THE SHOGUN

He was the effective ruler of Japan, the supreme general who held the military's highest rank. The *shogun* controlled the country from the twelfth century to the Meiji Restoration in 1868. During the period of the shogunate, the emperor was respected but had no real power.

THE MEIJI RESTORATION

The process by which Japan went from being a closed country controlled by *samurai* to an open one, controlled by Emperor Meiji. The year 1868 marks the beginning of the Meiji Period in the mind of the Japanese and Japan's entry into the modern age.

THE INTRICACIES OF THE JAPANESE LANGUAGE

Japanese is spoken by 130 million people all over the planet, and it's the eighth most spoken language in the world. Although it's used mainly in Japan, its usage extends to Hawaii, Guam, Palau, Taiwan, and certain areas in Brazil, where there are significant Japanese communities. It's an unusual language, and linguists have been arguing for many years over its classification and exact origins. According to the most accepted classification, it belongs to the family of Japonic languages, which comprises only Japanese and the Ryukyuan languages spoken on the Okinawa islands, south of Japan. This means that, although at first glance it may seem that Chinese and Japanese are similar, they are very different. They belong to completely separate language families but share some similarities. Many Japanese words have their origin in Chinese words, but over time their pronunciation has evolved and deviated from their Chinese equivalents.

The origins of Japanese are a mystery, but obviously Asian languages entering the north of Japan from China via the Korean peninsula were of great influence. The Malay languages to the south also contributed one of the bases of the Japanese language. The Japanese began to develop their own writing system around the fifth century CE, based on Chinese characters called *han*. They used the Chinese symbols to represent their own spoken language graphically, though the Chinese and Japanese grammars have nothing in common. Thus, Chinese was only a tool, providing ready-made forms to be able to start writing. These original characters gradually evolved into the *kanji* used in present-day Japanese. Later, during the tenth century, the syllabic writing systems know as *hiragana* and *katakana* were developed. Modern Japanese grammar began with these writing systems, and there followed a literary boom culminating in *Genji Monogatari* (The Tale of Genji) as its greatest achievement. This classic work is to Japanese what Shakespeare's opus is to English.

It is said that Japanese is one of the most difficult languages to learn. There are many reasons for this, but one of them is its complex writing system. In modern Japanese, up to four alphabets are used: a symbolic one (*kanji*), two syllabic ones (*hiragana* and *katakana*), and our Western alphabet, known in Japan as *romaji*.

> "The origins of Japanese are a mystery, but obviously Asian languages entering the north of Japan from China via the Korean peninsula were of great influence.... The Japanese began to develop their own writing system around the fifth century CE, based on Chinese characters called *han*."

THE RYUKYUAN LANGUAGES

Ryukyuan languages are used in the Okinawa island chain, south of mainland Japan.

Weeklies filled with manga stories are among the most read magazines. For students of Japanese, they are a recommended way to start reading.

One of the difficulties of the Japanese language is that it uses different alphabets depending on the context or the origin of the word. The Japanese also use our alphabet for some foreign words.

WRITING BASED ON KANJI

Kanji characters are the cornerstone of Japanese writing. They come from *hanzi* Chinese writing and are symbols that have one to several meanings, one to several pronunciations, and can be combined to form new words. This last point, while seemingly trivial, gives the greatest headaches to those studying this language and to the Japanese themselves, who must devote more than ten years to learning how to write them. There are more than 40,000 *kanji*, but the Japanese are required to know a list of "only" 2,136 official *kanji*, known as the *Joyo Kanji*. The Japanese learn 1,006 *kanji* during six years of elementary school and the rest in high school. Once you know the full list, you can read any Japanese text. Books and newspapers using *kanji* that are not on this list must write their transcription in the *hiragana* syllabic alphabet. Children's books also add this syllabic transcription for the most difficult *kanji*.

The first three *kanji* in the chart are the easiest, and you will probably remember those one, two, and three strokes for numbers 1, 2, and 3 from now on. But, when we get to number 4 it's another matter, and it's not so easy to remember. From 5 on, new forms appear, and understanding becomes complicated. The *kanji* for "rain" looks rather intuitive—it seems to represent raindrops. The one for "woman" hints at a woman's body, but in the second row things are not so obvious. The symbol for "north" doesn't suggest the concept of "north," though when the Japanese see this symbol they automatically think of that meaning. The symbols for "spirit," "electricity," "discuss," "warn," and "dig" don't seem motivated visually either, and their meaning isn't self-evident. If we went into the study of *kanji* in more depth, we would learn how they consist of several parts—patterns that are repeated and that might help us in memorizing them.

In Japanese, no spaces are used to separate words, so *kanji* characters are useful in defining where words start and end. Another characteristic of Japanese is that it has many homophones. If we wrote these words in our own alphabet phonetically, we wouldn't know for sure which word was meant, whereas with *kanji* we know at once what the written word or concept is, because these symbols transmit their meaning visually.

This writing system causes the Japanese to think in a different way from us. They organize concepts on the basis of *kanji*; they draw diagrams with structures that are difficult for us to understand; the order in which their writing flows is different; and, generally speaking, their minds work on the basis of images.

The following table is usually found in Japanese language textbooks for beginners. You can see here the original pictorial forms for kanji.

OLD FORMS	MODERN CHARACTERS	MEANING
	木	TREE, WOOD
	林	WOODS
	森	FOREST
	本	ROOT, ORIGIN
	日	SUN
	月	MOON
	明	BRIGHT
	山	MOUNTAIN
	鳥	BIRD
	島	ISLAND

"*Kanji* characters are the cornerstone of Japanese writing. They come from *hanzi* Chinese writing and are symbols that have one to several meanings, one to several pronunciations, and can be combined to form new words."

Let's see what some kanji look like and what they mean:

一	二	三	四	雨	女
ONE	TWO	THREE	FOUR	RAIN	WOMAN
北	気	電	議	警	掘
NORTH	SPIRIT	ELECTRICITY	DISCUSS	WARN	DIG

ROMAJI

Romaji simply refers to the transcription in our (Roman) alphabet of how a word sounds. For example, the word "house" is pronounced *ie* in Japanese, and therefore "house" written in *romaji* would be *ie*. It's that simple. We could write Japanese in our alphabet. For example *Eki wa doko desu ka* means "Where is the station?" The problem is that, while this seems convenient to us foreigners when we start learning Japanese, a Japanese person reading *romaji*—and this may strike us as amazing—will find it difficult to understand what it says. Japanese minds are designed to understand symbols and not letters. That's why, if it's difficult for us to learn Chinese or Japanese, they find it just as hard to learn our languages. *Romaji* is used in some Japanese beginners' books, it's used to transcribe train station names in urban areas where you might find foreigners, and it's also used on posters and advertisements as a device to attract lots of attention. Since *romaji* isn't normal for the Japanese, an advertisement in our alphabet arouses their curiosity.

The Japanese Constitution, created under American supervision after the war, has a version written in *romaji* because the Americans didn't trust Japanese symbols and wanted a version that they could at least read, even if they couldn't understand it.

THE HIRAGANA SYLLABARY

The 46 symbols in the *hiragana* syllabary represent the 46 possible consonant and vowel combinations in spoken Japanese.

As with *romaji*, we could write anything in Japanese using only *hiragana*, but the problem is that it would be difficult to understand because of the large number of homophones and also because spaces do not separate words. *Hiragana* is normally used for grammatical particles and verb endings. Verbs usually start with a *kanji*.

THE KATAKANA SYLLABARY

The *katakana* syllabary is used to write words of foreign origin that have been introduced into Japanese. It has the same number of symbols as *hiragana* and is quite similar. For example, the word "computer" is written in *katakana* and, when pronounced by a Japanese person, would sound something like "conpyutaa." This syllabary is used for new loanwords from English and the languages of other countries that have influenced Japan. Another use of *katakana* is to highlight words, more or less like using boldface type or capital letters in our language system.

A totally different language for a totally different culture. If you'd like to take on the difficult but rewarding challenge of learning Japanese, I recommend you start with Marc Bernabé's books *Japanese in Mangaland* and *Japanese in Mangaland 2*, or *Japanese for Manga People* by Maria Ferrer. To learn *kanji*, you can start with *Kanji De Manga* by Glenn Kardy and Chihiro Hattori. These are good tools that will teach you the basics of Japanese in a fun and enjoyable way.

THE ANCIENT BUSHIDO CODE: THE WAY OF THE SAMURAI WARRIOR

The *samurai* were the most powerful social class in Japan for centuries. From the twelfth century on, the warrior class, known in Japanese as *bushi*, began to have power within the social structure as well as political power. The *samurai* adhered to a way of life, an ethics, rules, and a code that over the years spread to all branches of society and even today affects the way the Japanese think. This code is known as *bushido*, its last character (*do*) meaning "way." So we have *bushi* (warrior) and *do* (way). This way of the warrior was based on a nexus of values such as loyalty, justice, self-sacrifice, and honor. Let's now explore in more detail all those aspects of the *do*. To begin with, *bushido* was much influenced by two religious disciplines: Zen Buddhism and Confucianism.

ZEN

Buddhism came from ancient China during the sixth century and since then has been fundamental in shaping Japanese culture. To be precise, a sect called Zen settled with greatest strength in Japan. Zen aims to achieve enlightenment through the liberation of the mind, by seeking the union of body and spirit, the state of spiritual peace that leaves your mind blank. A number of disciplines that help cultivate these principles or aims have developed from Zen Buddhism, for example, the tea ceremony (*chado*) and calligraphy (*shodo*). Notice how both words include the particle *do* ("way"). As for the *samurai*, the practice and understanding of Zen helped them stay calm and patient in battle, even in extreme situations, and not be overwhelmed by fear. This legacy remains today. Those who have met a Japanese person will agree that almost all are calm and patient people.

CONFUCIANISM

Confucianism too came from China, in the twelfth century. According to Confucianism, relationships between human beings are the basis of society. We must respect our ancestors, our relatives, and our superiors. The values of loyalty, justice, and honor are also central. Today, the Japanese still bear Confucianism in their minds, for they highly respect their superiors both in their own families and in their companies.

LOYALTY AND HONOR

Loyalty may be one of the most important values of the *samurai*. They aspired to be absolutely loyal to their feudal lord, risking their life for him every day. A *samurai* doesn't mind dying so long as he regrets nothing he's done in his life. That is, he must try always to be loyal and keep his mind free from any blemish. As far as honor is concerned, the *samurai* were terribly strict. "Better death than disgrace" was their philosophy. They tried always to be at the forefront in battle, and if they failed in an important mission they committed *seppuku* (or *hara-kiri*), ripping their belly open with their sword. Other *bushido* values are sincerity, compassion, courtesy, and honesty.

Nowadays, dozens of martial arts are practiced all around the world, and most of them are based on the philosophy of bushido.

BUSHIDO TODAY

From the Meiji Restoration on, the *samurai* ceased to exist in Japan, but many aspects of their way of viewing life are still present in society. Students are loyal to their teachers, workers are loyal to their companies, putting in long overtime hours, and even now there are Japanese who commit suicide to preserve their honor when they make a very serious error, thus trying to preserve their family's or company's reputation.

"*Bushido* is the code followed by the *samurai* to achieve their way of life. With the passage of time, it spread to all branches of society and even today affects the way of thinking of all Japanese people."

In conclusion, *bushido* is still very much present in Japanese society, in the Japanese mind, in families, companies, and Japan in general. The Japanese are loyal, honest, sincere, and disciplined at work. They follow rules and try to improve themselves every day, just as the *samurai* did in their time. Perhaps, following the country's destruction, *bushido* is one of the reasons Japan could rise again several times in the last 150 years.

As a complement to this text, I recommend the movie *Shichinin no Samurai* (The Seven Samurai). *Kakushi Toride no San Akunin* (Hidden Fortress) by Akira Kurosawa and Toshiro Mifune also contains many elements from *bushido*. This whole philosophy has reached the West through the martial arts. If you practice a martial art, you are following *bushido* in some way: *judo* (the way of flexibility), *aikido* (the way of energy), *karate* or *karatedo* (the way of the empty hand).

MEET THE REAL GEISHA

Many myths surround the concept of the *geisha*, such as the big question: are *geisha* prostitutes or not? *Geisha* are traditionally considered artists. Most frequently they perform dances and play the *shamisen* (a three-cord musical instrument that comes originally from Okinawa). Young women who want to become *geisha* when they grow up start as *maiko* (apprentices). When the necessary training comes to an end after many years of working as an assistant, a *maiko* becomes a *geisha*.

Geisha usually perform in private for men. Their role is to entertain them while they chat in social gatherings. Normally, after performing for a while, they sit at the table and engage with their customers, chatting and filling their cups with *sake* or similar liquors. That is, their work entails freeing their clients from the daily travails of life, even though very often drunkenness takes hold of the guests, who pay prohibitive prices for each drink.

GEISHA AND HOSTESS

Hiring a genuine *geisha* is generally very expensive, on the order of several thousand dollars at the current exchange rate. In present-day Japan, there are also hostesses, who are not artists like the *geisha* but do serve in the role of providing entertainment, theirs being a much cheaper service. These are casually dressed young women whose work involves sitting at the tables with customers, talking to them, entertaining them, getting them drunk, and so forth. Hostess bars can be found anywhere in Japan, and they charge around US $50 an hour (much more affordable compared to the several thousand a *geisha* costs). The opposite gender alternative also exists, where men known as *hosto* chat with women and entertain them. Working as a hostess or a *hosto* is considered a decent job and pays very well. Many university students do it to earn some extra money.

THE PROSTITUTION MYTH

Imagine what a group of drunken businessmen flush with money can ask of a *geisha* or hostess as the night draws on. Many *geisha* and hostesses do go on to prostitute themselves when they realize how easily they can earn huge amounts of money. This practice has given the *geisha* such a bad reputation, it has spawned a myth worldwide. After much controversy and many urban legends, "prostitute *geisha*" have come to be known within Japanese society as *onsen geisha*, to distinguish them from those considered genuine *geisha*. Thus, traditional *geisha* are trying to keep their dignity and status as true artists. Nowadays, these genuine *geisha* can be found in certain districts in Kyoto, but they are not easy to see if you're a tourist.

Geisha walking in the streets in Gion.

"Hiring a genuine *geisha* is generally very expensive, on the order of several thousand dollars at the current exchange rate. In present-day Japan, there are also hostesses, who are not artists like the *geisha* but do serve in the role of providing entertainment, theirs being a much cheaper service."

BAD REPUTATION

"Prostitute *geisha* have come to be known within Japanese society as *onsen geisha*, to distinguish them from those considered genuine *geisha*."

A geisha at a Shinto shrine purifying her hands with water.

A geisha in the Gion district of Kyoto.

WALKING AROUND THE GION DISTRICT

Kyoto is the quintessential traditional Japanese city, where many festivals and customs survive after having disappeared from the rest of Japan with the passage of time. In the Gion district, there are still nine working *okiya*, where *maiko* and *geisha* live. In the afternoon, they leave the *okiya* to work in a *ryotei*, a luxury restaurant, or an *ochaya*, a special teahouse designed for the enjoyment of *geisha* services. In the *ochaya*, *geisha* and *maiko* serve food and drink, converse, play music, and dance before their guests. Nowadays, it's unusual to see *geisha* and *maiko* walking around Gion. Most likely instead, you'll see groups of foreigners waiting for one to come out of an *ochaya* so they can snap a picture of her. Nevertheless, one traditional detail that can still be seen on the streets of Gion is the hustle and bustle of boys in kitchen caps transporting food by bicycle from restaurants to the *ochaya*. *Ochaya* have no kitchens but are conceived exclusively for their guests to relax comfortably in private rooms and enjoy the dancing of the *geisha* or *maiko*.

THE ICHIRIKI OCHAYA

More than 300 years ago, several *ronin* met at Ichiriki to plan the murder of the man responsible for the death of their *daimyo*, while they enjoyed the dancing and music of the *geisha*. Some 150 years later, the Ichiriki *ochaya* was also the place chosen by politicians and other powerful men to plan how to end the Tokugawa shogunate, which had been governing the country for generations. During the Edo Period, Ichiriki, in the heart of the Gion district in Kyoto, was one of hundreds of *ochaya* where people could enjoy the services of *geisha* and *maiko*. Today, Ichiriki is one of the hundred *ochaya* still operating in Kyoto, and it's first in terms of exclusivity and tradition. A night of fun at the Ichiriki *ochaya* costs around US $6,000 a head. And, even if you can afford that amount, admission is not for everybody. You can get in only if someone with direct contact with the owners has personally recommended you. It's impossible for tourists to get in, so if you're a tourist you have to content yourself with seeing a *geisha* go in or out and glimpsing for a brief moment that courtyard, which, oblivious to the passing of time, has to be crossed to gain access to the *ochaya*'s interior. How many prominent historical figures must have traversed that courtyard? Still, in compensation, we can choose to enjoy a coffee at the Starbucks next door and read the novel *Memoirs of a Geisha*; the

Ichiriki *ochaya* is one of the places where much of the action is set.

Ichiriki is easy to recognize, with its exterior walls built of sturdy black-and-red painted wood and decorated with bamboo poles, to recreate castle walls. It's the largest *ochaya* in Gion, and it's right at the entrance of the district's southern part, at the end of the street named Shijodori.

TAKAHIRO: FROM MAIKO TO GEISHA

The first time I saw Takahiro performing, I thought she was a *geisha*, but I was mistaken. Young women who want to pursue a career as a *geisha* start as *maiko* at the age of 14 or 15. For five years they must train in the *okiya* that sponsors them, until they become *geisha*. You can easily identify a *maiko* because they wear a long *obi*, as if it were a tail. Another difference between *maiko* and *geisha* is that *maiko*, unlike *geisha*, don't wear wigs.

There are two kinds of *geisha*: those who play musical instruments and those who dance. Takahiro is on her way to becoming a dancing *geisha*. When she is ready to become a *geisha*, Takahiro will be between 18 and 20 years old. A ritual called *erikaishi* will be held, in which Takahiro will change her *kimono* and her makeup and will start wearing a wig. Once she is transformed, the ritual will end with her first opening dance as a *geisha*.

A young dancer resting after a performance in a temple near the Gion district in Kyoto.

RELIGION AND PHILOSOPHY

Most Japanese don't believe in one specific religion but combine aspects of several religions in their daily lives, often unaware which one they're following. For example, it's absolutely normal to be baptized in the Shinto ritual, get married with a Christian ceremony in a church, and, finally, celebrate a funeral following Buddhist tradition.

All these religions are mixed up in their mind, without the Japanese knowing for certain which rituals and rules belong to one or the other. They simply follow certain traditions, ways of behaving and thinking that derive from different schools of thought and ancient religions.

BUDDHISM

Buddhism arrived in Japan in the sixth century via China and Korea. It quickly expanded all over the country and became integrated with Shinto. Buddhism seeks enlightenment through sacrifice and indifference toward material possessions. Many Buddhist concepts were introduced into the Shinto religion and Japanese daily life. The enormous patience of the Japanese, for example, might stem from Buddhism. Nowadays, most funerals follow the Buddhist ritual.

TAKUHATSU

Takuhatsu is a traditional way of begging for money, common to some Buddhist monks in Japan. Monks who practice *takuhatsu* usually travel and live only on donations, and are content with having enough to survive. In bygone days, they begged only for food, normally white rice, which they received in a bowl. The monks' only belongings are their clothes, their hat, and the bowl with which they receive alms of food or money. Some of them don't even have shoes.

Nowadays, you hardly ever see monks practicing *takuhatsu*. In Kyoto, they are found on the bridges; in Tokyo, they are usually in Ueno and in some more traditional neighborhoods; and in Nara, you can see them near the temples, but not inside.

CONFUCIANISM

Confucianism is not practiced as a religion in Japan, but it has greatly influenced the Japanese way of thinking. Confucian philosophy advocates a series of practices and behaviors in daily life when we interact with other people, with our family, our company, or the government. It places special emphasis on respect and loyalty to the system and on helping other people,

so that everything flows as it's expected to, creating happiness for others and for ourselves. This philosophy/religion was developed by the Chinese philosopher Kong Fuzi (known in the West as Confucius) more than 2,000 years ago, and it has influenced not only Japan but all Asian cultures now in existence.

SHINTO

Shintoism or Shinto (*o shinto* in Japanese) is a polytheistic religion that originated in Japan. Its thinking has thoroughly permeated Japanese society and is part and parcel of the Japanese mind. Life after death is not one of its concerns. Instead, it concentrates on seeking happiness in this life. There are no dogmas, there is no clearly defined way of praying, there is no spiritual leader or revered founder to emulate. It is perhaps more a philosophy or a way of life than a religion. Shinto is a collection of methods and rituals to improve human relations and ensure that there are no problems in the coexistence of human beings and nature. Respect for the members of one's family is another of its key points.

According to Shinto, nature is sacred. When we are in contact with nature, we draw closer to the gods. In Japan, many trees are considered sacred and it is said a god lives inside them. Under these trees people often hang *ema*—wooden plaques with their wishes written on them for the god to make come true. If your wish is granted, you must return and hang another *ema* to show your gratitude to the tree god.

Another curious example of the influence of Shinto on the Japanese way of being is that things that belong to you partake of your spirit. When you give a present, you are giving part of your spirit to the other person. That's why presents in Japan are so very important, even if they're small presents of no real value. This belief also has significance when you buy something second-hand. The Japanese are reluctant to purchase things that have belonged to someone else, maybe because the previous owner's spirit still lingers inside them. One of the advantages of this belief is that theft in Japan is almost non-existent: stealing something from someone would be like stealing part of their spirit.

In Chapter 3, we will review many key words and behavior patterns by the Japanese that have their origins in Shinto.

MATSURI AND NATIONAL CELEBRATIONS

The *matsuri* are festivals celebrating religious traditions throughout the year. They are mostly Shinto festivals devoted to

different gods and local traditions depending on when and where they are celebrated. During the celebration, the streets around the temple sponsoring the *matsuri* are closed to traffic, and people go out to dance, eat, drink, parade, and carry *mikoshi*—tiny portable wooden shrines that can be borne on people's shoulders. The *matsuri* are ideal occasions to witness the authentic traditional Japan. Their specific dates depend on the year, the season, and the location, so you should ask for information wherever you are staying. In any case, here is a list of the most important national celebrations throughout the year:

Seijin Shiki (Coming of Age Day): second Monday of January
Hinamatsuri (Doll Festival): March 3
Children's Day: May 5
Tanabata: July 7
O-Bon: August 13–15
Shichigosan: November 15

TOKYO'S IMPORTANT SHINTO FESTIVALS

Sanja Matsuri (at Asakusa Shrine, next to Asakusa Station): third weekend of May

"Most Japanese don't believe in one specific religion but combine aspects of several religions in their daily lives.... Shintoism or Shinto is a polytheistic religion that originated in Japan."

Kanda Matsuri (at Kanda Shrine, next to Kanda Station): closest weekend to May 15
Sanno Matsuri (at Hie Shrine, next to Nagatacho Station): June 15

While most Japanese don't believe in one specific religion and only 20 percent believe in the existence of gods, they do, generally speaking, and regardless of their specific faiths, embrace certain superstitions, popular beliefs, and the notion of fate. For instance, the most common activities when visiting a Shinto shrine are making a wish, buying protective charms, and buying *omikuji* (strips of paper that tell your fortune in the near future). Palmistry is also a very profitable business on the streets of Japan. Some palm-reading experts become famous, and you have to book months in advance to have your fortune read.

One of the traditions in Shinto shrines involves writing your wishes on a wooden plaque called an ema and hanging it next to the others.

A sacred tree with ema hanging around its base, posting wishes to be granted. This tree is at Meiji Shrine in Tokyo.

VISITING A TEMPLE OR SHRINE

Most religious temples in Japan are Shinto or Buddhist, corresponding to the two main religions in the country. Depending on the temple you're visiting, you'll see a series of symbols that distinguish one from the other. Sometimes, though, Buddhist and Shinto features appear in the same place, and then it's difficult to know which religion the temple belongs to.

Jinja is the Japanese word that designates Shinto shrines. The easiest way to identify a *jinja* is to look at the entrance. You will almost always find a large red wooden gate marking the entrance to sacred ground. In contrast, at the entrance to a Buddhist *o-tera*, there is usually a smaller dark-colored gate and walls separating the temple grounds from the outside.

When you go in, Buddhist temples are generally austere, while Shinto shrines are much more ornate, colorful, and full of decorations. As for figures, in Shinto shrines we see many different gods with animal forms, diverse faces, etc., whereas in Buddhist *o-tera*, figures are in the lotus position and they all look like Buddha, with long ears, eyes staring toward the horizon, etc.

A tiny Shinto shrine where you can see a torii gate, two kitsune, a bell, and even a small purification fountain to the left.

1 **Temizuya**: purification fountain
2 **Kitsune**: sacred foxes
3 **Shimenawa**: ropes
4 **Honden**: main building
5 **Saisenko**: offertory box
6 **Torii**: gate
7 Small bell rung before making a wish

THE MAIN ELEMENTS OF A BUDDHIST TEMPLE

The structure you encounter in Japanese Buddhist temples is quite similar to that of Buddhist temples in China or India. Let's look at some of their most common elements.

MAIN HALL

This is the place where sacred objects are kept, the most important of all being the figure of a Buddha usually placed in the center of the hall.

PAGODA

Pagodas in Japanese temples are an evolution of Indian *stupas*. They usually have three or five stories, although some of them have more. Each story represents an element: earth, water, fire, air, and void (very important in Buddhism).

A five-story pagoda.

GATES

Buddhist temple gates have a "building" structure. They are built of wood and they have a huge roof. There is usually a main gate directly facing the main hall, and then there are other secondary gates that provide access to auxiliary halls and study rooms.

BELL

In Japan, when the year ends, they don't ring the bell 12 times but 108 times, once for every earthly desire we humans have and must overcome to reach enlightenment. Each stroke quells one of these passions in the faithful, helping them to be happier. Remember Buddhism seeks "not to desire anything" as the means to reach wisdom and happiness.

Buddhist bells are rung using a big wooden log.

SENKO

Senko means incense in Japanese. Incense, which originally comes from India, is an element that has always been linked to Buddhist tradition. In Japanese temples, there is usually a sort of pedestal with sand where you burn your *senko* stick, and then you wave the purifying smoke toward your body with your hand.

KARESANSUI DRY GARDENS

Dry gardens (Japanese rock gardens)—*karesansui* in Japanese—are characteristic of Zen Buddhism. Their simplicity and harmony make them ideal for meditation.

Incense is burned for purification in a pedestal filled with sand at Buddhist temples.

Rocks on gravel. It can't be simpler than that. But within this simplicity lies great complexity. So much so that even today doctoral theses are still being written about dry gardens. The positioning of the stones is not fortuitous—it is very deliberate, so the space between the stones creates harmony and relaxes those who gaze on them.

The mystery of dry gardens is that nobody knows for sure what they mean or the reason they evoke such calm and peace in the visitor. One of the most accepted interpretations is that the main point when designing a dry garden is not the stones but the space between the stones. Zen emphasizes void, nothingness.

"What makes dry gardens so special?
The space between the rocks." —Alan Booth

The famous Ryoan-ji temple garden, which comprises a karesansui dry garden.

CEMETERY

Earlier I said that funeral rites are almost always celebrated following Buddhist tradition. That's why you will probably find a Buddhist cemetery next to an *o-tera*. Buddhist cemeteries are very different from what we are used to seeing in the West. After the Buddhist rite, the body is incinerated and the ashes are buried under the earth in a family grave. By the grave there is a plaque where the names of all the family members in it are written. Offerings that are made, besides flowers, include objects or food the deceased was known to like during his or her life. For example, it's not unusual to see a bottle of *nihonshu* or tea on top of a grave.

A closely packed Buddhist cemetery.

SHINTO SHRINES (JINJA)

The most beautiful Shinto shrines are usually in the middle of woods, surrounded by trees, forming part of nature.

TORII GATES

Once purified with water, you enter the temple through a gate called a *torii*. They are usually made of wood painted red or orange, and their shape is very characteristic. The largest *torii* is usually at the main entrance, and inside the temple there are many more at the entrances of each secondary hall.

TEMIZUYA FOUNTAINS

Temizuya are purification fountains found usually both in Buddhist temples and Shinto shrines. Normally, a few yards before the entrance of the temples there is a purification fountain. Following tradition, before you enter the temple and visit the deities, you must purify yourself by pouring water over both hands and rinsing your mouth. This process is known as *tesui*. Other purifying elements in Shinto are fire, sand, salt, and alcohol. In Buddhism, incense smoke is one of the most important purifying elements.

EMA FORTUNE TABLETS

Ema are small wooden tablets where you can write wishes. *Ema* tablets are hung near the main hall or next to a sacred tree.

MAIN HALL (HONDEN)

Normally, the main hall rises in the center of the temple and consists of one or several buildings. The most sacred objects are usually kept here, and there is an area where offerings can be made. You will recognize it by the long ropes hanging from the ceiling that are used to ring a bell. To pray, you first make your offering by throwing money into a box (*saisenko*), then you ring the bell to attract the gods' attention and make a request, facing the center of the temple.

KITSUNE FOX SPIRITS

Kitsune means fox in Japanese. It's one of the animals that appears most frequently in Japanese folklore. Foxes are believed to be messengers of Inari, the god of fertility. The more tails it has, the more powerful it is. The highest number of tails it can have is nine. There are many Shinto shrines devoted to Inari, and you'll be able to recognize them right away when you see a statue of a fox.

KOMAINU GUARDIANS

Komainu are figures of lions or dogs, normally in pairs, usually to be seen at the entrance of Shinto shrines. This tradition was imported from China, where *komainu* are known as *shi-zi*. In the West, they are often seen at the entrance of Chinese restaurants.

OMIKUJI FORTUNE PAPERS

In Shinto shrines, you can buy small envelopes that contain a strip of paper with your fortune written on it. Once you have read it, you must attach your *omikuji* to a tree branch. If you get a lucky paper, you will have good luck when you attach it. If you get an unlucky one, attaching it to a branch will cancel the bad luck effect.

SHIMENAWA ROPES

Shimenawa are thick ropes that mark the boundaries of the sacred grounds. They are usually coiled up around *torii* gates, trees, or sacred stones.

TOMOE SYMBOL

The *tomoe* is one of the most common Shinto symbols. *Tomo* was the name of a part of the armor used by *samurai* more than 1,000 years ago. It was a small circular piece made of iron, with curved blades, designed to be worn on the elbows to protect them from arrows. The *tomoe* symbol took its name from the *tomo* because of their similarity in form.

Among the *samurai* the symbol was popular because of its association with armor. Its form brings to mind a swirl of water, and it is believed that it helps protect against fire. In fact, eventually, besides being used in Shinto shrines, the symbol was used as fire protection on castle walls and even on the eaves of houses belonging to upper-class families. It is one of the most noticeable Shinto symbols, and you can find it almost anywhere in the country. There are several kinds, depending on the number of blades. The one in the photograph has three blades, and if you take a good look, you will see several one-blade *tomoe* to the right.

Used for centuries in family and clan emblems, the tomoe has appeared more recently in corporate logos.

CHAPTER 2

THE TRADITIONAL ARTS AND DISCIPLINES

美術

陳大道無名上德不
德玄功潛運 邦子臨

During the Edo Period, when Japan received almost no influence from foreign cultures, a number of unique arts or disciplines were developed. For instance, *kabuki* theater appeared as a consequence of the need to entertain an increasingly flourishing society with more and more free time.

UKIYO-E: THE FLOATING WORLD

Ukiyo-e literally means "pictures of the floating world." This printmaking art was developed during the Edo Period (1603–1868). For more than 200 years the country was closed to all foreign influences, so that life in the cities was fully devoted to pleasure and art.

Ukiyo-e were mass-produced thanks to the new printing technique. Numbered copies would be made—in greater or lesser quantities depending on the stature of the artist—and then the original block was destroyed in order to ensure that buyers owned something unique. *Ukiyo-e* prints usually represent typical scenes of the period, such as *kabuki* theater performances, portraits of *geisha*, *samurai*, *sumo* wrestlers, people traveling on the Tokaido route (from Kyoto to Edo/Tokyo), and rice harvesting with Mount Fuji in the background.

HOKUSAI AND HIROSHIGE

Two of the most famous artists are Hokusai and Hiroshige. They created thousands of original *ukiyo-e* blocks in the early nineteenth century. Moreover, thanks to the ease with which *ukiyo-e* copies could be made, their work arrived in the West and influenced painters of the time, such as Vincent van Gogh and Claude Monet.

Hokusai is said to have created more than 30,000 original pictorial works. He is particularly famous for the *Thirty-six Views of Mount Fuji* series, in which 36 prints, with Mount Fuji in the background, all depict scenes from daily life. Yet he might have achieved even greater renown with his work *Hokusai Manga* (1814), a series of caricatures and comic drawings that are considered the origin of the Japanese comics known the world over as *manga*.

EROTIC SHUNGA

Besides portraits, landscapes, and theater scenes, certain circles began using the same technique to mass produce *ukiyo-e* prints of scenes of explicit sex. These erotic prints are known as *shunga*, and they may constitute one of the earliest pornographic markets in history. Nowadays, erotic prints have practically disappeared, but there are erotic *manga* known as *hentai*, which share certain similarities to traditional *shunga*. If you travel to Japan, one of the best places to appreciate this art is the Ukiyo-e Museum, located next to Harajuku Station in Tokyo (see the Harajuku map, page 153).

UKIYO-E

A Japanese art developed during the Edo Period (1603–1868) consisting of woodblock prints that represented landscapes and typical scenes of the period.

SHODO CALLIGRAPHY

Shodo literally means "the way of writing." *Do* refers to the way of personal fulfillment and wisdom, and it draws on the same philosophical roots as did the ancient *samurai* warriors. *Shodo* is the art of writing with a brush and black ink on a special type of paper. It is taught in Japanese schools and is part of Japanese language learning. However, although it's still used in ordinary life for New Year's cards or special occasions when money is given in an inscribed envelope as a gift, it is no longer very common. There are true artists who do *shodo* professionally. It's said that to be really good at it you need several years of arduous training. Two of the most important rules are always to hold your brush perpendicular to the writing surface and follow the correct stroke order. Japanese children take compulsory *shodo* lessons in elementary school. In high school it's an optional subject for art students. If you're interested in taking your first steps in *shodo*, a basic kit costs between 3,000 and 5,000 yen, and you can find them in any specialized stationery store or in the Tokyu Hands department stores in Japan.

SHODO CONCEPTS
Fude: brush made of bamboo and horse hair
Sumi: ink that is placed on a stone container (*suzuri*)
Hanshi: special paper used to write in black ink
Shitajiki: protection placed under the paper
Bunchin: weight used to hold down the paper

(Above) *A shodo teacher doing a demonstration with hiragana characters.*

(Left) *An example of a scroll created by a professional shodo artist.*

"*Shodo* is the art of writing with a brush and black ink on a special type of paper."

JAPONISM, VAN GOGH AND UKIYO-E

The influence of Japanese aesthetics on the West began during the last quarter of the nineteenth century when Japan opened itself to the world, allowing trade in works of art. Several artists and collectors living in Paris were the first to take an interest in Japanese art. One of the forms that aroused the most interest in French circles was *ukiyo-e* prints. Buying up great quantities and bringing them to Europe was easy, and, thanks to this, they spread quickly.

When van Gogh was living in Paris, his apartment was only two blocks away from the gallery of Samuel Bing, one of the most prominent *ukiyo-e* collectors of the time. Van Gogh became friends with Bing, took an interest in Japanese prints, and began collecting them too. In fact, he liked them so much he started creating his own versions of some of the most famous prints by Eisen, Hokusai, and Hiroshige. For example, van Gogh's *The Courtesan* and *Flowering Plum Tree* are imitations of works by Eisen and Hiroshige, respectively. Besides imitating works by Japanese artists, van Gogh began to incorporate some of the techniques he liked from *ukiyo-e* prints in his paintings.

> **"Thanks to the ease with which *ukiyo-e* copies could be made, they arrived in the West and influenced painters of the time, such as Vincent Van Gogh and Claude Monet."**

Ukiyo-e prints so fascinated Western artists of the time because, despite ignoring strict perspective, creating completely asymmetric compositions that had no object of interest placed at the center, and omitting pictorial detail to the extent the work might seem unfinished, they were able to represent evocative and beautiful scenes that were full of energy. Japanese prints handle perspective through the manipulation of reality. Many use superimposed planes to evoke a false sensation of depth, and they hardly ever rely on shading. Among other common features of the prints are bright colors in flat areas, *wabi-sabi* asymmetry (see page 41), and irregularity in composition.

Other Western artists besides van Gogh were influenced by Japanese art, and this small movement came to be baptized Japonism by a French magazine. Impressionists and Post-Impressionists like Claude Monet, Edgar Degas, Paul Gauguin, and Henri de Toulouse-Lautrec each had their Japonist period, with Japanese prints and culture in general being a source of inspiration for them. For example, Claude Monet's famous painting *La Japonaise* depicts a woman in a *kimono* holding a Japanese fan. The style of Toulouse-Lautrec's posters also clearly shows the influence of *ukiyo-e*.

(Above) *"Night View of Saruwaka (Monkey) Theater Street" by Hiroshige shows what the entertainment areas of Edo (Tokyo) looked like 200 years ago.*
(Below) *"The Great Wave of Kanagawa" is one of the best-known Japanese works of art. It was created by Hokusai using traditional ukiyo-e printing techniques.*

CHADO: THE TEA CEREMONY

We again encounter the *do* ending, for *chado* literally means "the way of tea." Legend says that tea was brought to Japan by a Buddhist monk in the ninth century. It's now one of the most popular drinks in Japan. The tea ceremony is a ritual that originated in Zen Buddhism, which came from India via China toward the end of the first millennium. The tea ceremony is related to many elements from other traditional disciplines, such as *shodo*, the *kimono*, traditional pottery, incense, and *ikebana* (flower arrangement).

As with *shodo*, although it may seem simple at first glance, you need several years to learn all the steps in the tea ceremony. The preparation is laborious, and very precise steps must be followed. Even the angle at which objects are placed together is important. Another curious feature is that the ritual changes depending on the season of the year, and there are many different kinds of ceremonies depending on the festival day or the type of tea being used.

CHAGAMA

Chagama is the Japanese name for the traditional teapots used in the tea ceremony. These iron teapots were a multipurpose utensil in olden times. As well as being used to prepare tea, they also served to heat and humidify homes, since winter cold in Japan is usually quite dry. For the tea ceremony, water is boiled in the *chagama* until it reaches the ideal temperature. Tea isn't steeped inside the teapot, but instead hot water from the *chagama* is poured into a *chawan* (tea-cup with no handle), and the green tea is mixed in. The belief is that when you heat the water in a *chagama*, it absorbs iron particles from the pot, giving the tea a special flavor and providing extra iron for people's diet. Today, the *chagama* is also sold with a special enamel coating inside, which allows you to prepare tea directly in the teapot.

MATCHA

Matcha is one of Japan's most appreciated varieties of green tea and is the variety used in the tea ceremony. The main difference between *matcha* and other types of green tea is that, during the last weeks before harvest, the tea plants are covered so they don't get any sunlight. Moreover, only the best shoots are hand picked for *matcha* production, and unlike in other teas they are ground to an extremely fine powder. It is very rich in amino acids and antioxidants. When preparing the tea, you take a little bit of *matcha* powder and whisk it into the hot water using a special kind of whisk called a *chasen* until the powder is completely dissolved. It has a rather strong and bitter flavor, so it is usually served with sweets.

Matcha ready to drink, served with a salty cracker, or senbei.

It is very important to hold the cup at the correct angle before drinking.

Serving the right quantity of tea powder.

The position and movement of the hands are among the most difficult things to master.

The bowl must be held in both hands at all times.

The aesthetics and beauty of the tea ceremony lie in its simultaneous simplicity and precision.

KABUKI THEATER

Kabuki is a genre of very stylized traditional theater that also began in the Edo Period (1603–1868), as did most traditional Japanese arts. In *kabuki*, music, dance, makeup, and costumes are very important. One of *kabuki*'s distinctive characteristics is that all actors are men, even those in female roles. Moreover, all actors have their faces painted white, using a special makeup made from a white powder obtained from rice.

WHERE CAN WE SEE KABUKI IN JAPAN?

The two most prominent *kabuki* theaters in Japan are in the Gion district (Kyoto) and in Ginza (Tokyo) (see the Ginza map, page 158). Plays usually treat traditional subjects like quarrels between *samurai* families, wars, or thwarted love. During the performances, Old Japanese is spoken in a very unnatural, high-pitched voice that is unique to *kabuki*.

KABUKI

Kabuki is traditional Japanese theater in which music, dance, makeup, and costumes are very important.

RAKUGO, NOH AND BUNRAKU

Kabuki is not the only form of traditional theater in Japan. There are other, lesser-known genres. *Rakugo* is comedy theater. The comedian comes onstage, kneels on the floor, and proceeds to recite monologues to make the audience laugh. The best *rakugo* comedians usually achieve quite a lot of celebrity in Japan. *Noh* is closer to *kabuki* but with masks, more dramatic overtones, more music, and a much slower rhythm. *Bunraku* is a traditional form of puppet theater.

MY PERSONAL EXPERIENCE

I once had the opportunity to see a performance at the most important *kabuki* theater in Japan, located in Ginza Station in Tokyo. The play I saw was very entertaining because it was about the quarrels between two *samurai* families, so one or two battles were shown. However, the truth is, I understood almost nothing because they spoke in Old Japanese, which is difficult even for native Japanese. During the performance, the characters talked to one another in a peculiar way, as if they were screaming in a girl's voice.

Noh performances are spectacular because of the actors' costumes.

ZEN MEDITATION

Zen is the name of a Buddhist sect that stresses the search for wisdom through the meditation known as *zazen*. Zen developed in China and arrived in Japan more than a thousand years ago, becoming one of the Buddhist sects with the largest number of followers. Today, Japanese Zen is so well established there are several sects based on it.

A ZEN MEDITATION SESSION

During my first year in Japan, I had the chance to attend a Zen meditation session. First, we were given a brief theoretical introduction to its Buddhist origins, and then we undertook a 35-minute practical session in which we had to try to free our minds of all thoughts. That is, the aim of this kind of meditation is to not think about anything—as those who have read books devoted to this subject will already know. The fact is, we had to remain seated in an uncomfortable position without moving a muscle for more than half an hour while we stared at a white wall. If we made the slightest movement, the monk would come over with a stick and whack us between the shoulder blades. The worst part was, you never knew when the blow would fall because you were staring at the wall. When the session was over, the monk said that to understand the true meaning of Zen you needed to practice meditation several times a day. Then he told us a story, or *koan*:

"A long time ago, a student tried every day to understand the true meaning of Zen, and, because he couldn't work it out, his teacher hit him constantly with the stick. The day came when the student decided to leave and travel in order to try to understand what Zen was. A few years later, he came back to see his teacher, who asked him, 'Do you now know what Zen is?' Then the student answered, 'Yes, this is Zen,' as he took the stick and hit his teacher."

Buddhist monks practicing zazen meditation.

Along with koan and meditation, Zen rock gardens are designed to calm the mind and help it to switch off, meditate, and reach one step further.

ZEN KOAN

Koan are brief stories in the form of riddles or fables that Zen teachers use to teach lessons to their students. According to Zen doctrine, the nature of Zen can't be taught with words, and therefore it is the student who must teach himself. This means that in the teacher-student relationship the teacher acts as a guide for his student. One of the tools for this is the *koan*. *Koan* may seem to contain no information in themselves but they help the student inadvertently reach a higher understanding of the universe. It's like trying to communicate something without saying it in a direct way. This too informs the Japanese mind, and is especially evident in Japanese writers.

> "According to Zen doctrine, the nature of Zen can't be taught with words, and therefore it is the student who must teach himself."

us closer to understanding that the universe is unchanging, while our mind interprets it in its own way:

> *Two monks were arguing about a flag. One said, "The flag is moving." The other said, "The wind is moving." The sixth patriarch happened to be passing by. He told them, "Not the wind, not the flag. The mind is moving."*

When we finish reading a *koan*, we're left with a bittersweet aftertaste. We're surprised and briefly dumbfounded. When we're in a state of perplexity, our brain starts thinking in a non-logical way, our thoughts become confused, and, thus, according to Eastern philosophies, we are better able to advance toward enlightenment.

> *Doko came to a Zen master and said, "I'm seeking the truth. In what state of mind should I train myself so I can find it?"*

KOAN

A *koan* is a brief story in the form of a riddle or fable that a Zen teacher uses to teach lessons to students.

SOME OF THE BEST-KNOWN KOAN
Sekishunokoe 隻手の声（せきしゅのこえ）
Perhaps one of the best-known *koan* is "What is the sound of one hand clapping?" Let's now consider a *koan* that tries to bring

The master said, "There is no mind, so you cannot put yourself in any state. There is no truth, so you cannot train yourself to reach it."

Doko replied, "If there is no mind to train nor truth to find, why do those monks meet here before you every day to study Zen and to train themselves through this study?"

"But there isn't even an inch of room here," said the master. "How could the monks gather? I have no tongue, so how could I call them or teach them anything?"

"Oh, how can you lie like this?" said Doko.

"But if I have no tongue that allows me to talk, how could I lie to you?" answered the master.

Then Doko said sadly, "I cannot follow you. I cannot understand you."

"I cannot understand myself," said the master.

And to conclude, one last *koan* that will totally disrupt the logic in our thinking.

Joshu asked the teacher Nansen, "What is the true way?"

Nansen answered, "Every day's way is the true way."

Joshu asked, "Can I study it?"

Nansen answered, "The more you study it, the further you will be from the way."

Joshu asked, "If I don't study it, how can I know it?"

Nansen answered, "The way does not belong to the things we can see nor to the things we can't see. It does not belong to the things we know nor the things we don't know. Don't look for it, don't study it, don't mention it. To reach it, open yourself as wide as the sky."

(The three classic *koan* above are adapted from the book *Gödel, Escher, Bach: An Eternal Golden Braid.*)

IKEBANA

Ikebana means "live flower," although you can also call it *kado* (the way of flowers, see page 42). It's a Japanese art that seeks beauty using flowers as its main element and stems from a Buddhist practice that first appeared in Japan in the sixth century. Besides its decorative function, it's also used as a method for meditation. Simplicity, the evocation of the flow of life, the seasons, and even enlightenment are sought through the positioning of the flowers. Nowadays, *ikebana* is a hobby practiced by many Japanese, and it's spreading to the United States and Europe.

Ikebana is another ritual that combines many elements of the most traditional Japan.

A exhibition of kendo involving combat with wooden sticks.

Shizuoka, kendo champion.

THE MARTIAL ARTS

Martial arts were developed within the Confucian and Hindu-Buddhist philosophical traditions in Asia and arrived in Japan during the feudal period (see pages 18–19). They combine the essence of many Eastern philosophies and religions with the codification of systems of single combat. They are based on teacher–disciple training and the practice of *kata*, or models. In the past, the main purpose of the practice of martial arts was to train for real battle. Since the beginning of the Meiji Period, toward the end of the nineteenth century, the fighting arts have been practiced for different reasons: sport, personal development, discipline, strengthening of character, and self-esteem.

Most Japanese martial arts aim at self-defense and are based on techniques that minimize the risk of injuring an opponent. Some of the best-known martial arts that originate in Japan are *judo*, *sumo*, *karate*, *aikido*, *shorinji*, and *kenpo*, which involve hand-to-hand combat; *iaido* and *kendo*, which involve combat with swords, and *kyudo*, which involves archery.

Martial arts are usually classified in three general groups: grappling, striking, and weaponry. There are also a few disciplines that combine elements from different groups.

STRIKING MARTIAL ARTS

In the striking group, we find *tae kwon do*, which originally comes from Korea, and *karate*, which originally comes from the Okinawa islands, south of Japan.

Karate (空手 "empty, hand"), arose from the influence of the Chinese martial art *kenpo* on indigenous traditions from the Okinawa islands, which had been developing for several centuries with little contact with the rest of the world. When Okinawa became Japanese territory in 1872, *karate* began to spread to the rest of the country. Then, after World War II, it spread all over the world, mainly due to the fact that the islands were full of American military bases, as they continue to be. Many soldiers who learned *karate* while stationed there decided to found *karate* schools when they returned to the United States. At the end of the 1960s, there were already several thousand schools on the other side of the Pacific. Today, *karate* is one of the best-known Japanese martial arts, along with *judo*.

"The ultimate aim of karate lies not in victory or defeat but in the perfection of the character of its participants." –Gichin Funakoshi, father of modern karate

GRAPPLING MARTIAL ARTS

Judo, *jiu-jitsu* (or *jujutsu*), *sumo*, and *aikido* are Japanese grappling martial arts.

Jiu-jitsu (柔術 "softness, technique"), or *jujutsu*, is a martial art developed by the military castes (*samurai*) to allow them to defend themselves without arms when facing armed enemies. Though it was intended for use in conflict situations or on the battlefield, it continued to develop during periods of peace, and many different schools and even other martial arts have emerged from the original forms of *jiu-jitsu*. Its aim has gone from one merely of fighting to a higher and more spiritual level.

Judo (柔道 "softness, the way"), the way of softness, is the quintessential grappling martial art. It was developed from *jiu-jitsu*. One of the basic concepts of *judo* is the search for ways of using the enemy's strength against him or her. This martial art has achieved wider international renown since it was included as an Olympic sport in the 1964 Tokyo Olympic Games, which were held at the Olympic stadium in Harajuku (see map, page 153).

Sumo is also in the grappling group and is one of the most popular sports in Japan. After baseball and horse racing, it may be the sport that occupies the most pages in the country's newspapers. Dating from more than 2,000 years ago, it's the oldest Japanese martial art. *Sumo* is based on Shinto traditions and in its present form still preserves many of its religious trappings. For instance, the referee in each match dresses like a Shinto monk, and, at the beginning and end of each match, the wrestlers perform certain Shinto rites, such as clapping their hands and hurling salt to scare away bad spirits.

Sumo wrestlers are known as *rikishi*. Each year's champion is proclaimed *yokozuna* and becomes a sort of national hero. The rest of the competitors also become well known, thanks to the *banzuke*—the official ranking—which is published in

A sumo wrestler leaving the stadium at Ryogoku, the main sumo stadium in the country.

Practicing judo in a park in the middle of Tokyo on a Sunday morning.

newspapers and posted in many bars and restaurants around the country. Some of the wrestlers even end up in commercials or on television programs.

Aikido (合気道 "union, vital energy, way") is a rather modern martial art. It was developed by Morihei Ueshiba from 1930 to the end of 1960 and began to spread worldwide after World War II. The main aim in *aikido* is to find the best way to neutralize conflict situations. It does not seek the enemy's defeat but harmony, personal growth, and control of the *ki* (vital energy).

WEAPON MARTIAL ARTS

In the weaponry group, we find *kendo* and *kyudo*. In **kendo** ("the way of the sword") you fight with wooden sticks. The origins of *kendo* date back to the time of the *samurai*, who used *bokken/bokuto* (wooden swords) to train with.

Kyudo ("the way of the bow") aims for spiritual development through archery. How you hold the bow and all the steps you follow up to the point where you release the arrow are very strictly determined and require many years of arduous training to master.

THE GOAL IN PRACTICING MARTIAL ARTS

The practice of any martial art is a way to seek perfection, spiritual peace, and the evolution of the relationship between teacher and disciple. These are typical values not only for those who practice martial arts but for any Japanese person. In schools, for instance, respect for teachers is very important. Children are taught to bow before the teacher (a gesture common to all martial arts as well), and they must pay attention to their teachers' words above anything else. In Chapter 3 we will learn more about relationships in Japanese society.

Through the practice of martial arts we seek improvement on several levels: physical, mental, emotional, and moral. In this sense, the practice of a martial art is not limited to the time spent in the *dojo*, or arena, but goes beyond, extending into the daily lives of those who undertake it.

The goal of its practice is self-improvement, the feeling of fulfillment, improved self-esteem, and personal growth, with the aim of becoming a calmer, more stable person. It is said that those who practice martial arts are, generally speaking, happier than those who don't.

This is the standard position you must adopt before you shoot an arrow in the martial art called kyudo.

CHAPTER 3
THE UNIQUE JAPANESE CHARACTER

In Chapter 1 we saw how Japan as a country existed for centuries in almost total isolation. This led to the formation of a unique culture, a unique way of thinking, and a unique language. To understand how the Japanese think and how they communicate, we must understand a series of concepts that are deeply rooted in their society. We will call these concepts cultural keys, and these are generally words that are difficult to interpret, having no exact or clearly defined translation. For this reason, we must look to their origins in history in order to grasp their true meaning and the influence they have in present-day Japan.

HONNE AND TATEMAE

Honne can be defined as the wishes, opinions, and true feelings every individual has, whereas *tatemae* refers to social obligations and opinions that have been adapted or adjusted to society's.

Alcohol is the most common means to go from tatemae to honne.

Co-workers eating and drinking after work, an important practice for communicating in Japanese companies.

HONNE AND TATEMAE

Honne and *tatemae* are two important terms for understanding Japanese behavior. *Honne* can be defined as the wishes, opinions, and true feelings every individual has, whereas *tatemae* refers to social obligations and the opinions that have been adapted or adjusted to society's.

Tatemae is evident when words and true intentions don't fully coincide. What is expressed orally by the individual is *tatemae*, and what he really thinks is *honne*. This may be a fact of life in every country around the world, and if we wanted to settle for a crude translation we could call it something like hypocrisy. This has negative connotations in Western countries, but in Japan expressing *tatemae* occurs on a daily basis, and it doesn't have a pejorative meaning, far from it. Knowing how to express *tatemae* and *honne* at the right time is considered a virtue.

From the Western point of view, concealing the truth may be looked on with disfavor. In Japan, however, preserving harmony is more important, and that's why true thoughts (*honne*) are not usually expressed in a straightforward way for fear of hurting people's feelings. We could say *tatemae* serves as a lubricant in human relationships. It is also used in business, where established conventions have to be followed.

SOME PRACTICAL EXAMPLES

Let's suppose we're invited to tea at a Japanese home, and as dinner time draws near our hosts ask us, "Would you like to stay for dinner?" This is *tatemae*, something one must do out of social obligation. The proper answer would be something like, "I'm not hungry, thank you." This behavior might seem really stupid and confusing, but that is how Japan works. For foreigners living in the Land of the Rising Sun,

understanding what a Japanese person really wants to say to them can be complicated.

Imagine you want to buy a ticket and there are no seats left. The ticket salesperson won't give you a straight answer, such as, "There are no tickets left." Instead, he will probably keep you waiting, pretend he's looking for something on his computer, and start making weird faces and saying *chotto* (see page 40). He might even consult his boss. And in the end, when you're feeling you've completely wasted your time waiting there, he will say something like, "Finding seats is difficult, *chotto....*" This is *tatemae* at its best.

WHEN TO USE HONNE AND TATEMAE

Honne is normally used among friends outside one's place of work. There is even a kind of party known as *nomikai*, where co-workers go to an *izakaya* (Japanese traditional bar) to chat, eat, and drink. On these occasions, you're supposed to show your *honne* and talk about your problems at work or in the family so that your colleagues can help you. This is the moment to complain about your boss or the pest from another department. You might infer that alcohol is crucial for shifting from the *tatemae* manner to the *honne* manner. That's why I always say that a Japanese who has drunk a couple of beers is a completely different person from one who is sober.

The most extreme case I've ever experienced was when I joined the head of another department for a company dinner. It was all very formal and tense until he drank a couple of beers and started telling me that he had gotten divorced the past weekend. Just as if I were a lifelong friend! At that instant I recalled all the books on Japanese culture I had read precisely in order to know what to do and say next.

THE VIRTUE OF HUMILITY

Modesty and humility are essential values for conducting oneself correctly in Japan. The Japanese are humble by definition, no matter what their social class, talent, studies, or job. They are simply expected to behave with modesty. One factor that reinforces humility as fundamental is language, for the Japanese language has honorific forms that serve to extol our interlocutor's virtues and other forms or formulas to lower our own status before someone who is our superior.

The most typical way to show our humility is by diminishing our own achievements while praising those of others. For example, if the head of our company tells us our work during the last few weeks has been perfect, we must answer that the credit is not ours, that the latest successes have been achieved thanks to his teachings and to what the company we work for has taught us.

Another example is when it comes to giving presents. Let's suppose we're giving our boss some cookies. At the moment we do, we must say, "Sumimasen, tsumaranai mono desu ga." This may be translated as "Pardon me for giving you such a petty thing." In using this expression, we are praising our boss by making him understand that he really deserves a much better present. The same expression would be used the other way around, if our boss gave us a present. No matter what one's status, everybody in Japan must be humble to respect their way of being. Sometimes it happens that someone is too ambitious and flaunts his power too much, and he ends up being ostracized by his company and society. There are books about cases where a person of great promise has ended up cleaning the company bathrooms because he was too ambitious and his superiors got scared. The Japanese see ambition as a threat to the inner balance of the system, which might bring them down in the future.

"There are books about cases where a person of great promise has ended up cleaning the company bathrooms because he was too ambitious and his superiors got scared. The Japanese see ambition as a threat to the inner balance of the system, which might bring them down in the future."

MY PERSONAL EXPERIENCE

I have met Japanese people with impressive careers behind them and who are much older and more experienced than me, who treat me on equal terms, tell me about their achievements only if I ask, and are always playing them down and telling me how the credit for their successes belongs to the people around them. The 70-year-old president of a company on Okinawa said to me, "When you are young, you fight vigorously to carry out your projects and dreams, you think you can conquer the world on your own. But when you are in your later years, you think about everything you have done and realize that everything you have achieved in your life has been thanks to the people around you."

The extreme humility of the Japanese might be one of the reasons there are not many media leaders. If we compare the world's great economies, how many Japanese businessmen have you heard of? And how many American businessmen? Right now, two of the most famous businessmen in Japan are the presidents of Sony and Nissan, but in fact neither of them is Japanese: the first one is American and the second one is French.

In this connection, there are a couple of very well-known sayings in Japanese:

"Nou aru taka wa tsune wo kakusu" — Talented eagles hide their claws.
"Deru kui wa utareru" — Stakes that stick out can be hammered.

In Japan, humility is one of the bases of professional success. When you greet someone, you must not shake hands or kiss. The standard greeting is a bow. Depending on the social status of the person you're greeting, you must bend your body to a greater or lesser degree.

THE CONCEPT OF GIRI

Concepts such as *honne* and *tatemae* are deeply associated with the Japanese *samurai* tradition. Another concept that is closely related to *bushido* is *giri*, something that is always present in the minds of the Japanese. *Giri* is a difficult word to translate. It's something like "obligation" or "social duty," the obligation to care about those who have given you something in life so that you are indebted to them. The Japanese feel a profound duty to return gratitude for what they have received, even if they have to make sacrifices to do so. *Giri* is present in the relationships between teacher and student, man and woman, friends, family members, business associates, and so on.

The origin of *giri* is ancient, but it became widespread through the influence of the *samurai* class in the feudal era, who would feel *giri* toward the lord protecting their families. *Giri* forces us to return favors, to preserve harmony in human and social relationships so that some measure of peace is maintained in society. Today, the concept of *giri* is very much a part of Japanese customs. There is an extensive tradition of giving presents on special occasions and, if you receive a gift, you must always give something of the same value in return. This might seem a matter of common sense in any other culture, but in Japan the amount of gift giving can be extravagant. According to one study, the same amount of money is spent on presents in Japan as Americans invest in justice. It so happens that Japan is the developed country with the least expenditure for justice per person in the world. Perhaps *giri* does help the Japanese preserve harmony to some extent and avoid having to resolve conflicts through the legal system.

GIRI AND PRESENTS

All over the world, the practice of giving gifts seems to be growing because of the pressure of excessive consumerism. In Japan, gifts are very important within the system, and there is a series of unwritten rules that, when broken, can cause social "unease." The basic rule is that a gift must be no more nor less valuable than the relationship between the two people. If you buy something too ostentatious for someone you've just met, the other person will probably feel offended and be obligated to you from that moment. The *giri* balance in the relationship has been upset. To solve this problem, the other person must give you a present of equal value because of *giri* pressure.

> "In Japan, the amount of gift giving can be staggering. According to one study, the same amount of money is spent on presents in Japan as Americans invest in justice."

There are dozens of kinds of gifts in Japan: for births, birthdays, weddings, deaths. They even give presents to commemorate death anniversaries. A wedding is considered a very important moment in life, when new connections are made between two families. The amount that is usually given is between 20,000 and 100,000 yen, depending on how close you are to the couple getting married. Incidentally, a gift of exactly 40,000 yen is almost forbidden, because, according to Japanese tradition, the number 4 brings bad luck. This is due to the pronunciation of 4, which sounds like the word meaning "death" in Japanese.

Another funny thing is that gifts are usually given to the doctor and nurses who deliver your baby. And when we start working at a company, on our first day we must bring a small gift for the boss and something to eat (cookies or something similar) for our co-workers.

A SPECIFIC CASE, GIRI ON SAINT VALENTINE'S DAY

Testimony to the West's influence, Valentine's Day is celebrated in Japan. On this lovers' day, women are supposed to give chocolate to men, and this is a tacit obligation not only to the man you love but also to all the men who are close to you. Thus, chocolate on Valentine's Day is divided into two kinds: "*giri* chocolate" (given by women as a social duty) and "true chocolate" (given to the man you love). If you are a man and you work in a Japanese company, on Valentine's Day you will probably eat a lot of chocolate. Unfortunately, this doesn't mean all the women in the company are in love with you. After receiving the chocolate, the men are morally indebted to the women. To solve this following the *giri* system, one month later they celebrate another day, when men give women white chocolate.

These examples give you some idea of how powerful *giri* and social obligations are in the Japanese way of being. An extreme case of the power of *giri* are the *kamikaze*, who volunteered in World War II to commit suicide in conformity with the code of honor, obedience, and duty toward their government and country.

A shop selling chocolate cookies for Valentine's Day. Tradition dictates that women must give men chocolate on Valentine's Day.

MAN-WOMAN RELATIONS IN JAPAN

Over the course of history, relations between men and women in Japan have changed depending on the period. In ancient times, men and women shared the same rights of succession within the family, and both men and women acted as leaders. Beginning with the Nara Period (710–794), men within the aristocracy started to have more power, and, as years went by, women started to lose the right of succession within families.

THE IE SYSTEM

During the same period, we see the development of the system of social organization known as *ie*, a concept that is usually translated as "house" or "household," although it has a much broader meaning and could be more conveniently interpreted as "clan." The *ie* system creates a whole hierarchy within the family, from the servants to the head, who would normally be the father or grandfather. In this system, the first born son was the heir and would become the new head of the *ie*. Women's role was limited to having children and creating links between *ie* by marrying leaders from other families.

CONFUCIANISM

With the arrival of Confucianism and on through the Edo Period (1603–1868), women were pushed further to the side in this system. According to Confucianism: "Women in home, and men outside." This way of thinking took root in Japan and still persists to a certain extent. Today, Japanese businessmen usually work very long hours, then they go out for dinner with their co-workers and return home when their children are already in bed. We might say that many Japanese fathers take part in family life only on weekends.

THE INTRODUCTION OF WESTERN IDEAS

Starting in the Meiji Period (1868–1912), Western ideas began to flow into the country and the education system changed. Still, for women, the idea was to mold them to be good mothers and little else. The final change was adopted with the end of World War II, when a new constitution was written, guaranteeing the same rights for men and women.

Even so, these days women's social status in Japan, as compared to other developed nations, is quite low. This is partly because many beliefs from the Edo Period and the influence of

Confucianism remain strong in the Japanese mind. Even the language reflects some of these ideas. Let's look at a few examples from simple, everyday words:

主人 MAIN PERSON	家内 HOUSE INSIDE	WOMAN 妻 BROOM
These are the symbols that represent the word *husband*. They mean "main person."	These are the symbols that represent the word *wife*. They mean "inside the house."	This symbol also represents the word *wife*. If we break it down into parts, the meaning is "woman" and "broom."

OMIAI

Another interesting topic is the two types of marriage in Japan: arranged marriages, called *omiai*, and marriages for love. As we mentioned before, arranged marriages have traditionally been considered unions between families and not solely as the relationship between a man and a woman. In the past, *omiai* was quite common, and all decisions regarding the marriage were made by the parents on both sides. Today, *omiai* marriages still occur but there is more freedom. Parents simply organize an appointment for their son and daughter and if it works, good, but if they don't suit each other, nothing happens. There's usually not much pressure. Nevertheless, one out of every ten marriages today is of the *omiai* kind.

MEN-WOMEN SEPARATION

Another curious phenomenon is that men and women very often split off into separate groups. At work, men go out for lunch together in groups, and women form other groups. It's unusual for guys and girls to mix. In my present company, I tried to bring the groups of men and women together to some extent. We sometimes would go out for lunch together, but I realized they don't feel totally at ease and tried to avoid it. So, I've gradually stopped making an effort and am adapting to the Japanese method, joining a group of guys. If I joined the girls, they would look at me as if I were from another planet.

I'M SORRY, EXCUSE ME

The Japanese usually apologize for every little thing and all the time. In the Japanese language there are dozens of expressions for apologizing, and the best known is *sumimasen* ("I'm sorry/excuse me"). But *sumimasen* does not mean exactly the same to the Japanese as "I'm sorry" means to us. Normally, we use our expressions to show we're sorry for something wrong we have done, whereas *sumimasen* is used to relax the tension in a conversation. It's like a sign that says you understand the other person's feelings. The meaning of *sumimasen* is more like that in "I'm sorry for the death of your dog." It's not our fault the dog has died, but by saying this we're implying we understand the other person's feelings. To give you an idea of the proportions of this phenomenon, the other day I counted 23 *sumimasen* in a one-minute conversation. Keep in mind that the Japanese seek harmony above all else and try not to confront or clash with others.

Another use of *sumimasen* that you'll find helpful when you travel to Japan is to start a conversation, just as we say "Excuse me" in English. You approach someone and say, "Sumimasen…," wait for an answer, and then you toss in your question, "Eki wa doko desu ka" (Where is the station?).

THE CULTURE OF CHOTTO

As with *sumimasen*, *chotto* is another handy word to avoid confrontation. *Chotto* is a mysterious Japanese word. If you look it up in a dictionary, it is translated as "a little, a minute, a moment." One of the first expressions you learn in Japanese is "Chotto matte kudasai," which means, "Wait a minute, please." You can also use this word whenever you want to answer a question such as "Do you like rice?" You can respond, "Chotto," which means you like rice a little bit. But you will gradually realize this word has more to it than meets the eye, and maybe, when we answer the rice question with *chotto* we are not really expressing the same concept of "a little bit" that we have in the West.

DISCOVERING THE MEANING OF CHOTTO

I will now tell you how I discovered the real sense of this word. We were looking for a hotel to spend the night in Nikko (see pages 180–181 for how to get to Nikko), and it was quite late, so finding a room was difficult. We entered the reception area at the first hotel and asked if they had any rooms available. The girl looked at us with a smile, turned around and started searching for something on her computer, made weird faces, turned to face us again, moved her neck to one side, and said, "Chotto," followed by a silence and then more talk in Japanese. To us, this literally meant "a bit." How can there be "a bit" of room available? The fact was there were no rooms, but the girl never said so using the negative *iie*.

On another occasion, when we were trying to buy a ticket for the Shinkansen (bullet train), the man who was serving us also made that neck movement, holding his ear closer to his right shoulder, and he then let out the feared "Chotto," followed by a tense silence. Can you guess? Indeed, there were no seats available on the Shinkansen, but the man never said the word *iie*.

I also remember a time I asked someone if I could take a photograph of him and he answered with "Chotto." "I can take a photograph of you a bit?" is what I understood. But what that person really meant was that he didn't want his photo taken.

As we've already seen, the Japanese really dread confronting other people, and that's why they hardly ever use the word "no," resorting instead to other, more subtle and gentler words like *chotto* or non-verbal language like the neck movement. Answering with *iie* is very curt and you hardly hear it, except in really tense situations. Think about how often you hear the word "no" in English in any one day. In Japan, the day you hear *iie* can be counted as something extraordinary.

Besides *chotto*, there are many ways of saying "no" delicately, depending on the situation. For example, my boss at work usually says, "This is very interesting," "Uh-huh," "Yes," "This is complicated, but…," or "We will study your proposal" when, judging by the face he's making, he's really saying "NO," "NO," "NO…." So you must pay careful attention to people's expressions in Japan. If you see that they look indecisive, that there is something that leaves them unconvinced, they are probably shouting "NO" at you, but you don't realize it because they are saying things like, "Perhaps I'd like to go to the movies with you," or something similar. Be careful, because the dictionary very often comes up short when we're dealing with cultures so different from our own.

> "*Iki* and *wabi-sabi* have many things in common, and together they constitute the basis of aesthetic ideals in present-day Japan as well as Japanese behavior."

AESTHETIC VALUES

Japanese aesthetic values are very different from ours and they have been developing for centuries, gradually influencing the rest of the world. *Ukiyo-e* printmaking, for example, influenced Western art movements as prominent as Impressionism and Fauvism. Even the architect Frank Lloyd Wright was a great fan of *ukiyo-e*. But *ukiyo-e* is not the only Japanese thing that fascinates the West. There are the *geisha*, Japanese gardens, literature, *haiku* poems, *bonsai* trees, *manga*…. What do all these have in common? Why do people like them?

Have you realized that whenever you look at the pages of a Japanese book, spend some time in a Zen garden, read a couple of *haiku*, or taste quality *sushi*, you experience a similar feeling? Though seemingly very different, they are all paths to the same state of mind, just as watching a hundred different suspense thrillers would lead us to a similar state, and playing any group sport would put us into more or less the same state of excitement. There are certain values that help explain the uniformity of Japanese aesthetics. Two of the most important ones are *iki* and *wabi-sabi*.

IKI

Iki is a term born during the Edo Period. It was used first in *samurai* circles to designate men of worth and elegance who followed the code of honor. The term began to spread and took on the meaning of "elegant, distinguished but not arrogant or flamboyant." The Japanese have always valued sobriety. We could say a person or thing is *iki* if he, she, or it is original, calm, refined, and sophisticated without being perfect or complicated. In English literature, this is often translated as "chic."

To cite an example, an Audi 8 would be *iki*, whereas a four-wheel-drive vehicle would not. As for people, the typical rich guy would not be *iki*, while an educated man with a good career and who stands out not because he forces the situation but because the environment makes him stand out would definitely be *iki*.

If we apply this to the Japanese world, *geisha* are *iki*. They are beautiful and sophisticated, but have no intention of standing out. Japanese avant-garde architecture is *iki*, and so are the interiors of Japanese houses with *tatami* mats, Haruki Murakami's novels, eating *sushi*, *ukiyo-e*. Whenever we come in contact with any of these things, we attain a similar state of mind.

Iki is a value that still prevails today, and people tend to use this word to describe certain people. If they say you are *iki*, you are being praised, whereas its antonym—*yabo* or *busui*—would mean something like "vulgar, rough, coarse, or simple."

WABI-SABI

Wabi-sabi represents imperfection and incompletion. *Wabi-sabi* derives from the Zen Buddhist concepts of impermanence and constant flow. *Wabi-sabi* also emphasizes simplicity and sobriety, just like *iki*. For example, a chipped teacup is *wabi-sabi*, and so is an old sculpture, a castle in ruins, and an asymmetric glass. In the Japanese world, *shakuhachi* music, *ikebana* flower arrangement with its asymmetric forms, Zen gardens with their eroded rocks and raked gravel representing the constant flow of things, the art of *bonsai*, poems, and the tea ceremony are *wabi-sabi*. All these "imperfect" arts produce a similar state of mind of melancholy and harmony with the environment.

Iki and *wabi-sabi* have many things in common, and together they constitute the basis of aesthetic ideals in present-day Japan as well as Japanese behavior. Don't you have the feeling when you face something that is *iki* or *wabi-sabi* that it's trying to communicate wisdom through silence? When you read a Japanese short story or when you see a Japanese movie, very often at the end you ask yourself where the moral is in its message. It's not handed to you on a platter, but imperceptibly it has reached your mind. This is what you find in any work by *mangaka* Jiro Taniguchi, any book by Haruki Murakami, and any movie by Akira Kurosawa.

Sand and rock gardens are an example of wabi-sabi.

> **IKI**
>
> *Iki* is a term born during the Edo Period and is used to designate people, things, or situations that are original, calm, refined, and sophisticated without being perfect or complicated.

> **WABI-SABI**
>
> *Wabi-sabi* derives from the Zen Buddhist concepts of impermanence and constant flow, and emphasizes simplicity and sobriety.

DO = THE WAY

In Chapter 1 we talked about the importance of *do* and its relationship with *bushido*. In Japanese, Chinese, and Korean, there are many words and expressions that contain the *kanji* character *do*, which translates literally as "way."

DO IN JAPANESE VOCABULARY

Many names for Japanese traditional arts include this character, as do martial arts or words that express some philosophical or religious knowledge. Let's examine now a brief list of words with the character *do*:

神道   Shinto = The "way" of the gods = Shinto

道教   Dokyo = The "way" of faith = Taoism

道徳   Dotoku = The "way" of virtue = Ethics

道理   Dori = The "way" of logic = Reason

悪道   Akudo = The "way" of evil = Bad, evil

道楽   Doraku = The "way" of comfort = Entertainment

道路   Doro = Road

大道   Daido = Avenue

道場   Dojo = The place of the "way" = Training hall

茶道   Chado = The "way" of tea = Tea ceremony

武士道   Bushido = The "way" of the warrior

剣道   Kendo = The "way" of the sword

弓道   Kyudo = The "way" of the bow = Archery

華道   Kado = The "way" of the flower = Flower arrangement/ikebana

合気道   Aikido = The "way" of the union of spirit and mind

柔道   Judo = The "way" of flexibility

跆拳道   Tae kwon do = The "way" of stamping and punching (Korean)

These are just a few examples, but the dictionary contains hundreds of entries with the character *do*. These words are in everyday use in Japan, Asia, and even the West. *Judo*, *tae kwon do*, *kendo*, and *aikido* have achieved some popularity in the United States. The difference is that in Japan it's not merely a character but a whole philosophical concept and a way of life that has been deeply rooted in Japanese thinking for centuries.

THE ORIGINS OF DO

Do originated in China five or six centuries before Christ. It was Laozi (or Lao Tzu) who developed *tao* or *dao* (the Chinese pronunciation of the character 道. Tao or Taoism is the Chinese word usually placed on the covers of books written to explain Eastern philosophy to Westerners, but the basic idea is the same, and what matters is that the character is the same in both Chinese and Japanese, 道. Laozi wrote about the importance of following a way, a doctrine, a code to unite man and nature, to unite sky and earth. According to Laozi, there is a *tao* or *do* that is a sort of universal spirit with which we can come into contact just by following the way. It is said that *tao* cannot be understood or explained. It will simply reach your inner self if you follow the way and the teachings of a teacher who has already achieved it.

Japanese students and workers must follow strict rules and methodical systems that originate in do. For instance, in all the schools in Japan, wearing a uniform is compulsory for students.

Laozi's ideas spread throughout Asia, arriving in Japan by way of Zen Buddhism (see pages 18–19), which incorporates many of his basic ideas. In Zen Buddhism, for instance, absolute truth cannot be communicated. You must attain it by yourself. Instead of saying that *tao* is a universal spirit that lives within each one of us, Buddhists say that it's Buddha who is inside all of us.

In Japan, strict systems of meditation were developed through which you could get to know the nature of Buddha and absolute truth, and by means of which the teacher could help students to progress while always allowing them to find wisdom for themselves. Over the centuries, a system evolved so that the student could become like his teacher, so that the student could understand the 道. This learning or apprenticeship system spread to different aspects of Japanese life and has survived to the present day.

THE APPRENTICESHIP SYSTEM

Basically, the apprenticeship system in any discipline following the 道 Tao-Zen philosophy consists of three steps:
1. Establishing a series of patterns, models, or forms known as *kata*.
2. Repeating the *kata* for many years.
3. Perfecting and searching for beauty in the *kata*, "joining" them in a sort of enlightenment.

Those who practice any martial art will be very familiar with this system of repetition. Teaching martial arts usually involves repeating the teacher's *kata* movements and always showing respect and obedience to him or her. This teacher-student relationship based on respect is very much present in today's Japan and is known as the *senpai-kohai* relationship (see page 66). The aim is that through repetition, the student will not be able to lose concentration, as if under a sort of hypnosis. Always imitating the teacher will create discipline. Through many, many repetitions, the student will reach the *mushin* "no-mind, no-spirit" state. This "no-mind" state makes us accept the world as it is, and it's one of the training keys in any *do* discipline.

This apprenticeship system of learning by doing repeatedly came out of Buddhist schools and the martial arts and was introduced into some traditional disciplines, such as flower arrangement (*ikebana*), calligraphy (*shodo*), and the tea ceremony (*chado*), where, though you may find this hard to believe, it takes several years to master all the ceremony *kata*. But this method of "repetition without thinking," followed in a strict, systematic, and perfectionist way, has ended up permeating many of the daily work routines of the Japanese.

THE INFLUENCE OF DO IN MODERN JAPAN

The Japanese seek perfection in some tasks (*kata*) as a means to acquire spiritual satisfaction in their lives. It's impressive, for example, to see how serious the Japanese get when they practice their hobbies. It looks as if their lives depended on those hobbies and as if they're not really enjoying themselves. But if you ask them afterward, it's not like that at all. They enjoy them even more than we do.

The Japanese learn through repetition at school and in college. They are hardly given any option to think for themselves. They tend to be satisfied with established rules, following the set path without making life difficult for themselves, instead of seeking to be original or creating new ideas. At work, they mold themselves in their companies through the repetition of certain patterns, and they develop the same task throughout their lives. They get to be very good at what they do, probably much better than anyone else doing the same thing in another part of the world, but it is also very difficult for them to depart from their routine. We might call them super-specialized.

CRITICIZING DO

Many people accuse the Japanese of not having their own thoughts, of following rules like mere ants. One of them is Kenzaburo Oe, Nobel Prize winner for Literature, from whom we now quote some remarks made in an interview with the Spanish newspaper *La Vanguardia*:

"War, made by armies, is the greatest expression of violence and ignorance. Japan, for example, has a pacifist constitution and yet the government violates it by sending troops to other countries such as Iraq. I'm not only against all those who use violence to defend their ideals, territory, or ideology, I'm also against the army consciousness itself, people who don't act on their own initiative but follow the orders they receive. Unfortunately, in present-day Japanese society, it's not only the armed forces but also people in offices who think like this. There are fewer people whose conscience is their own."

Do has made the Japanese polite, strict, methodical, hardworking, and perfectionist, and this has led them to become world leaders in technology, among other things. But, on the other hand, it has turned them into little "non-thinking" ants who simply copy and improve what they see. Might *do* have something to do with the fact that for most of the time since the end of World War II the country has been governed by virtually the same people?

LIVING WITH DO

At a cohabitation level, I can assure you that the Japanese are generally quite stubborn and not at all open-minded. They al-

"The Japanese learn through repetition at school and in college. They are hardly given any option to think for themselves. They tend to be satisfied with established rules, following the set path without making life difficult for themselves, instead of seeking to be original or creating new ideas."

ways follow the set path, they follow the *kata* or the procedures they learned or those that are written. If a piece of paper says A must be done following the B procedure, the Japanese will always use the B procedure without ever considering that there could be something better. If you explain to them that the C procedure is better than B, they will give you a doubtful look, as if suspecting something, and they will probably keep on using the B method. In the business world, they would change to the C procedure, but they would change all the pieces of paper and do an in-depth study of the change that could take several months or even years. This makes Japanese companies slow but safe.

Another manifestation we can spot right away if we travel to Japan is that in any shop, restaurant, supermarket, or hotel they will greet you with the same words and gestures. They all follow the same *kata* and the same rules, as if they were robots. You will be welcomed everywhere with the shout "Irasshaimase!" and a bow. When they serve you at the cash register, there is another protocol, a series of set phrases, a set order for taking the money, giving the change, putting things in bags, finished by another bow. When you leave, the entire staff will say goodbye to you. This happens everywhere! The sales clerk at the 24-hour convenience store in the center of Tokyo will behave exactly the same as a sales clerk in Chiba or Saitama. You'd think nobody had their own personality. Expressed in this way, it may not seem particularly interesting, but if you go to Japan, pay attention to this aspect. I'm sure it will surprise you.

The concept of seeking an apprenticeship in order to learn seems to have permeated society deeply, but somehow it has been misinterpreted to the point of limiting the freedom of thought of the Japanese. Is this good or bad? Is specializing good or bad? Has the spirit of repetition of *kata* and following the way to perfection helped Japan become one of the world's leading economies? You still haven't understood what *do* is? Don't worry, it's something you can't explain. A Japanese teacher would say that it's something you must grasp by yourself through the search for wisdom in your field by repeating your *kata* every day.

AMAE

AMAE

Amae is a concept used to describe the way we act when we wish to be loved or seek attention, when we want to depend on someone else with a certain sense of submissiveness.

Amae is a concept used to describe the way we act when we wish to be loved or seek attention, when we want to depend on someone else (your father, your wife or husband, or even your boss) with a certain sense of submissiveness. A person with strong *amae* would be someone who makes himself desirable and who acts capriciously so that others pay attention to him. Children are the most obvious example of the manifestation of *amae*.

There is *amae* all over the world, but it's funny how in Japanese there is a specific word to describe it. They even have the verb *amaeru*, "to wish to depend on other people's kindness." The fact is that in Japan *amae* is somewhat exaggerated, and you find 40-year-old women who act like teenagers and this is considered *kawaii* (cute). Japanese men prefer women with a girlish face who behave submissively and act like girls. They are not attracted to elegant women who look as if they have a lot of personality. Men, boyfriends, and husbands like playing the role of protectors.

PRACTICAL EXAMPLES OF AMAE

A universal example of *amae* in practice is the boy who carries the girl's books in college. She could easily carry them herself, but she likes to be taken care of and the man likes to feel he's taking care of somebody. Another manifestation of *amae* would be when you act capriciously so that your protector will let you get away with something. A boy pretends to be tired so that his mother will yield and allow him to go to bed without putting his clothes in the washing machine. An example of *amae* for a man would be when the husband arrives home drunk and his wife, instead of telling him off, helps him into his pajamas and puts him to bed—a typical scene in Japanese soap operas. These examples are quite normal, but there are also exaggerated instances of *amae*, like that of a woman who works with me, who tells me at lunch how much she would like our boss to be her elder brother so he could take care of her, because he would be the ideal brother (see *sempai-kohai* relationship on page 66).

Japanese culture is full of examples of *amae*: any *shojo manga*; Japanese pop music, which all sounds like it's written by teenagers; the always extremely high-pitched voices of girls in movies, commercials, and television; and even erotic movies, where submissiveness is a recurrent theme. *Amae* plays an essential role in a collectivist society, where individualism is frowned upon and group power in general is encouraged because it helps create harmonious links within the family, the company, or in groups of friends. Again, remember how the Japanese avoid confrontation or conflict at any cost. *Amae* is a tool used to preserve harmony and peace, the *wa* (peace-harmony) in Japanese society.

> "*Amae* plays an essential role in a collectivist society, where individualism is frowned upon and group power in general is encouraged because it helps create harmonious links within the family, the company, or in groups of friends."

By Western standards, Japanese children are usually very spoiled.

SOTO-UCHI

In Japanese thinking, there is a big difference between the way you treat people in your family and circle of friends (*uchi*) and the way you treat other people (*soto*). We can find this differentiation all over the world, since we don't treat people who are close to us the same way as we treat those we don't know so well. For example, have you noticed how in your society it's difficult to become part of a group of friends if you are the last to get there? Still, we do what we can to integrate people in our gang. In Japan, this is even more complicated. Becoming part of a group you don't belong to, no matter how much effort you put into it, is almost impossible if they don't accept you. Let's examine in more detail the sharp dichotomy between *uchi* and *soto*.

IE SYSTEM (HOUSE)

内
UCHI

外
SOTO

In the past, Japanese life was centered around the *ie* system, that is the family nucleus. The head of the family was usually the eldest man, whose responsibility was to supervise everybody in the household and keep them in harmony. As the members of the family married members of other families, the branches of the family *uchi* group expanded.

Another very important consequence of the *ie* system is that individual opinions had little value. All members had to consider

> "Being treated as *soto* doesn't mean they treat you badly. They will probably be more attentive to you than your Western friends."

The movie "Go" illustrates rather well the relations between native Japanese and Korean immigrants.

family harmony above everything. This still prevails today and is one of the reasons Japanese companies are considered the slowest in the world, because everyone must agree before anything is done. The benefit of such a democratic system is that, in the end, decisions are normally correct and workers don't usually go on strike.

A PRACTICAL EXAMPLE

The need for all *uchi* members to agree on something can be exaggerated to an unbelievable degree! I remember a colleague of mine whose CD drive broke down. One of the bosses spent half an hour analyzing whether it had really broken down. Next day, four bosses held a meeting to discuss the problem and look for a solution and, in the end, they decided to replace the CD drive. However, they also decided to order additional replacement drives and try other brands so as to avoid similar problems in the future. Faced with a problem, no matter how insignificant, all *uchi* members have to agree on the way to proceed, then the necessary measures are taken so that it doesn't happen again.

DEGREES OF UCHI AND SOTO

Uchi and *soto* and the differences between them can fade into one another quite a lot. At the first *uchi* level we find our family unit, followed by families "connected" to us. Then, we have friends, followed by our company, and last, we have our country. Thus, foreigners in Japan are about as *soto* as you can get. That's why they say that, no matter how long you live there, you will always be treated as a *gaijin*. The Japanese will treat you as *soto* simply because they unconsciously believe you are some sort of threat to their *uchi* harmony, and that is one of the reasons Japan is such a closed country.

INTEGRATING INTO JAPAN

It is probably the most advanced country with the lowest immigration in the world, although lately the Japanese are cracking open their doors a bit more. The largest minority is Koreans, whose problems integrating into Japanese society can be seen in the film *Go*.

But don't misunderstand me. Being treated as *soto* doesn't mean they treat you badly. They will probably be more attentive to you than your Western friends. The problem is, you feel as though there is some sort of barrier. This also comes through in the use of both verbal and non-verbal cues, which clearly denote whether you're entering their *uchi* or not.

By reason of everything I've told you, they say that making friends with a Japanese is difficult, but if you do, he or she will become a true friend who will never fail you. Remember that he or she will always go to great lengths to preserve harmony inside the *uchi*. Those who have a Japanese friend can confirm this.

CHAPTER 4

CURIOSITIES AND SYMBOLS

伝

Walking around Japan, you will probably see many things that look strikingly different and you'll wonder why. We'll now examine some of the things that most arouse our curiosity.

ANIMAL FIGURES

The *tanuki* is a typical animal in Japan, although it's difficult to see in the wild. When you go on a mountain excursion, you might glimpse a real one if you're lucky. What is certainly easier is spotting *tanuki* statues, since they are a ubiquitous symbol of good luck.

THE REAL TANUKI
Considered a member of the dog family, it's usually mistaken for a raccoon. It's native to Japan and Manchuria, but during recent decades it has spread to Eastern Europe.

THE TANUKI MYTH
We find thousands of stories about *tanuki* in Japanese folklore. According to their traditions, the *tanuki* can transform itself and adopt any appearance. Nowadays, outside many Japanese restaurants there is usually a *tanuki* statue. In his left hand he's holding a bottle of *nihonshu*–his favorite drink–and in his right hand he holds an accounts book. The *tanuki* figure is said to bring good fortune and prosperity.

Another characteristic of *tanuki* statues is their oversized testicles. If you take a close look at the photograph, at the base

The tanuki figure is said to bring good fortune and prosperity.

of the statue you don't see its feet but its *kin-tama* (literally "gold balls"). These large attributes are a symbol of good luck, and in many stories about *tanuki* they use the skin of the scrotum to play the drum or even as a parachute. The use of the "gold balls" as a drum can be seen in the Ghibli movie *Heisei tanuki gassen pompoko*. This is a typical example of Japanese humor at its purest.

SUPER MARIO TANUKI
As a matter of fact, the racoon suit in Super Mario Bros 3 is actually a *tanuki* suit that confers on its wearer the superpowers associated with this Japanese mythological figure. Moreover, when you're wearing the *tanuki* suit, you can turn into an invincible statue.

THE LUCKY CAT
The *maneki neko* is a Japanese traditional sculpture that brings good luck to whoever owns it. It's a figure of a cat that moves one paw and is usually placed outside Japanese businesses, mainly restaurants. It's supposed to make the business prosper.

If the cat (*neko*) raises its left paw, it means it's trying to attract customers, and if it raises its right paw, it's attracting money. There are many kinds of *maneki neko* to entertain yourself with when you go to a Japanese restaurant.

THE MAMBOU FISH
This is a very popular fish in video games. These meek animals can weigh more than 4,000 lb (1,800 kg) and usually live in temperate ocean waters. In Japanese, it's called *mambou*–sunfish in English–and its scientific name is *Mola mola*. They are famous for being very clumsy and useless, and in Japanese culture they frequently appear in company logos, video games, etc. From a scientific point of view, part of its interest is that it's the largest fish with a bony skeleton, so it's probably one of our distant cousins.

The maneki neko is the popular figure of a cat with a raised paw that brings good luck and prosperity to businesses.

The mambou fish's mysterious shape is fascinating.

SAKURA CHERRY BLOSSOMS

Sakura is the name of the Japanese cherry tree and flower. At the beginning of April, the blooming of the *sakura* is quite an event. In fact, there is a word, *hanami*, which means "to see flowers", used to refer to the act of gazing at cherry tree blossoms.

When the time is near, experts on television will look at the trees and forecast when the flowering will take place. There is even a map on Yahoo showing the days this will happen in every area in Japan. There are also signs in the streets indicating parks with *sakura*, tourist maps showing the best spots to view *sakura*, and even travel agencies offering special packages to see the blooming trees.

THE HANAMI TRADITION

Going to *hanami*, in other words, going on an excursion to see flowers, is a centuries-old tradition in Japan. In times past, the Japanese believed gods lived inside *sakura* trees, and just before the rice-sowing season offerings were made under the trees. One of these offerings involved drinking *nihonshu* (*sake*).

Today, the *hanami* tradition involves sitting under a *sakura* tree with your family, your friends, or the people at your company. In the case of families, it consists of the typical barbecue or Japanese-style picnic. Generally, young people and companies go a little later to drink beer, *nihonshu*, or any other liquor. It's like a big party on a national scale. The main problem is the lack of room. Yoyogi and Ueno Parks (see maps, pages 153 and 161) are jam-packed, and that's why someone from the company usually goes early to scout out a place and save some room under a tree. There are apparently people who will even sleep under a tree that's expected to flower the next day so they'll be able to enjoy it with their colleagues from work.

> "In times past, the Japanese believed gods lived inside *sakura* trees, and just before the rice-sowing season offerings were made under the trees."

Sakura in full bloom in a Japanese park.

WHY DO PEOPLE WEAR FACE MASKS IN JAPAN?

Many people wonder why so many Japanese wear a mask on the streets of Tokyo. One of its uses is to avoid contagion when you have a cold. But its main purpose is for pollen allergies, and that's why its use increases in the spring.

The truth is that this practice can be somewhat depressing and off-putting as the sight of so many people wearing masks is a little scary at first. You also may feel uneasy talking to someone who is wearing the famous mask, but you have to understand that the problem of allergies in Japan is very serious. Let's have a look at its origins.

THE PROBLEM OF KAFUNSHO

Allergy to pollen is known in Japanese as *kafunsho*, and it affects 20 million people in Japan. This allergy is mostly caused by cedar (*sugi*) pollen. The fact is that after the destruction of Japan in World War II, wood was in high demand for building and whole forests of fast-growing Japanese cedar trees were planted to meet this demand.

Forests planted with cedars now cover 12 percent of the total land area of Japan, more than 11 million acres (4.5 million ha). These trees start generating pollen when they are 30 or 40 years old. It's not surprising that the increase in the production of pollen coincides with the recorded increase in the number of people affected by this allergy. Moreover, importing wood from overseas is cheaper at present than felling cedars in Japan. Over the last several years, pollen levels have broken all records. It seems global warming is also one of the reasons for this increase. Faced with this situation, the

Japanese people protect themselves against pollen by wearing masks.

Japanese Ministry of Health considers *kafunsho* one the worst health threats for the Japanese. Of course, many companies are making a profit from the production of masks, medicines, air filters, and other devices. What some people are choosing to do is to move to Hokkaido, an area where cedars are scarce and people are not so affected by this allergy.

THE JAPANESE BATH

Ofuro could be translated as bathtub, but really it has a broader meaning. To begin with, Japanese bathtubs are somewhat different from ours. They are wider, deeper, and shorter. Besides that, the *ofuro* is usually located in a fully plastic-lined small room, separate from the bathroom. There is a part of the room where you take a shower, and once you're clean, you get into the *ofuro* filled with very hot, limpid water to relax.

The Japanese are immensely fond of getting into the *ofuro*. In fact, most of them spend an average of 30 minutes a day in the water, usually just before going to bed, because they say it helps them relax and stimulates blood circulation. Moreover, in families, small children join their parents in the *ofuro* every day, and it's considered an important moment of family communication.

Where does this habit of taking very hot baths every day come from? It might have to do with the changing temperatures in Japan over the seasons. In summer, a bath helps you rid yourself of sweat, and in winter it helps you warm up. Another explanation could be that, because of the large number of volcanoes in Japan, constructing hot water bathtubs where everyone in town could bathe was easy in earlier times.

> "In families, small children join their parents in the *ofuro* every day, and it's considered an important moment of family communication."

THE SENTO

During the Edo Period (1600–1868), public baths (*sento*) began to spread all over the country. In Tokyo, with a population of little more than a million, there were more than 600 of them. People usually didn't have a place to wash at home, and they simply went to the nearest *sento*, paid a small fee, and used the facilities to take a shower and a bath in the *ofuro*.

Today there are still many *sento*, although their numbers have decreased because almost every home now has a private bath. However, many people prefer going to the nearest *sento* because it's like a social gathering place where you can chat with people from the neighborhood while you soak in the water.

Organization of a Sento

Traditionally, men and women bathed together, but from the Edo Period it was forbidden by law. Nevertheless, the law was relaxed on several occasions and nowadays mixed *sento* are completely legal, even though in practice they are scarce and it's really difficult to find baths without separation of the sexes.

When you go into a *sento*, you pay and they give you a key for a locker. You go to the appropriate side depending on your sex, leave your shoes outside, take off your clothes inside, and leave them in the locker. Then you go to the bath section where you take a bucket and a stool, go to a shower that's not taken, and sit down. You shower sitting down and finish off by pouring very cold water over you with the bucket just before you get into the *ofuro*. It's time to take your relaxing bath. You ease in little by little because the water is extremely hot, normally at around 115 °F (45 °C), and you let water cover you up to your neck. You can relax for a while, but be careful not to overstay. If you stay in for too long, you could even faint when you get out. This is the reason you pour a couple of buckets of cool water over you just before getting in. They say it helps prevent dizziness when you get out of the *ofuro*. Once they're out, people don't usually pour water over themselves again so as to allow the minerals from the *ofuro* water to remain on their skin. The basic rules for avoiding making a spectacle of yourself are: enter the bath area completely naked, be careful not to splash your neighbors when you're taking your shower, and finally, go into the communal *ofuro* completely clean and with no soap traces so as not to sully the water.

THE ONSEN

An *onsen* is like a *sento* but more luxurious. Its water is taken directly from the mountain, so it comes imbued with the natural minerals from the volcanic area where the *onsen* is located. They are usually situated in mountain tourist areas, and the *ofuro* is usually outdoors. The rules to follow in an *onsen* are the same as in a *sento*.

In Japan there's little seaside tourism. What they like best is going to *onsen* in different volcanic areas in the country and enjoying good food. The typical Japanese vacation could be three days at a mountain hotel close to a good *onsen* and eating at good restaurants specializing in the region's typical cuisine.

The ofuro or Japanese bath is a basic element in Japanese culture.

Showers in a sento. You sit on a stool and shower sitting down, so you can get into the ofuro afterward.

This is a rotenburo (open-air ofuro) in the countryside.

THE TRADITIONAL KITCHEN

Irori is the name for those Japanese traditional kitchens that were usually located in the center of the living room and were used both for cooking and heating the house. In the center of the *irori* there is a *jizaikagi* or pot hook, where you hang the cooking pot or kettle. Notice how on the sides there are pieces of bamboo full of *nihonshu* (*sake*) to keep them at the ideal temperature. Furthermore, *nihonshu* heated inside a bamboo cane has a very special flavor.

A Japanese traditional kitchen. You hardly see them anymore.

PACHINKO

Pachinko are the Japanese pinball machines par excellence. They are machines with small balls that you fire and, depending on where they fall, you win money or you don't. When you play, in most models all you can control is the speed at which the balls are fired, and therefore the game is quite simple, though addictive.

Japan is full of *pachinko* game centers, where the Japanese have a wonderful time. These centers are usually packed with people, the noise of the falling balls is unbearable, and the music is blasting to encourage people to keep playing. If you want to experiment with *pachinko* one day, the way you do it is to buy the balls at the entrance and sit at the machine you like best. If you're lucky, you might even leave with more money than you had to begin with.

Gambling is illegal in Japan; for instance, there are no casinos. So, how can *pachinko* parlors exist? There happens to be a legal loophole that allows *pachinko* parlors to operate. If you end up with more balls than when you started your *pachinko* game—which means you have won—these won't be exchanged for cash. Usually, you get some sort of object, like a small, cuddly toy. Next, you go with your cuddly toy to another location, usually in a back street near the *pachinko* parlor. In these premises—controlled by a company associated with the *pachinko* parlor—they'll exchange your cuddly toy, or whatever object you've been given, for cash.

In the beginning, *pachinko* machines were 100 percent mechanical, but nowadays they include all kinds of electronics and some of them even have screens in the center that show you animated sequences related to what is happening to the *pachinko* balls when they fall. Legend has it that professionals study their chances of winning with each machine in a given parlor. But they also say that the parameters of each machine are changed nightly so as to prevent people from cheating.

Some pachinko parlors are huge.

Although huge, most of the time parlors are filled with people playing.

NIO PROTECTORS

The *nio* are two protectors who are usually at the entrance of Japanese temples, placed on each side of the gate. They are easily recognizable because they have a clearly threatening appearance so as to scare away evil spirits, devils, and thieves. Some legends say the *nio* accompanied the historical Buddha and protected him when he traveled around India. The open-mouthed *nio*, called Agyo, is pronouncing the sound *a*, which means "birth." The closed-mouthed *nio* is called Ungyo and is pronouncing the sound *un* (which can be pronounced with your mouth closed), meaning "death." As it happens, *a* is the first sound in the Sanskrit and Japanese alphabets, and *un* is the last sound in both alphabets.

(Above) *Agyo in the temples at Nikko (see page 180 for how to get there).*

(Left) *Nio protectors in the temples at Nikko.*

THE MANJI SYMBOL

Many people are shocked when they realize Japan is full of swastikas, particularly around temple areas, but there is an explanation for this. In the past, the *manji* was used as a good luck charm and to repel evil spirits. Apparently, the symbol was already in use around 2,000 BCE in areas near the Indus River. During the following centuries, it spread all over Asia, becoming a symbol of life associated with the image of Buddha. On Japanese maps, there are usually *manji* indicating the location of Buddhist temples.

In the *manji*, the vertical axis represents the union of heaven and earth, the horizontal axis represents the union of *ying* (darkness) and *yang* (light), and the four arms represent the continuous movement of the elements, thus forming an image of the universe in eternal harmony and constant change.

The manji is an ancient Buddhist symbol full of spiritual meaning.

SHACHIHOKO MONSTERS

Shachihoko is the name for an ancient Chinese sea monster with a tiger head and carp body. Legend says its body is covered in poisonous scales, and it can turn into a tiger when it has to move around on solid ground. For more than 500 years, the Japanese have been using *shachihoko* figures to decorate and protect their castles.

A shachihoko on a roof at Osaka Castle.

THE NARUTO PHENOMENON

Naruto is a *manga* created by Masashi Kishimoto and adapted for television as an *anime* series. The main characters are *ninja* with special powers, who fight to keep peace in their village against threats from other *ninja* clans. The *manga* was first published in 1999 and soon became a bestseller. To date, it has sold more than 100 million copies in Japan alone. The hero in the series is Naruto Uzumaki, an ambitious young *ninja* with a pure heart and a very rebellious personality.

Naruto Uzumaki is not a typical Japanese name, so let's investigate what makes it such a curious choice by the author. The fact is, *naruto* is something you eat. It's one of the ingredients in *ramen*, the hero's favorite food.

The white part of the *naruto* is made of crushed fish paste, and the spiral is made with different aromatic herbs. It is also called *narutomaki*, which means literally "rolled *naruto*" or it could also be translated as "*naruto* cake." The word *naruto* doesn't really have any other meaning, but thanks to the spiral decorating the food it has ended up acquiring a meaning of "spiral" or "whirlpool." Doesn't that remind you a bit of the personality of the character Naruto Uzumaki?

There is also a marine region in Japan called Naruto, famous for the whirlpools formed when the tide rises and falls, so we are back to whirlpools and spirals. If we translate the

Naruto Uzumaki   *Typical ramen dish with naruto*

kanji character for this sea literally, they mean "roaring gate." This is due to the sound the water makes when the whirlpools form. There is a bridge crossing this whirlpool zone that is also called Naruto.

As to Uzumaki, it could also be translated literally as "whirlpool." Now think about the number of spiral symbols in the series. Look at the clothes the hero wears or at the *chakra* lines provided by the nine-tailed fox. And by the way, doesn't the fox remind you of the legend of the *kitsune* (page 23)?

BLOOD TYPES

In Japan, people ask what your blood type is in the most unexpected situations. They usually ask you on registration forms on the Web, whenever you enroll in an association, at job interviews, or when you start working at a company. Sometimes when you meet someone, they ask what your blood type is before asking you how old you are. My co-workers know everybody's blood type, and they talk about it very often. They are somewhat obsessed with this subject.

The fact is, many people believe in a host of superstitions and pseudo-scientific theories that associate blood types with character. It all began with an article written by a Japanese psychology professor in 1916 titled "The Study of Temperament Through Blood Type." In spite of little evidence to back up the article, the theory quickly spread and was even used by the nationalist government to recruit soldiers depending on their blood type. According to this theory, people with group O are more aggressive and passionate and would, therefore, be better soldiers.

In the 1970s and 1980s, many books were written on this subject and they were very successful, so that it became a phenomenon nationwide. Books that tell you how to choose your partner by calculating the compatibility level of blood types and magazines with a "horoscope" section based on blood types are very common.

Generally speaking, Japanese "theories" characterize blood types as follows:

Type A:
Perfectionist, punctual, shy, intellectual, patient, stubborn
Type B:
Does things in a practical way, great capacity for concentration, individualist, thoughts above feelings.
Type O:
Energetic, social, extroverted, leader, arrogant
Type AB:
Mixes characteristics from all groups, plus a cool person.

And here are the compatibilities that tell whether you can get along with someone depending on your blood type:

A is compatible with another **A** and with **AB**.
B is compatible with **B** and with **AB**.
AB is compatible with **AB**, **B**, **A** and **O**.
O is compatible with **O** and **AB**.

About 40 percent of Japanese people have blood type **B**.

WHY DO JAPANESE WOMEN COVER THEIR MOUTHS WHEN THEY LAUGH?

Anybody who has met a Japanese woman will have noticed how they tend to cover their mouth when they laugh. Depending on the person, this is done more or less exaggeratedly. Some don't even let out a smile without covering it. For centuries, a woman showing her teeth or her open mouth has been considered more or less indecent in Japan.

In the Nara Period (710–794), a new custom began that was known as *ohaguro* (お歯黒, "black teeth"), which required a woman to dye her teeth black. At first it meant a girl had become a woman, but during the Edo Period (1603–1868) it became an essential sign that a woman was married. For more than 200 years, many married women blackened their teeth.

Thus constrained by society, women didn't feel particularly comfortable with dyed teeth, and when they laughed they unconsciously covered their mouths. This custom has passed from one generation to the next until our time, even though today nobody practices that tradition any more.

This seems to be the main reason for the Japanese woman's tendency to cover her face when she laughs. Another reason might be directly related to *amae* (see page 44) and the "immaturity" and "infantilism" implicit in the way of being of Japanese women. Sigmund Freud said that covering one's mouth when laughing is childish behavior.

IS ROARING WITH LAUGHTER BAD MANNERS?

Covering your teeth with your hand is seen as a sign of good manners in Japanese women. Shamelessly showing the inside of your mouth when you laugh can be seen as a sign of bad manners.

Sometimes the gesture is so exaggerated it covers almost the entire face.

BIG EARS, GOOD LUCK AND MONEY

In the West, a big-eared person is not generally considered attractive, but in Japan having huge ears is a symbol of good luck and money. Popular belief says that those who have big ears, especially ears with long lobes, will be lucky in life and have plenty of money.

Buddha (Siddhartha) was born with big ears. During his childhood and youth, he lived surrounded by wealth in the bosom of a noble family. Siddhartha dressed well and wore lots of gold jewelry. Among his favorite jewelry was a pair of heavy gold earrings, which eventually deformed his ears and made them even bigger than before. The moment came when Siddhartha decided to relinquish all his material possessions, and he stopped wearing those huge gold earrings. However, his ears remained deformed all his life.

Siddhartha reached enlightenment through meditation and "became Buddha." Since then, people with big ears have been considered good at listening to nature around them and at hearing the advice of the gods. Making money and being lucky in life have to be easier when you can hear the gods and the world around you better than anyone else.

The former prime minister of Japan, Yasuo Fukuda, has rather big ears. Were those ears what brought him to power in Japan? Or did the subconscious of the Japanese people tell them to elect him when they saw his big ears?

A buddha statue with big ears near a temple in Hakone.

THE SEVEN GODS OF FORTUNE

The seven gods of fortune (*shichifukujin*) form a group of very popular deities in Japan, but only one of them, called Ebisu, originally comes from the Land of the Rising Sun. Daikokuten, Bishamonten, and Benzaiten come from India, while Hotei, Jurojin, and Fukurokuju come from China. All of them originate in Taoist and Shinto beliefs.

EBISU

Ebisu is the god of good luck as well as of fishermen. He is usually depicted with a fish in his left hand and a fishing rod in his right hand, although this last item can vary. Being the fish lovers they are, the favorite god of fortune of the Japanese is Ebisu.

Toward the end of the nineteenth century, Japan Beer (a company that would eventually change its name to Sapporo) launched a beer called Yebisu (an archaic spelling for Ebisu) in honor of the god. At the time, Japan Beer had most of its factories in the southwest area of Tokyo, and they decided to build a train station called Ebisu to improve their distribution system. Today, Ebisu Station is the next one after Shibuya on Tokyo's Yamanote Line (see map, page 148).

Besides being the god of fishermen, Ebisu has also become the god of merchants and farmers, who usually have an Ebisu figurine in the kitchen next to Daikokuten.

JUROJIN

A god of longevity from China, he is the oldest of the gods of fortune. His statues usually have a long beard and a scroll where the dates when all living beings will die are said to be inscribed.

DAIKOKUTEN

A god originally from India and adapted to Japanese tradition in order to improve wealth, commerce, and, more specifically, to see to the kitchen, Daikukuten is believed to bring food to the family. He is usually depicted atop two bales of rice and holding a good luck mallet in his right hand.

"SUPERSTITIOUS JAPAN?"

The Japanese believe your blood type determines your character to a great extent. People are very superstitious, and religions are based on superstition.

BENZAITEN

She is the only woman among the seven gods of fortune. She is the patron goddess of music and fine arts in general. Temples honoring Benzaiten are found near the sea (there is one in Enoshima), and representations of her usually show a very beautiful woman playing the *biwa* lute next to one or several white snakes. According to legend, the goddess Benzaiten can turn herself into a snake. Many Japanese believe that if a white snake appears in your dreams, it symbolizes good luck.

HOTEI

He is the god of happiness and derives from Chinese beliefs. Fat and smiling, he is depicted with a sack full of stuff for the poor.

FUKUROKUJU

The god of wisdom and longevity, Fukurokuju usually appears near the figure of a turtle.

BISHAMONTEN

The god of war and warriors, he has the power to heal. He usually wears armor and has a sword in his right hand.

CONCLUSION

Pay attention when you travel to Japan. You may come upon a surprise around any corner: a little pile of salt, a fountain with ladles, or even a small *ofuro* with warm water to soothe your feet after a long walk.

KARAKURI: THE ORIGINS OF THE JAPANESE PASSION FOR ROBOTS

Karakuri are mechanized puppets or automata created by Japanese traditional artists beginning in the seventeenth century. They may be considered the ancestors of today's humanoid robots, which the Japanese were the first to create.

KARAKURI IN SOCIETY

Karakuri figures are automata that lack any sort of (artificial) intelligence and usually conceal some sort of mechanism or trick to captivate an audience. In olden times, their manufacture was an art in itself. They were used in religious festivals as well as in theater and are said to have influenced *Noh*, *kabuki*, and *bunraku*. It is thought they are one of the reasons the Japanese have come to accept robots as friends and not enemies. Notice how in American movies robots always end up rebelling and trying to destroy the world, whereas in *anime* series and *manga* robots are very often superheroes. They have feelings and even behave as if they were human. Doraemon and Astro Boy, for example, are robots who feel emotions and always try to do the right thing, helping the humans around them.

Today, there is only one artist left in the world who still produces hand-crafted *karakuri*. His name is Shobei Tamaya IX, and he seems reluctant to accept the advances of technology. Nevertheless, several toy companies do offer designs inspired by *karakuri*.

"The art of *karakuri* is considered one of the origins of present-day robotics and one of the reasons the Japanese perceive technology as something friendly."

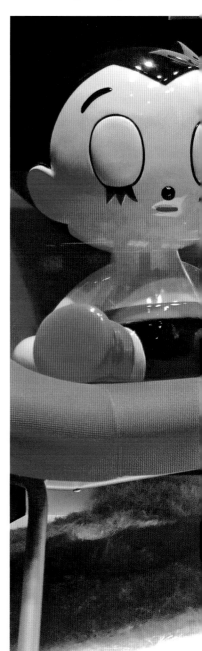

A typical mechanized karakuri.

A passion for automata led the Japanese to being the first to create a humanoid robot.

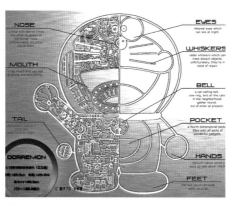

The cosmic cat Doraemon is a robot who always tries to help Nobita.

This photograph shows a 160-year-old karakuri created by the founder of Toshiba. The robot can do shodo with a brush and can write four different characters—for pine tree, bamboo, plum, and happiness. You can find this machine in the Edo-Tokyo Museum.

KARAKURI

Karakuri are mechanized puppets or automata created by Japanese traditional artists.

Tetsuwan Atomu (Mighty Atom), or Astro Boy, an icon of the Japanese passion for robotics.

CHAPTER 5
THE JAPANESE AT WORK

社

Japan has had a substantial business tradition for centuries. In fact, the oldest surviving company in the world was founded by a prince in the south of Japan more than 1,400 years ago, and it's still operating today. It's a building company called Kongo Gumi and is run by direct descendants of that prince, the founder, more than a millennium ago.

This example illustrates how closely connected company and family are in this society. The company you work for is viewed as part of your life. People become part of the company as the company becomes part of your family. This is one of the reasons most people stay at the same company their whole lives, from the time they leave college until they retire. It's also probably one of the reasons overwork, and what we would consider workaholism, are normal. The Japanese give everything for their company and they don't mind working overtime even if they don't get paid for it. In this chapter, we will examine the inflexible structure of the typical Japanese company and the behavior you have to exhibit to be just another Japanese person.

THE JAPANESE ECONOMY AFTER WWII

The Japanese economy is said to be one of most difficult to understand. The truth is, it *is* mysterious and often acts just the opposite of the way one would expect. When World War II ended, Japan was bankrupt. In Tokyo, some accounts say scarcely 10 percent of the buildings were left standing, and the same was true in other cities, like Hiroshima or Nagasaki. But only 20 years later, Japan had become the world's second largest economy and it remained so until it was passed by China in 2010. At present, it still produces about 60 percent of the GDP of the whole Asian continent.

THE SECRET OF SUCCESS

The American government helped Japan greatly during the 1960s and 1970s with business agreements and injections of funds. In addition, the Japanese government adopted protectionist and other policies to encourage private industry to emerge from the postwar crisis. During the first years after the war, there was also a surge of new methodologies, concepts, and work patterns in the business world that have survived until today. For example, the *keiretsu* concept is considered one of the keys to the miracle of the postwar Japanese economy. *Keiretsu* are groups of companies that work together, trying not to compete with one another and cooperating in order to make more money together. The companies in one *keiretsu* always help each other to stay afloat. Moreover, many of the companies in the group usually share part of their social capital.

CREATING A KEIRETSU

To create a *keiretsu*, you normally have a bank that helps all the companies participating in it by means of investing, creating new lines of business, etc. Another role of the bank is to protect the companies in the group when faced with a possible hostile takeover bid. After the war, six main *keiretsu* were formed: Sumitomo, Fuyo, Mitsui, Mitsubishi, Dai-Ichi Kangyo, and Sanwa. Some of the companies in the Mitsui group, for example, are Toshiba and a big bank called Mitsui-Sumitomo.

After many years of this sort of collaboration, Toyota has become the world's number one automobile company. Toyota's lead is so strong it made five times more money in 2006 than the sum of the profits made by its eight most direct competitors. One of the secrets of Toyota is that, besides being protected by a *keiretsu*, it applies a strict continuous improvement system, called *kaizen,* at all levels.

Subsequently, many foreign companies have "copied" the *keiretsu* model in some way or other. For example, various airline alliances, General Electric, and conglomerates formed around banks are built on more or less the same concept, although in Japan collaboration is much closer and financial details are totally different. Japanese *keiretsu* are unique.

Over the six big *keiretsu* (each of them controlled by one important bank) is the MITI (Ministry of International Trade and Industry). The MITI is considered the ministry with the greatest direct influence over the country's economy because it has the standing to give direct orders to certain *keiretsu*, asking them to double their production for the following months or to help this or that sector emerge from a crisis.

The mental image you should have of the country's economic structure right now is of the Japanese government, led by the MITI and with special assistance from the United States, controlling the whole of Japanese industry through the six *keiretsu*, which include the biggest companies and banks in the country. You could say that they all banded together to lift the country out of poverty, with an interventionist and protectionist government controlling the prices of imports (they had the power to do it) and facilitating exports.

KEIRETSU

Keiretsu are groups of companies that work together, trying not to compete with one another and cooperating in order to make more money together.

Skyscrapers in Shinjuku's financial district

THE IZANAGI BOOM

During the 1960s, an especially large injection of money arrived due to the Vietnam War, and from 1965 to 1970 there was an economic boom known in Japan as Izanagi. During the Izanagi Boom, the GDP grew at an annual rate of 11–13 percent. At the end of the boom, the Japanese GDP was 70.4 percent higher than at the beginning. The keys to this were increases in production and indiscriminate exportation. After the Izanagi Boom, the economy kept growing, though at a more moderate rate (4–6 percent), mostly due to the oil crisis. However, Japan surpassed the United States, whose growth was hovering at around a 3–4 percent during those years.

THE HEISEI BOOM

Toward the end of the 1980s, there was a second big economic boom called the Heisei Boom. One of its keys was the production and exporting of cars and electronic devices. In 1990, the Japanese economy rocketed. Japan had the highest income per capita in the world. You could breathe wealth in Tokyo. The oldest people around say there was not one beggar on the streets, lower classes almost disappeared, and the price of 900 sq ft (84 sq meter) apartments in Tokyo rose to several million dollars at today's value. The Japanese had money and spent their time going from one party to another and traveling all over the world with brand-new cameras produced by their own country. Tokyo became the city with the highest GDP in the world, ahead of Paris and New York, as it is today.

But it all began to collapse in the early 1990s when the stock exchange started to plummet. In 1992, the GDP began to drop too, wages decreased, foreign investors lost confidence, and Japan entered a crisis. This crisis situation gave way to a phenomenon little known in advanced societies: deflation. Toward the end of the 1980s, a beer cost 500 yen in the center of Tokyo and today it still costs around 500 yen. The price of houses also started to come down and kept coming down for 16 years in the Tokyo area. In 2006, real estate prices rose again for the first time.

THE CRISIS OF THE NINTIES

The last 50 years in Japan have been marked by two economic booms and one deep crisis: the Izanagi at the end of the 1960s, the Heisei at the end of the 1980s, and the great crisis of the 1990s. Let's look in more detail at what happened during that crisis and at the current slow economic recovery. At present, Japan is trying hard to keep up with globalization and a fast-changing world. The problem is that the rate of growth is very slow and people still feel pessimistic after a decade of crisis. Therefore, domestic consumption is at rock bottom.

During the Izanagi period, exports were the basis for economic growth. In contrast, the Heisei was based mainly on a spectacular increase in domestic consumption, because the Japanese believed that they earned good wages and had lots of extra money (disposable income) and therefore wished to live better. This increase in domestic consumption forced Japan to import a lot and to process and create new technologies in order to sell them to the Japanese, who were eager to satisfy their craving for consumption. Everything worked fine while the Heisei lasted—wages kept rising, demand increased, companies grew. A colleague, overcome by emotion, told me how, at the end of the 1980s, his wages were raised annually, the company paid the rent on his house, and they hired new people every few months. During the 1990s, they had trouble firing people, and they even offered employees fresh fruit every morning for breakfast.

Things unraveled very quickly at the beginning of the 1990s when certain movements in the stock market started to shake confidence in large corporations, which had a lot of debt at the time. Wages stopped rising, and this brought about a decrease in domestic consumption, resulting in a total imbalance in trade. In 1992, Japan already had a supply excess, and the equilibrium was not restored by demand until 2005. Another of the main reasons for the crisis is that Japan had maintained its protectionist policies, not allowing the free entry of foreign capital, a strategy that had worked very well during the Cold War. Japan's traditional methods for managing its economy had a very negative effect, just as new rules were starting to prevail in the globalizing world.

RECOVERING FROM THE CRISIS

In the year 2000 certain laws changed and the doors to foreign companies were finally opened. Capital from American investment banks (and from other countries) started to flow in, and in 2001 Japan began to pull through. During the crisis years, wages kept going down, interest rates dropped until they reached zero point something percent, and the excess in supply provoked a never-ending fall in prices.

The decline in interest rates and the new measures taken to help the Japanese market open itself to the globalizing world seemed to produce the desired effect. In 2001, the GDP grew by 0.1 percent, and the percentage kept rising until it reached 2.7 percent in 2007. At present, the GDP is growing at an annual rate of between 0 and 3 percent, unemployment is around 4 percent, company profits have increased, and laws have been introduced to help create new companies to the point that, right now, you can set up a company in Japan with an initial investment of only 1 yen. But the Lehman Shock crisis affected Japan a lot, making Japanese companies, the government, and the people despair of real economic recovery. Some say that Japan has entered a chronic economic crisis it cannot recover from, but the Japanese people have learned to live happily with it.

JAPAN TODAY

It does appear, however, that ominous clouds are undermining the confidence of the Japanese. Wages are still falling, and they have fallen more than an average of 10 percent since 1997. The average Japanese wage right now is about $2,700 a month, although in Tokyo it's much higher and is now around $4,200 a month. These are relatively low wages compared with a few years ago, and therefore people are still reluctant to spend. The level of public anxiety continues to grow and the index of consumer confidence is collapsing. The current Japanese economy helps companies but not people. As a result, the distribution of wealth is getting out of balance for the first time in decades, and citizens no longer trust their government or the pension system. The population is growing old very rapidly, and the government doesn't have a specific plan to solve this problem. Moreover, Japan is more in debt than ever before.

To conclude, here are some economic data for Tokyo, the city where I've lived for six years and which never stops impressing me. Tokyo has more technology companies than Silicon Valley, the GDP in the Tokyo area is higher than in the whole of Spain, and it is the city with the largest number of Fortune 500 companies in the world. In Tokyo, there are 52 companies in the ranking, ahead of Paris with 27 and New York with 24. As you can see, the Japanese economy is growing, but there are certain trouble spots that have yet to be solved.

JAPANESE AGRICULTURE

Japan is an archipelago with a surface area equivalent to Montana's. The problem is that because of its volcanic origin it's almost entirely covered by mountains, while plains are scarce. Only 15 percent of Japan can be used for farming.

Nevertheless, the Japanese are very efficient, and they're able to obtain a surplus of rice, which they export to much larger countries like China or the United States. There has been a strong rice tradition for centuries; they've been cultivating it for more than 2,000 years. It's one of the staples in their diet, the equivalent of potatoes or bread for us. Moreover, rice is used to make all sorts of other foods: liquor, cakes, sweet things, snacks, etc.

Rice is one of the only foods the Japanese are able to overproduce. Everything else is imported from Australia, the United States, and China.

THE INVISIBLE HAND IN JAPAN

Japanese people work selflessly for their community, their company, and their country. According to Adam Smith's classic metaphor, when an individual pursues his self-interest, an invisible hand will automatically help with the interests of all society. This metaphor is strictly followed in individualistic societies like the United States, where most people do things for their own benefit, eventually bringing prosperity to consumers and society. In Japan, on the other hand, this metaphor applies in the opposite direction. The Japanese give their utmost in their work in order to serve consumers and society. In this way, they automatically obtain benefits for the society and achieve their individual aims.

Both visions are equally valid: individualism focused on personal interest, automatically obtaining benefits for society and consumers; or, on the other hand, giving everything to society and your company and, thus, automatically obtaining personal benefits.

MY PERSONAL EXPERIENCE

In my experience, one of the advantages of the Japanese system is that when I go to a shop or a restaurant I always feel very well taken care of. Customers are treated like gods; you feel loved by the salesclerks. Whenever you go into a Japanese shop, they will welcome you with the shout "Irasshaimase!" and when you leave, whether you have bought something or not, they will send you off with a bow.

An extreme example of this special treatment and care for other people was the day I went to a post office 10 minutes before they opened. I sat on the steps at the entrance. The staff were getting the office ready to open, but two minutes later I noticed five of them looking at me and talking among themselves. Suddenly, one of them comes out, bows, welcomes me, points at the piece of paper I'm holding, and tells me it's a special delivery paper and I can go to a sort of 24-hour office hidden at the back of the building. I had no idea my paper was special, but inside the office they had worried about me, checked what I was holding from a distance, conferred, and, realizing I could use the 24-hour office, decided to help me. They took me to the office through a back door and helped me until I got my package. At the end, they saw me to the door and bowed to say goodbye.

This kind of thing can happen to you every day in Japan. It's a consequence of the Japanese invisible hand that helps you have an easier life and with which you help others have a better life. Moreover, it also benefits companies and the Japanese economy in general.

> "In Japan, people give their utmost in their work in order to serve consumers and society. Thus, they automatically obtain their own personal benefits and they achieve collective aims."

KAIZEN: CONSTANT IMPROVEMENT

KAIZEN

Kaizen literally means "a change for the better" and is used in Japanese business culture to express the need to improve constantly, to do things the best you can, using the fewest resources and creating the highest value.

Kaizen literally means "a change for the better." This word is normally used in Japanese business culture to express the need to improve constantly, to do things the best you can, using the fewest resources and creating the highest value.

To understand the real meaning of the word *kaizen*, we must go back to the 1950s. After its defeat in World War II, Japan was virtually destroyed. The capital, Tokyo, had been bombed many times. In Okinawa, hundreds of thousands of civilians had died, Hiroshima and Nagasaki had been devastated by atomic bombs, and generally speaking, the country was in total ruin.

But thanks to American money and the Japanese character, Japan reached the summit of the world economy. During the 1950s, the War Department of the United States created a program specifically aimed at reviving Japanese industry. This program introduced new ideas about quality control as well as the concept of the Shewhart cycle.

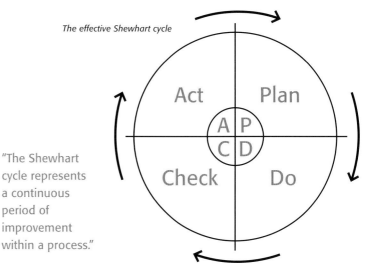

The effective Shewhart cycle

Act · Plan · Check · Do

"The Shewhart cycle represents a continuous period of improvement within a process."

THE SHEWHART CYCLE

The Shewhart cycle represents a continuous period of improvement within a process. Basically, the idea entails looking for a process that needs to be improved, preparing and planning how the problem can be solved, proceeding with what has been planned, studying whether the process has improved or worsened, determining the causes, and starting all over again.

From the Shewhart cycle and other concepts introduced from within Japanese culture, a business culture was developed that involved looking for constant improvement—the *kaizen*—trying to eliminate tasks that add cost but not value, seeking harmony in the company, learning while you work, standardizing processes, and so on.

TOYOTA, THE QUINTESSENTIAL MODEL

One of the companies that has used *kaizen* with greatest effectiveness over the last decades has been Toyota, famous for being the company with the best production system in the whole world. They are the best at manufacturing quality cars in little time and with minimum cost. To achieve this, they've spent decades applying the Toyota Production System (TPS) developed by the company's founder and his son. This system is based on the elimination of redundant tasks and a focus on correcting faults, overproduction, and excess or needless transport and waiting time. As you can see, the Toyota Production System sounds very much like "kaizen," and *kaizen* is, in fact, one of its main components.

代官山デジタルゲートビル9階
~Central Park~

Digital Garage Group

"Japanese companies
really take care of
their employees,
and the employees
really love their work
above everything else,
because it constitutes
an essential part of
their life."

THE STRUCTURE OF A JAPANESE COMPANY

The structure of Japanese companies is very rigid. There is a whole standardized system at all levels that is the rule in the majority of them.

Analysts say this system is too inflexible and leads to changes being carried out very slowly. For example, to decide about a matter X, you must fill out forms A, B, and C and hold meetings with people D, E, and F. Moreover, in Japanese society all sides must reach a consensus in order to avoid confrontation, so if someone says he doesn't agree with this or that, even if it's one against 20, notice will be taken of what he says and people will try to find a solution that satisfies everybody. This can sometimes be extremely exasperating and slow.

This system has the advantage that, even if it's slow, the decision has to be weighed over and over again, with the issue passing through many hands, until the decision that is finally arrived at is usually the best.

HIERARCHY IN A JAPANESE COMPANY

Shacho: He is the president of the company. Above the *shacho* there is only the *kaicho*—the company's main investor—although he doesn't usually work for the company and is only its owner.
Bucho: They are the heads of each department (human resources, sales, research and development, etc.). The *shocho* (managers of individual factories of the company) and *shitencho* (managers of individual branches of the company) also belong to this group.
Kacho: They are right below the *bucho* and they are the chiefs of each subsection within the departments. To become a *kacho* you normally need 15 years or more of commitment to the company.
Kakaricho: They are the supervisors in charge of assigning specific tasks to lower-level employees. Normally they are in charge of groups of five to ten people.
Kaishain: They are the lowest level employees in a company.

The usual process in Japan involves joining the company as a *kaishain* when you finish college. When a company hires you right after you've obtained your degree, their aim is to have you with them forever. That is, as soon as you leave college, you already have a permanent job for virtually your entire life.

After a few years of work and commitment, employees go from *kaishain* level to *kakaricho*, then to *kacho*, and finally, if they're lucky, at the age of 50 they can become *bucho*. If you have influential contacts and loads of money, you can even become a *shacho*.

In short, Japanese companies really take care of their employees, and the employees really love their work above everything else, because it constitutes an essential part of their life.

HOW A JAPANESE COMPANY WORKS

In Japanese culture, as we have seen, there is a sharp dividing line between people who are inside a group and those who are outside the group. Behavior when interacting with other people varies greatly depending on whether it's one of "yours" or not. A person's social position depends very much on the group he or she belongs to. For example, when you introduce yourself for the first time, you must say your name followed by your company name to indicate the group you belong to. This concept can be applied on many levels, for relationships between companies, between departments, between groups within a department, and so on.

The general rule when interacting is that you can exchange opinions, information, etc., with people from your closest group, but to communicate with people from other groups you must follow a protocol. As far as the company is concerned, this protocol involves filling out a form for your group or department head, who then passes it on to the other group or department head to see whether your request is legitimate. This process is very slow, especially when the form must climb up a few levels and then climb down. This is one of the reasons Japanese companies are slow but safe. Everybody must give his or her approval for any changes to be made and, even though this slows down the making of decisions, it's also good because it corroborates several times over that what they intend to do will really benefit the group.

The philosophy in Japanese traditional companies consists in there always being a correct way to do something following a method. Their aim is to minimize friction between groups and to keep everybody informed about what is being done. Besides, if something goes wrong or well, there is always documentary evidence, in writing, of everything that has been done.

RELATIONSHIPS IN A JAPANESE COMPANY

Let's look now at how a graduate begins work at a company. Normally, as soon as they arrive at the company every new *kohai* (worker) is assigned a *senpai* (tutor), who takes charge during the first several months of teaching the freshman the essentials of the job. This is the basic process of job training in business in Japan.

Another type of relationship is *joshi-buka* (boss-subordinate). After the training period, the subordinate is supposed to know his boss very well and, therefore, he must know what his superior wants without the need for explicit requests. This is a typical form of Japanese communication; it involves "understanding 10 from hearing 1." This means that if the boss says "we could do A," then the subordinate does A, B, and C. So, to be competent at work, you must know your boss very well. Another typical aspect of this relationship involves going out together for a beer. This is when you'll be able to complain openly about any matter. Eventually, if everything goes well, your boss will rise to the next level in the company hierarchy and so will you. Normally, the system is very strict, and you climb up levels simply on the basis of seniority. There is no risk of being surpassed by some super-clever rookie.

Japanese companies tend to have huge rooms full of cubicles and papers, and they are in complete disorder.

These two types of relationships are of the vertical kind, but there are also horizontal relationships known as *doki* ("of the same period"). The term *doki* is used to refer to all the employees who joined the company in the same year. They will all start going out for a drink together (*nomikai*) and exchange opinions, complain about what their boss said, and so on. As we've seen, it's not usual to exchange strong opinions at work, so as not to disrupt the harmony among the group. One's true opinion (*honne*) comes out at the *nomikai* (gathering in a bar to drink and talk). This kind of gathering between *doki* eases the flow of unofficial communication between departments.

AN EXAMPLE OF DECISION MAKING

Let's suppose you are part of the research and development department in a car company and you have found the way to improve the production time of component X, so you want to ask someone in the production plant if it would be possible to make changes Y and Z in the production line. The correct way to proceed is to fill out a *rishingo* (an official form) that will go to the higher levels of the department and then be sent through other departments until it reaches the production plant, where the form will go through several levels until it reaches the person in charge of the production line. The form must be read and signed by each of the people it passes through. It might take more than a month to reach the person in charge of the produc-

> "In a Japanese company, everybody must give his or her approval to any changes to be made. This is slow, but it's also good because it corroborates several times over that what they intend to do will really benefit the group."

tion line and then another month to come back with an answer. If the answer is no, we have probably wasted two months waiting. How can we get the information quickly and avoid waiting two months for nothing? The most intelligent way involves talking during a *nomikai* with some *doki* who works at the production plant and discussing the matter with him. Your contact will take care of discussing it with the people in his department, and he will ask if changes Y and Z are possible. If the answer is yes, then you know you won't be wasting your time if you send the *rishingo*. However, you must still fill out the form, since you can only use the unofficial contact technique to make sure you won't be wasting your time filling out papers, but not to initiate the actual change.

FOLLOWING THE SYSTEM

In Japanese society, everything must be in writing; to progress in your professional life you must go out drinking with your colleagues and your boss (*nomikai*); and the way to proceed inside the company is clearly defined, even in supposedly informal situations.

In Japan, there is a whole established system. Following their normal procedure, every year large companies hire hundreds of new employees just out of college, and they keep training them for years until they become essential components of the company. In other societies, we don't find such a clearly defined system; everything is more chaotic. When you start working right out of college, you don't really know what will become of you in 20 years' time, but the Japanese do know.

However, this system also has its problems, as we can see in the bad results obtained by traditional Japanese companies such as Mitsubishi. Faced with this situation, some companies are starting to look for balance, and they are adopting certain organizational models based on American (Toyota) or European (Nissan) philosophies.

TECHNOLOGY AND SCIENCE

Together with the United States, Japan is the most technologically developed country in the world. In many fields, they are way ahead of the Americans, as for instance in automobile technology, in robotics, and in microelectronics, to mention a few.

Japan has an excellent educational system. According to statistics, when the Japanese finish high school they are the best in the world in math, and they are nearly the best in arts. Japan also has world-leading universities, such as Tokyo University and Waseda University.

The Japanese are not behind in the scientific field either. They have an aerospace program, a nuclear physics laboratory that includes the world's best neutrino detector—the Super-kamiokande—and they possess several agencies and organizations for the promotion of science and technology.

Japanese companies also invest a large part of their budgets in basic research, developing new technologies that eventually invade the world, like for instance the compact disc, the result of the collaboration between Philips and Sony; the DVD, also promoted mostly by Japanese companies; the legendary Walkman; hybrid cars, etc. Just think about the devices you use every day and you'll realize how many of them have Japanese brands, and although you can't tell this from the outside, they almost certainly will have a Japanese chip inside.

"Traveling to Japan is like being transported into the future."

The Telecom Center in Odaiba, one of the most technologically advanced places in Japan, where a visit will make you feel like you've been transported into the future.

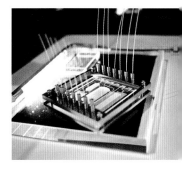

A field where they especially stand out is robotics. In Japan, there are almost more robots than in the rest of the world. A great enthusiasm for them began more than a century ago when the Japanese started creating *karakuri* (see page 56). Later, they were the first to create a humanoid robot, with a private company, Honda, leading the research. The most recent success in this field is the pet robots developed by Sony, with their famous Aibo. In Japan, robots are seen as friends and not as enemies. In movies, novels, and cartoons, the robot is almost always someone kind, who helps and has good feelings. By contrast, in our Western tradition robots are usually seen as apocalyptic enemies with chips that go crazy, so that they want to kill the human race. From this, we might conclude that the Japanese were the first to accept machines in their lives. It's amazing to see the ability elderly Japanese have with computers or remote controls, for they've had a lot more practice than us. The technological revolution started earlier in Japan than anywhere else in the world.

IS JAPAN THE FUTURE?

Japan is the country with the highest percentage of air conditioners installed in homes (over 98 percent). Watching television on the Internet or on mobile phones has been common since 2004. It's also the country with the highest rate of ownership of microwave ovens in the world. In 2005, Internet connections at 1 Gbps were already being offered at reasonable prices. They are also leaders in the penetration rate of car navigation systems. They have the most advanced mobile phone network in the world and the cheapest data transfer rates. Traveling to Japan is like being transported into the future.

During the last decade, Japan has been facing competition from other Asian countries, but they are swiftly adapting through research, delegating the manufacture of their products to China, and then exporting technology all over the world.

"In the long run the Japanese always end up obtaining the best results because they are extremely perfectionist."

An eight-wheel electric car capable of reaching 170 mph.

THE JAPANESE AUTOMOBILE INDUSTRY

In the *kaizen* section, we talked about one of the methods used by the Japanese automobile industry to achieve the best production system in the world. If we add the fact that they are world leaders in robotics, we will have the main keys to their success. The Japanese automobile industry has a long tradition and began to stand out in the 1950s during the recovery of the Japanese economy after World War II. Legend has it that when he began in a small garage in 1948, the founder of Honda predicted, "Honda will be the largest manufacturer of motorcycles in the world." A few decades later, they achieved it. Toyota, Nissan, Daihatsu, Mitsubishi, and others managed by the year 2000 to raise Japan to second place in the world in car production.

Today, Chinese competition is forcing Japanese companies to reorient their businesses so they focus more on research and development in car electronics. The efforts of the industry and the government have already made Japan the world leader in this area.

THE SECRET TO SUCCESS

The perfectionist character of the Japanese enables them to manufacture cars with extraordinary quality that are among the most perfect in the world. Over the last several years, European companies have been copying Japanese methods and obtaining similar results, although in the long run the Japanese always end up obtaining the best results because they are extremely perfectionist and they never leave anything to chance. As we've begun to appreciate, to bring about a change, no matter how small it may be, they normally need the agreement of all department members; the head is not the only one making decisions. For slightly more important changes, they need the agreement of several departments, and everybody must sign their approval. If someone objects, he is asked to set out his reasons. They analyze them and they search for a solution acceptable to all involved.

SHINNYUSHAIN-KENSHUU

This is the training period for the *shinnyushain* (new employees), when they learn about the company's internal functioning, how to behave, formal Japanese, and so on.

Things may advance very slowly this way, but they advance safely, since the entire community's agreement is sought. Japanese companies are a bit like big families where everybody collaborates, seeking what's best for their common prosperity.

THE SHINNYUSHAIN TRAINEE

The fiscal year in Japan starts in April. At the beginning of the month, the school year starts, new employees, or *shinnyushain,* join the companies, new laws go into effect, etc.

Traditional Japanese companies usually have a training period for the *shinnyushain*—known as the *shinnyushain-kenshuu*—when they learn about the company's internal functioning, how to behave, formal Japanese, and so on.

The *shinnyushain-kenshuu* is a whole tradition in Japan. At Mitsubishi Motors, for instance, the training period lasts four months, during which the trainees go to some mountains near Mount Fuji and must perform different teamwork tasks. One of these tasks involves building a Mitsubishi car almost from scratch. Even those who will be doing office work must learn how to build a car and how it works. Presumably, this will help them attach a higher value to the real essence of the company.

During my training period, I learned about the structure of my company, how to speak formal Japanese in meetings with clients, about simulating the setting up of a company, how to speak on the phone, and how to bow at the right angle depending on the client you are talking to.

WORKPLACE MANNERS

The Japanese are extremely cautious and respectful with their fellow men. That's why individual behavior and personal treatment are key features in the labor life of a company.

THE IMPORTANCE OF THE MEISHI

Meishi means "business card," and it's an extremely important element when starting a conversation with a stranger, a client, or another company. Because it is so very significant, you must treat it with the utmost care, as if it were part of the other person. This great respect for a simple object is due to the influence of Shinto (see page 18), according to which any object that belongs to us contains a bit of our souls. Mistreating or tossing a *meishi* on the table as if it were any old piece of paper is bad manners.

HOW TO TREAT THE MEISHI
- Do not fold it.
- Do not stick it in the back pocket of your pants.
- Do not write on it.
- Take it with both hands.

Meishi are an essential tool in the life of Japanese people, who attach much importance to the contacts they make and treasure their cards. Later on, if they need something from someone, they can use the card and ask for a favor, propose a deal, etc. If you have given your *meishi* to someone, you are supposed to have some *giri* regarding that person (see page 38). There are people who will contact someone via *meishi* when they haven't been in touch in years. By the same token, if you have someone's *meishi*, contacting them is not a problem. My president told me that using *meishi* is like playing cards. You collect them, and when you need something, you "play" the most suitable one for the occasion.

HONNE AND TATEMAE

In Chapter 3 we discussed the importance of *honne* and *tatemae* in Japanese relationships (see page 36). Within the company you must always use *tatemae* to avoid causing conflict. If something bothers you or you want to complain, it's always more sensible to tell one of your colleagues via *honne* outside the office, over a coffee or dinner.

SUGGESTING SOMETHING TO YOUR CO-WORKERS

If you want to ask something of your co-workers, you must always do so in a roundabout way. Your boss, for example, will always ask you indirectly to do things. If he says, "It would be convenient to get the cover of that magazine finished," it's his way of saying, "Finish that damn cover right now, we are running out of time!" At first, this indirect way of asking things is confusing, but it's something you encounter every day. Instead of asking or demanding, they always suggest.

OMIYAGE GIFTS
When you go on vacation and you come back to work, you must bring a small gift, normally something sweet, to share with your colleagues. In the office, there is usually a place where the *omiyage* is left, often near the coffee machine. The way to proceed is to go to every one of your co-workers, offering each one of the sweets and telling them where you vacationed. When you finish, you leave the box with its remaining sweets in the usual place.

Doraemon and Hello Kitty omiyage, suitable for fellow workers.

HANDLING THE MEISHI

Meishi are nothing more than business cards, but in Japan they are an extremely important element when starting a conversation with a stranger, a client, or another company. Because the *meishi* is so significant, you must treat it with the utmost care, as if it were part of the other person.

During the meishi exchange, it's very important to make a bow at the same time and to hold your card with both hands as you tender it.

THE IMPORTANCE OF NEMAWASHI

Nemawashi is an essential concept for understanding the Japanese business world. It defines the process through which decisions are made that involve changes to the company. Originally, the word *nemawashi* 根回 was used by agricultural workers when they had to transplant something: 根 "root," 回 "turn." The literal meaning is "to turn the roots," that is, to dig around the roots of the plant or tree before transplanting it. Let's examine its current meaning.

Suppose a Sony employee has the brilliant idea of eliminating a redundant chip from one of the company products. For this to happen, the process in a Western company varies depending on the procedures of each company, but the decision would probably be made through a series of proposals and meetings among the various executives of the company and their superiors. In Japan, the process is much more complex, and it's quite standardized and similar across all companies.

Before making your proposal, you must make sure that all the employees around you agree. This is the process called *nemawashi* (it's usually translated as "prior consultation"). But this consultation yields numerous advantages. If all agree with your proposal, you have an almost 100 percent chance it will be accepted, and if people don't accept your proposal, you can improve it so as to include everybody else's suggestions. Also, if your idea is a bad one, you won't make a fool of yourself since you haven't made a formal proposal. The *nemawashi* process itself will make your proposal disappear if it has little chance of success.

The Sony employee will consult all his department co-workers, and, once he has made sure his proposal is accepted by everyone, he will talk with his *kakaricho* (immediate superior). His superior will then do a *nemawashi* among the other department heads, and once they have agreed, the process will continue until the idea reaches the highest spheres at Sony. Notice how, if the *nemawashi* process fails somewhere along the line because someone is totally against it, the idea never flows to the top of the pyramid. If everyone agrees or if some modifications are introduced along the way as the idea spreads, the process continues.

Once the *nemawashi* process has been completed, the department that initiated it can make a formal proposal in a meeting, where it will obviously be accepted. They can then go on to implement the new idea/process/product/deal without losing decision-making time in the meeting, because it has all been previously decided. The *nemawashi* process thus allows people to preserve group harmony and also avoids strong disagreement, something very important for the Japanese. Everyone has to be in agreement.

The problem in all this is slowness. Japanese companies are famous for doing things well but slowly. Making decisions is very hard for them. Few changes are made, and everybody must agree, often even on insignificant matters. For example, I'm amazed when I suggest to my co-workers that we change the type size on the main page for some of our services and they look suspiciously at me and ask, "Who decided that change is needed?" And I answer, being funny, "I decided." Then they laugh, because they know me, and they look at me as if thinking, "This foreigner here has no idea about *nemawashi*." Next, I have to get all my co-workers to approve it, then I have to talk with my superior, then with my superior's superior, and if we all agree we propose the idea at a meeting with the board of directors, who already know about the proposal because my superiors have informed them through *nemawashi*. If everything comes out all right, we will be able to change the type size on the main page. This whole process may last a couple of weeks before we can get down to work. The secret is to get a jump on ourselves and start the *nemawashi* process as early as possible.

To some extent, you could view *nemawashi* as a sort of democracy taken to the extreme. But thanks to this, Japanese companies seldom make mistakes and are always taking steps forward and improving ceaselessly, if slowly. *Nemawashi* is a tool for *kaizen* (see page 64). In addition to companies, *nemawashi* process is also used in politics, something that has been criticized because it looks like matters have been decided before the official meeting.

In large Japanese corporations, change is hard to bring about. Normally, procedures such as nemawashi are followed to be able to improve things.

NEMAWASHI

To some extent, we could see *nemawashi* as a sort of democracy taken to the extreme. Thanks to this, Japanese companies seldom make mistakes and are always taking steps forward and improving ceaselessly, if slowly.

DAILY LIFE IN A JAPANESE COMPANY

I was once in a coffee shop with two co-workers, while two other co-workers were at another table and the president of our holding company was sitting at a third table. The president was the first to finish, and he passed by our table to say hello but he didn't bow. He was right above us, so it was my co-workers and I who bowed to him and made a couple of remarks. As he passed by the other table, the president didn't recognize his own employees, so he didn't even greet them. As it happens, the president dropped his wallet near the table of the employees he didn't know. One of them picked it up and took it to the president, who was at the coffee shop door. The president, seeing that a "stranger" (actually, one of his employees) had helped him recover his wallet, started making 90-degree bows (showing the highest respect). This was the first time I ever saw the president make a 90-degree bow! If he had known that the person returning his wallet was one of his own employees, he wouldn't have bowed at all, for he mustn't bend down before a lower-level employee under any circumstances. He would simply have looked surprised and said thank you. In this situation, we clearly see the role played by *uchi* and *soto* in Japanese daily life (see page 45), and it's also an example of how your level/rank in society, a company, or a group is extremely important in Japan.

A friend of mine who works for Kodansha, the largest publishing company in Japan, told me about the process they followed to close down a magazine that wasn't generating enough income. To fire the employees, they "suggested" that they look for another job several months before the department was to be eliminated. As the date of the planned closure was drawing near, Kodansha went on to suggest that employees of the magazine leave the company of their own free will. In the end, they achieved their aim. All the employees in that department left voluntarily, and no one had to be fired, thus saving all the costs this would have entailed. This is an example of employees, through their behavior, declaring their "support" for their company's problems, assuming their responsibility in the magazine's failure, and undertaking their duty—*giri* (see page 38)—to leave voluntarily so as not to damage the company any further. Doesn't their behavior seem incredible to you? If this had happened in an American or a European company, I can imagine disgruntled employees and labor unions making noise, even going on strike. This is an example of how the Japanese avoid conflict by every possible means and of the role played by the *giri* sense of duty when decisions must be made.

It's funny how, after working for more than two years with the same people every day, getting along with them wonderfully and considering them as though they were part of my family, they still bow and use formal language before asking me for anything at work. I think this might be easier to understand with an example.

Western company: After years of mutual trust and a very good atmosphere: "Hey, man, have you finished what I asked you to do two days ago? If we don't finish it today, the bosses are going to get really mad, ha, ha."
Japanese company: After years of mutual trust and a really good atmosphere (I'm giving a rather literal translation, though it may sound weird): "Excuse me for interrupting at such a busy time, Mr Hector, but regarding what I mentioned two days ago.... Do you think you might be able to finish it? (bow)"

What I wish to illustrate with this anecdote is the great difference between being in a work environment and being somewhere else in Japanese society. The very same people can act in radically different ways in different environments, and the same worker who addresses me as Mr Hector at the office will treat me as if I were his lifelong friend when we are in a restaurant.

Manners, language, and the way co-workers relate to each other are very different at work from what they are away from the office.

Saying goodbye like this would have never happened inside the company's offices. This photograph was taken outside a karaoke club, far from the work environment. That's why they felt comfortable waving their hands to say goodbye instead of using the traditional Japanese bow. The same people act very differently depending on the environment.

CHAPTER 6
JAPANESE SOCIETY AND DAILY LIFE

Young people relaxing during a break.

Japanese society is like an ant's nest.

POSITIVES AND NEGATIVES

In previous chapters we've looked at specific features of Japan that together constitute a way of living and a society completely different from ours, full of mysteries, surprises, and new things to learn. In this chapter, we will try to form a general picture of Japan and what daily life is like in one of the most advanced societies in the world, with its advantages as well as its disadvantages.

In Japan, everything works almost to perfection. People do what they're supposed to do, trains run well, everybody has a job, everybody has money to live. In fact, extreme poverty is virtually non-existent, children study (and, according to the latest OECD research, they are the second best in the world), Japanese companies are all over the planet and the Japanese economy is the third biggest in the world, their technology could be considered the most advanced in many respects, and Tokyo is the cleanest city I've seen in my life despite being the largest urban area in the world. If you go walking in the most prominent districts of the capital at night, you realize that people enjoy life. Tokyo, like New York, is known as a city that never sleeps.

At first glance, it seems a perfect place. How have the Japanese achieved this? What are the disadvantages? When you begin to meet Japanese people, to talk with them, and they tell you that they work 13, 14, or even more hours a day because they want their company to do well, you realize that something's wrong. Or is it? In Japan, there is a culture of admiration for companies. When people introduce themselves, they often say the name of the company they work for first and then their own name. Their company is the most important thing. You must give everything for your community and you must follow their rules to the letter. In short, the Japanese do what they must do without hesitation.

When they work for a company, nobody ever complains, nobody creates something new for fear of getting into trouble, and people hardly ever go on strike. By the way, the "Japanese-style strike" is an urban legend. There is no such thing. Company structure is very rigid, and everything must be done following written rules. Still, thanks to this system, there are usually no conflicts because the Japanese avoid direct confrontation above all. Employees simply go to work every day, don't complain, arrive punctually, and never leave on time. They usually work overtime,

> "The Japanese avoid direct confrontation above all. Employees simply go to work every day, don't complain, arrive punctually, and never leave on time. They usually work overtime."

and this becomes more an obligation than an option. In fact, a true "Japanese-style strike" might entail not working overtime.

One of their favorite ways to complain or to criticize some aspects of their company is when they are out drinking at a *nomikai*. When you go out for a drink or for dinner with your colleagues and superiors, once you are inside the bar you are officially drunk. It doesn't matter if you drink water or wine, you can say almost anything you want because everybody is in a "party mood." This is the time to express your *honne* (see page 36).

Normally, the Japanese consume a lot of beer and end up picking on their boss right to his face. It's a good system to deal with stress. What I'm telling you is absolutely normal, however much it may surprise you. There is another unwritten rule. On the following day you must not talk about anything that happened the previous night. That's why nothing will change. The boss will keep on doing what he must do, as usual, and the workers will too, even if there are things they don't like. Making changes in Japan is difficult. Everything is slow, there is a lot of paperwork, everybody must agree, and there are tons of meetings. But when things are done, they usually work to perfection—everything goes well.

How do you do things? Fast and well? Fast and poorly? Slow and well (Japan)? Slow and poorly? The Japanese usually say they must work overtime to help the economy. They must help Japan come out of the crisis and give everything for their country and their company. It becomes a kind of obsession.

The conclusion is that in Japan no one deviates from the river's course, no one rocks the boat, bureaucracy is very rigid, and everybody strictly follows the rules. When everything works to perfection, as usual, it's impressive, but there are always things that can be improved. Yet, for fear of being rejected by society or the company, no one does anything to change things. There are many problems, like overwork, child prostitution, the yakuza, and suicide, just to mention a few examples. Almost nobody says or does anything. They act as if nothing happened, as if it were normal. They merely follow the set path, without making life difficult for themselves. Some anthropologists say the Japanese are like ants, because they always follow the same steps in an organized way and everything generally goes off without mishap. The great problem is that, if a big stone falls on the ant's nest, it will bring total chaos.

"Making changes in Japan is difficult. Everything is slow, there is a lot of paperwork, everybody must agree, and there are tons of meetings. But when things are done, they usually work to perfection—everything goes well."

SAFETY IN JAPAN

Japan is one of the most advanced countries with the lowest crime rates in the world. In the Land of the Rising Sun, 1.3 thefts are committed per 100,000 inhabitants, whereas in the United States the rate is 233 per 100,000. The difference is incredible!

Walking around any street in Tokyo and at any time of day or night is completely safe. One of the things we foreigners living here like best is the feeling of security you have when you go about the big city. Here, I don't have to worry if I leave my mobile phone and wallet on the table in a coffee shop while I go to the bathroom, because I know nobody will touch them. Moreover, nobody uses PIN numbers in mobile phones. They come deactivated by default when you buy one. They are not necessary because theft of mobile phones is virtually non-existent.

WHY IS THERE SO LITTLE CRIME?

Some of the reasons for the low crime rate are legislation restricting the sale and use of firearms, severe penalties for committing a crime, and not much trafficking in drugs, so little crime is generated by that problem. However, deep down, the lack of crime is due to a great extent to the Japanese people's way of thinking. In Chapter 3 we spoke of the importance of groups, and how the Japanese are not individualists but act in a group and think as such. Accordingly, if a Japanese person commits a crime, he will feel guilty and ashamed for having done this to his group. In Western society, we tend to look out for ourselves, and that might be one of the reasons why petty theft is so common in America and Europe. The thief doesn't care about his society's reputation. What matters to him is getting a bit of money for his own benefit.

A low crime rate doesn't mean that everything isn't well monitored and that there aren't policemen everywhere. What strikes you is the number of small *koban* (police buildings) secreted everywhere in the country. In every *koban* there are two or three cops ready in case you need them. The truth is, they don't have much serious work to do, and they are almost always giving directions to passersby in the area. If you get lost walking around Osaka or Tokyo, one of the simplest ways to get back on the right track is to go to a *koban* for help.

"In Japan, I don't have to worry if I leave my mobile phone and wallet on the table in a coffee shop while I go to the bathroom, because I know nobody will touch them."

Japanese woman asleep with her handbag open and no fear of being robbed.

This is a typical koban. They are very easy to recognize because they have the same logo all over the country.

LIFE OF A FAMILY

The importance of ancestors, respect for elders, the power of men, the eldest brother becoming the head of the family, the *samurai*, the youngest son driven to the point of killing his older brother in order to gain power, the spirits of the ancestors coming back to visit the family during the Obon festival, celebrated every summer to honor the dead.... These would be the essential elements needed to portray the classic Japanese family of tradition. The whole family—three generations—used to live under the same roof, but this is now impossible due to the high cost of housing. Families and clans would merge, and even an entire village could become a single family unit. To achieve these unions between families, *omiai*, or arranged marriage (see page 39) was one of the most common tools.

Nowadays, families are much more fragmented, and it's difficult to have more than the basic family unit under the same roof. In most cases, the mother is still in charge of running the household and the father brings in the money. Women in this country seem to like this system and they don't usually complain. The typical Japanese family lives in a big city, in either the Tokyo-Yokohama-Chiba or Kyoto-Osaka-Kobe conurbations (50 percent of the population of Japan lives in these two city conglomerates), with all that goes with it.

Even though at first family life in such large cities might seem difficult, the Japanese urban model does facilitate things somewhat. Normally, people live in houses (not apartments) that spread across large residential areas built around train stations. In these areas, there is usually a hospital, a school, a high school, and even a college or university campus, making family life easier. If you have ever watched *Doraemon* or *Shin-chan*, you probably have some idea of what these residential areas look like. The one who has to make the greatest effort is the father, since most companies are located in the city center or in outlying industrial parks. He will normally have to travel between 40 and 80 minutes to go to work.

> **"The daily life of a family is determined by the father's work addiction level."**

Usually, the family unit—father, mother, and one or two children—lives under the same roof. In the morning, they all breakfast together on *miso* soup, rice, and some fish. The father and the mother go to work while the children go to school. The children eat lunch at school in special dining rooms, where they themselves clear the tables and do the cleaning up. In the afternoon, after-school activities and especially homework are very common. School is extremely competitive and parents always want their children to be the best. The mother will probably get home early and she will have dinner with the children, then they will get into the *ofuro* together (see page 50) before going to bed. Normally, the father is the bigger earner, and he almost always works till late, coming home when the children are already asleep. The fact that the father works long hours is looked on favorably, and when he finishes work he usually goes out for dinner and drinks with his workmates. At these dinners in *izakayas*, he and his colleagues exchange opinions and

> **"In most cases nowadays, the mother is still in charge of running the household and the father brings in the money."**

discuss company problems, speaking in the *honne* manner (see page 36), and very often they also talk about sorrows or worries in their private lives.

The man of the house arrives home at around midnight, with the last trains. Back home, his wife and a good *ofuro* are waiting for him, and then off to bed to start all over again with renewed energy the following day. We might conclude that the daily life of a family is determined by the father's work addiction level, which in most cases is a lot higher than you might imagine.

DIARY OF A FAMILY

On weekdays: The father works overtime almost every day, so he arrives home very late with hardly any time to see the children. The mother takes the kids to school in the morning and then does some *arubaito* work (part-time) to earn extra money.
On weekends: Trips to visit the grandparents, on either the father's or the mother's side. Or family trips to a famous *onsen* (spa) or popular tourist spot.

Retired women enjoying a day at the park.

LONGEVITY

The Japanese are the longest lived people on earth. The life expectancy for men is around 80 years and for women is 85. In Okinawa prefecture, the life expectancy for women reaches 90 years of age. Moreover, Japan holds the world record for being the country with the highest percentage of centenarians.

The Japanese are stressed by work, there are lots of smokers, and they are very heavy drinkers, but the key seems to be their diet. They eat very little fat and a lot of fish and seaweed, and they drink lots of green tea, which contains antioxidants. In addition, they don't usually stuff themselves but eat just enough to fill their stomachs without overeating. For instance, the fixed-price restaurants in business areas usually serve no desserts. Besides lengthening their lives, this good diet means there are very few obese Japanese, and almost everyone has a nice figure, even though they aren't very tall.

The problem is that, if in addition to this information we bear in mind that their birth rate is one of the lowest in the world, with only 1.3 births per couple, the population of Japan is in danger. In fact, the year 2006 was the first in Japan's modern history to register a fall in population. This trend is expected to continue. In a few years, one in every five Japanese will be over 60 years old and this will have very serious economic consequences. The number of young workers won't be enough to support the population pyramid. Exacerbating this, Japan is a country quite closed to immigration, whereas immigrants could be the solution to this problem.

Another fundamental aspect of this problem is that, at their present working pace in Japanese companies, where overtime is the norm every day, people have little time to raise children. More and more couples are deciding not to have children or to

Life expectancy in Japan is higher than any other country.

have one child at most. Business, the government, society, and the system in general do not provide any incentives to have families.

The consequences of the inversion of the population pyramid are becoming increasingly obvious. Many hospitals and social services can't cope, many pensions are insufficient for retirement, and many people are still working at 70, 75, or even 80 years old. And, all in all, the government does only the minimum for the system not to collapse like a house of cards.

Many companies are delaying the age of retirement, but at the same time young people, seeing the poor prospects in pension schemes, are refusing to pay into them. In short, enjoying good health is a plus for the people in the country but it's also a double-edged sword for the economy. The Japanese will have to make changes and keep close watch on how they go so as to not slip further as an economy.

LIFE OF A RETIREE

Japanese people consider work the essence of their lives. Perhaps that's the reason they are famous for being such hard workers. They always seek perfection in everything they do, and they give everything for their company, not so much to climb the corporate ladder as for their own satisfaction. That's why, when they retire, many people look for another, easier job so as not to feel useless and so their life still has meaning. On the other hand, people in high positions hold on to them and keep working until virtually the end of their days. Many who reach retirement age keep working at the same company but in a more relaxed way, simply attending some company meetings, socializing, and taking care of their families. In other societies, if a 70-year-old man continued working at his company, it would not be considered proper or correct, but in Japan the opposite is true. For the Japanese, it's like having access to a treasure trove of knowledge, who, though he may not perform like a 25-year-old man, can give advice based on a lifetime of experience.

The proportion of retirees in Japan is the highest in the world and keeps growing every year. This is the most serious problem the country faces in the twenty-first century, and it's a steady

> "Age in Japan is directly proportional to respect, and young people must address their elders in very formal language."

topic of debate in politics and daily life. Supporting the pension system with a rapidly aging population is not easy.

Japanese retirees are highly respected. Age in Japan is directly proportional to respect, and young people must address their elders in very formal language. The older you are, the more money you earn and the better position you hold in a company. From the age of 50 on, everybody usually has a responsible position where no big effort is required. The most difficult jobs are left for young people, who are supposed to work hard if they want to be respected in the future.

DIARY OF A RETIREE

On weekdays: In the afternoon, they go visit their family businesses or their lifelong companies, attend some meetings, and then have dinner with company colleagues. As to retired women, they enjoy home life, walk around the neighborhood, and so on.
On weekends: Family life.

THE DELIGHTS OF JAPANESE CUISINE

The Japanese are authentic gourmets. They are very demanding about food, and when they travel they always think more about tasting some local dish than visiting monuments or museums. Japanese travel guides look more like a catalog of restaurants than anything else.

On Japanese television, there are lots of programs that just show people eating while they talk about how good or bad everything is. In other words, these are food shows about *eating* food, not preparing it. Even on programs that have nothing to do with food, the characters may suddenly go into a restaurant and sit down to eat. And when a restaurant appears on a television show, it garners a great deal of prestige. There are also many books, guides, and magazines on food and dining. Some books go into such detail they only focus on a small district in some large Japanese city, analyzing each and every one of its restaurants.

Around the world, *sushi* is Japan's most famous dish. But, as with all things "typical," people tend to think that's the only thing Japanese eat, just as they think Spanish people eat paella every day. If you travel to Japan, try sampling a bit of every sort of food and don't be too intimidated to go into any restaurant you come across. The less well promoted restaurants are usually the best, but we travelers, not being in the know, tend to be timid and opt for safe bets.

Tokyo is the city with the biggest accumulation of Michelin stars, and it's widely considered the city with the best restaurants in the world. Japan also has the most restaurants per capita in the world.

In Japan, people eat out a lot, and dining out is relatively inexpensive. In America as in Europe, shopping at a supermarket and preparing dinner at home can be much more economical than dining at a decent restaurant with average prices, whereas in Japan there isn't such a big difference. Products in supermarkets are slightly more expensive than in other countries, but the food in restaurants is cheaper. As a consequence, many people, especially in large cities, almost always end up eating out. So too, restaurants work well, and their numbers keep increasing. However, the profit margins in this kind of business tend to be a lot smaller than in other countries.

Another characteristic of Japanese restaurants is their specialization. There are restaurants specialized in almost any kind of dish, and some of them only serve the dish in which they specialize, for instance, only *takoyaki* or only *gyoza*. Consumers like this because, in their eyes, *sushi* prepared in a restaurant that serves only *sushi* has to be better there than in a restaurant where many other dishes are served.

Finally, typical of some Japanese restaurants is that they are not designed for people to sit there eating for a long time. The most common example is *ramen* restaurants where they start frowning at you if you linger for more than 20 minutes. Usually, though, these are very small restaurants that barely fit 10–15 people, and therefore they really depend on turning over the largest number possible in the shortest time. Customers must rotate quickly for their business to work.

The two basic ingredients in the diet of all the Japanese are white rice and *miso* soup. They are almost always included in fixed-price menus in traditional restaurants. During the work week, people usually have fish, rice, and *miso* soup for breakfast. For lunch, the usual thing is to buy a *bento*—a ready-made boxed lunch—and eat it in your office or go to a fast-food restaurant for *ramen* or some type of *donburi*, a rice bowl dish. At night, dinner is more elaborate, as are meals on weekends.

BENTO
Ready-made lunch boxes sold at specialized stores and 24-hour convenience stores.

TEMPURA
Fish, shrimp, and vegetables in a special batter

SUSHI
Raw fish on rice or rolled with *nori* seaweed and rice

SASHIMI
Raw fish

SOBA
Thin spaghetti that can be served in thousands of different ways: cold, hot, in soup, in salad, etc.

HIYASHI CHUKA
A typical summer dish. Chinese noodles with cucumber, ham, and tomato

RAMEN
Noodles prepared in different soups depending on the Japanese region

UNAGI
Eel in a special sauce

UDON
Like *soba* but thicker spaghetti, also cooked in many different ways. For example, *sumo* wrestlers usually eat *chanko*, a sort of stew with lots of meat and vegetables and *udon* as the main ingredient.

YAKITORI
Skewered meat or vegetables

DONBURI (DON)
This means it's served on rice. Thus, *katsu-don* is pork on rice, *gyu-don* is veal on rice, *una-don* is eel on rice, and so on.

YAKI-NIKU
Grilled meat

GYOZA
Meat dumplings that originated in China, usually eaten with *ramen*

ONIGIRI
Rice balls

SAKE, AWAMORI, AND SHOCHU

Sake is probably one of the most internationally recognized Japanese words, and its most accepted meaning is "Japanese clear spirits made from rice." But when you arrive in Japan, you realize that *sake* means "alcoholic drink" in general. Thus, if you drink beer, you are drinking *sake*; if you drink whiskey, you are drinking *sake*; and if you drink rum, you are drinking *sake*. So, when we order *sake* in a Japanese restaurant outside Japan, what is the specific name for the drink they serve us? It will probably be *nihonshu*, which is the Japanese word used to refer to the alcoholic beverage obtained from rice. But we could also be drinking *shochu*, another drink with a very similar appearance that is made from sweet potato, barley, or rice depending on the distillery and the area where it's produced. Or we could be drinking *awamori*, an Okinawa drink that looks like *shochu* but is distilled using Thai techniques. The fact is, there isn't only one kind of *sake* in Japan. There are hundreds of varieties of *nihonshu*, *shochu*, and other drinks in a tradition that stretches back thousands of years. If you come to Japan and want to make a somewhat better impression than the typical tourist, try this: when you go to a restaurant, instead of ordering *sake*, stick to the words *nihonshu* or *shochu*, and savor it.

For example, a good Japanese dessert involves drinking a couple of shot glasses of warm *nihonshu*. In the past, they used the technique of warming *nihonshu* when it was of low quality to hide its flavor. Over time, warming the liquor has become customary, and there are even specific words to indicate the temperature you prefer. If you ask for *atsukan*, they will serve it at about 120 °F (50 °C); if you ask for *nurukan*, it will be at about 105 °F (40 °C); and if you don't want it warm, ask for *hiya*. If you pull out the words *atsukan* or *nurukan* in a shabby restaurant full of old people, you'll be a big success!

Nihonshu is used in Shinto purification rituals. It's considered the drink of gods, and even children drink it in religious rituals and in special celebrations. We've also seen that it is a favorite drink of *tanuki* (see page 48).

"When you arrive in Japan, you realize that *sake* means 'alcoholic drink' in general. Thus, if you drink beer, you are drinking *sake*; if you drink whiskey, you are drinking *sake*; and if you drink rum, you are drinking *sake*."

Alcohol smooths social relations in Japan.

The president and shareholders of my company breaking a cask of sake known as taru sake to celebrate the arrival of the New Year.

PERSONAL RELATIONSHIPS IN JAPAN

To summarize a little what I've been saying in these last chapters and illustrate how different we are from the Japanese, let's imagine a situation in which five Westerners meet for the first time and, by way of comparison, how five Japanese people would behave in the same situation.

THE FIVE WESTERNERS

They shake hands as soon as they meet and begin a conversation. The word *no* will be heard as many times as the word *yes*, or more. Instead of respecting "rank," after no time at all a 25-year-old guy will address a 40-year-old man by his first name. People will start to clap their counterparts on the back or touch their arm or shoulder to reinforce the points they're making. They'll talk loudly and a lot, and they'll emphasize every idea by gesticulating broadly. Most likely, after a while they will be all taking part in a lively discussion, talking at the top of their lungs, laughing, and so on.

THE FIVE JAPANESE PEOPLE

When they first meet, silence and a slight tension invades the participants for a few seconds, until one of them introduces himself, offering his *meishi* (business card) to the others. The *meishi* exchange (see page 69), including bows and some questions, will take about five minutes. When the five people have exchanged their cards, given the name of the company they work for, stated their position in it, and said their own name, they will feel comfortable enough to talk. The secret is that after the exchange ritual all those present know exactly who is the one with the most experience, who has the highest rank, and who works for the best company. Once they know the position held by everybody present, they also know what language register they must use. Japanese is a language with many levels of usage, and speaking in the appropriate register for the person or people you are addressing is very important.

They will talk slowly, with long pauses, and they will make sure everybody agrees with what they are saying. During the conversation, hearing the word *no* is almost unimaginable. They will seldom argue, and they will do all they can so that everyone is in agreement. If someone wants to introduce a different point of view, he will always do so in the most indirect possible way, without disrupting the harmony.

People will apologize all the time during the conversation, they will maintain their distance, and they will speak without moving their hands much. They will always show a friendly smile, but they will try not to roar with laughter. Once formal introductions have been made and the conversation has begun, they will use *sake* to relax the tension and to personalize their relationship.

> "When some Japanese men meet for the first time, silence and a slight tension invades those present for a few seconds, until one of them introduces himself, offering his *meishi* to the others."

Once formal introductions have been made and conversation has begun, the Japanese use sake to relax the tension and to personalize their relationship.

JAPAN'S TRAIN CULTURE

Japan has the best railway network in the world in all respects: modernity, frequency, number of stations, punctuality, etc. The only problem is that traveling by train is rather expensive, although the excellent service makes up for this. Railroad tracks extend to the most remote places in the country and their on-time percentage is unbelievably high.

The rail sector has been privatized and there are many train companies competing with one another. The most important is JR (Japanese Rail), which has the Shinkansen lines (the famous Japanese bullet train), the railway system with the highest average speed in the world at more than 140 mph. However, the most impressive thing is seeing how high-speed trains arrive in and leave Tokyo Station almost every minute, bound for different places in the country. Furthermore, the average delay for Shinkansen trains over the last 20 years is less than 54 seconds.

The Japanese bullet train (Shinkansen) is famous for its punctuality. Its average delay over the last 20 years is less than 54 seconds.

THE MAIN LINES

JR tracks in Tokyo usually run one or two levels above the ground. Their most famous line is the Yamanote, which forms a circuit and is characteristically represented as a circle on maps and diagrams. The Yamanote is very convenient for moving around the capital because it has stations in most important districts (Ueno, Akihabara, Shinagawa, Shibuya, Shinjuku). The trains on this line run every two minutes and carry over four million people a day, the same number of commuters carried in one day by all New York subway lines put together. That is, a single line with 29 stations is used by the same number of people as are the 26 lines and 468 stations in New York City. This should give you an idea about frequency, punctuality, efficiency, and use of trains in Japan.

Another of the leading companies is Tokyo Metro, run by the city council and with all its lines underground. At most stations you can choose between JR or Tokyo Metro. It all depends on whether you prefer traveling among the buildings and enjoying the view or going on the subway, underground.

There are other, minor companies, such as Disneyland Resort Tokyo or the Monorail line that goes over buildings and over the sea to the artificial islands in Tokyo Bay.

WHERE DOES IT GET CROWDED?

If Yamanote is the line carrying the most passengers a day in the world, Shinjuku Station is the world's busiest station. An average of 3.5 million people use it every day and it has approximately 200 different exits. If you take the wrong exit, you might get out more than a half mile from where you intended.

Most Japanese people are city dwellers: more than 50 percent of the population lives in the Kanto and Kansai regions (the Kanto region includes Tokyo). In these urban areas, the train is the axis of all activity. The average Japanese person spends an average of two hours a day commuting by train, meaning that some people reside even more than two hours away from work. The key to enduring this lifestyle is having comfortable and punctual trains and finding ways to entertain oneself during the journey. People sleep, read *manga*, newspapers, or books, play video games on portable consoles, listen to music, surf the Internet on their mobile phones, send emails, and so on. Trains, you might say, become a second home.

> "Trains on the Yamanote Line run every two minutes and carry over four million people a day, the same number of commuters carried by all New York subway lines in one day put together."

URBAN LEGENDS

EVERYTHING IS EXTREMELY EXPENSIVE

False. Maybe the difference was greater in the 1990s but today prices are comparable to those in America's biggest cities or in any major capital city in Europe. Aside from transport, which certainly is rather expensive, everything is affordable and sometimes even cheaper. For instance, everyday restaurants are cheaper than in San Francisco or New York. The three most expensive things in Japan are transport, housing, and education.

EVERYBODY READS MANGA

False. There is a myth about all Japanese people always reading comics. It's true that you sometimes see old people reading superhero comics in the subway or kids reading the adventures of Naruto Uzumaki, but this doesn't mean they are all *manga* fans. However, the comic phenomenon is indeed much stronger here than anywhere else in the world. There are entire buildings full of *manga* stores.

THEY ALL PLAY VIDEO GAMES

False. While it's true that the legendary Nintendo and Sega are Japanese, and most video game companies are also Japanese, and there is a huge domestic market, this doesn't mean that all Japanese are obsessed with the games and are always playing them. When they do play, they have very different tastes in subject matter and have a fondness for the role-playing ones as well as the giant robot Gundam type.

WHY DO THE JAPANESE COMMIT SUICIDE?

Japan has the highest rate of suicide of all advanced countries and the fourth highest rate of suicide among all countries. Why? Answering this question isn't easy, but let's look into some of the possible reasons.

First, we have to understand a little better the way the Japanese think. The religion that most influences people's everyday behavior in Japan is Shinto (see page 18). You might say that according to Shinto you must do the "right" thing at all times and you must follow the "set path." Going back to the *samurai* era, if a *samurai* warrior failed on a very important mission, he would feel, when he faced his superior again, that he hadn't done his duty and so would commit suicide. Something of this mentality has survived in our times.

Today, if the father of a family cannot repay a loan or cover the cost of his son's or daughter's wedding, he may resort to suicide in order for them to receive the money from his life insurance. On the other hand, if you work for a company and you make a very serious mistake that may cost them millions, one of the options taken by many Japanese is suicide. For young people, suicide can come after failing an important exam, usually the one that is taken to go to college. These appear to be the most common reasons the Japanese commit suicide. It's almost always when a person cannot do what he or she should have done. This explanation may be summed up with the concept of "social pressure," which is commonly used to describe the situation in Japan.

SUICIDE GROUNDS

The favorite spot for the Japanese to commit suicide is Tokyo's railroad or subway tracks. Just as in the United States, where the Golden Gate Bridge is one of the most popular places to commit suicide, in Japan it's the famous Chuo Line, the same one that goes right through the heart of Tokyo and is used by more than 20 million Japanese every day.

This practice results in huge losses to the train companies, so if investigators identify the suicide victim, it could mean ruin for his or her family. It is said that you have to pay fines of up to 100 million yen (about one million dollars) to cover the cost of cleaning services and delays across all the lines.

> "Today, if the father of a family cannot repay a loan or cover the cost of his son's or daughter's wedding, he may resort to suicide in order for them to receive the money from his life insurance."

Apparently, the Chuo Line is ideal for suicide because trains go very fast inside the city (at more than 60 mph) and there's little visibility, which makes it more likely that the train driver won't be able to apply the brakes in time. Another factor is that the line is run by the state, and therefore families of suicide victims pay smaller fines. That is, it's the line that guarantees a cleaner and cheaper suicide. Another reason is the "call effect." Appearing in the media as the site with the highest number of suicides gives it greater appeal, similar to what happens with the Golden Gate Bridge in San Francisco.

Leaving aside these curious facts, for the last few years the number of suicides has been so high it has started to affect population growth and, consequently, the economy. The government is now becoming aware of the problem and is starting to take steps. We will see if the situation improves in the future.

The Chuo Line is famous for the high number of suicides committed there by people jumping in front of oncoming trains.

EVERYTHING IS EXTREMELY CLEAN

False. Although, generally speaking, everything is neat and tidy and you don't see garbage on the ground, there are areas where things look old and neglected. Very often they don't replace old things but keep using them side by side with new ones. It's a good philosophy but it can make houses and streetscapes look pretty weird.

EVERYBODY SPEAKS ENGLISH

False. Nothing could be further from the truth. Does everybody speak English in Europe? Well, in Japan they don't either. In addition to the difficulty we Westerners have studying a foreign language, the Japanese have the added difficulty of learning a new writing system, completely new vocabulary, and totally different pronunciation rules. Still, almost everybody can say "hello," "goodbye," and a handful of other words.

Prices in Japan are not as high as one would expect. In this photograph, you can see that half a liter of Coca Cola costs 100 yen, which at the current exchange rate would be about a dollar.

CHAPTER 7
JAPAN TODAY

Japanese city architecture is both chaotic and ordered with unique aesthetics.

JAPANESE CITIES AND ARCHITECTURE

CITY STRUCTURE

The first-time visitor to Japan, accustomed to the symmetry and order of our European cities, might find Japan to be chaotic in the way its cities are structured. Cities generally have a downtown area with narrower and more complex streets than on the outskirts where parks and residential zones in blocks are the norm. Japanese cities don't have a defined center. Instead, there are tall buildings mixed with small cottages. Cities in Japan are a kind of chaos, a sort of expanding symmetry, which in the case of Tokyo approaches infinite proportions. Is beauty to be found in chaos or in order? Or perhaps in an order within chaos?

The Tokyo urban district is a kind of ameba of colossal dimensions where nearly 40 million people live. In the West, cities were formerly built around churches, so that we have ended up with cities whose activity is centered on a few main streets and their adjoining squares. In Japan, the city center wasn't a sacred place. Shintoist and Buddhist temples tend to be near parks or neighboring areas, and normally in wooded zones. But the Japanese did create a kind of square or central street where the town's market was located. In the big cities, a castle was situated in the center, or in the case of Kyoto or Tokyo, the Imperial Palace.

More than 90 percent of the houses and buildings in Tokyo were destroyed during World War II. Reconstruction was carried out very quickly, and what had been the city center up until then—the eastern zone of the emperor's palace—ceased to be so. The city's center of gravity moved quite a way toward the west, and especially toward a series of very busy train stations, mainly Shibuya and Shinjuku. Tokyo thus acquired multiple centers of activity. Hundreds of train and subway stations were built and around them appeared supermarkets, shopping malls, squares,

parks, etc. The Tokyo urban district became a kind of mega conglomeration of train and subway stations. The Imperial Palace continues to be the geometric center of Tokyo, but a five-minute walk along the streets adjacent to the palace is enough for you to realize it's a dead zone with hardly any activity compared to train stations like Shinjuku or Shibuya.

The greater part of the surface area of Japanese cities is occupied by small two- or three-story single family units. They are residential zones that appear not to be within a city. In these zones, the height of the buildings increases the closer they are to a train station. Around the stations is where the construction of tall buildings is permitted and where commercial activity is humming. The train stations are the centers of micro-cities that in turn make up large cities.

An exception to that rule is Kyoto, which fortunately was not destroyed in World War II and has a more European organization since its town planning was strongly influenced by China in ancient times and by Europe during the Meiji Restoration.

Don't judge Japanese cities by their appearance, or their lack of symmetry or order. Consider that Japanese cities evolve and change very quickly, adapting to the needs of their inhabitants and trying to make life easier for them. For example, the hypermarket model never worked in Japan. People prefer small grocery stores near their homes. The naturally decentralized structure of Japanese cities distributes supermarkets, businesses, and 24-hour stores in practically any location. This allows people to settle many everyday matters without having to go very far. Having to travel to work is an exception as the major companies remain centralized in certain business zones of Osaka, Nagoya, and Tokyo. According to several rankings, Tokyo, despite its immensity, Tokyo is considered to be one of the easiest and best places to live in the world.

Another factor to take into account when you are walking around Japan is that on average the houses and buildings tend to be demolished after 25 years. This helps the cities' continuous metamorphosis, but it is also another reason for the chaos. It's the most normal thing in the world to see a 20-year-old single-story wooden house next to a newly built three-story prefabricated house, beside a 10-year-old brick house right in the center of Tokyo. A real mix! By contrast, in Europe, London for example, houses last on average for more than 100 years, the streets are much more uniform, and you can guess the period in which all the houses in a neighborhood were built. Strolling around the center of Paris or Barcelona will also give you the feeling of harmony as that the houses and adjoining buildings match architecturally.

To go to my workplace in Tokyo, for two years I walked along the same 2,600-ft (800-m)-long street every day. I saw six buildings demolished and 15 houses replaced by almost identical new ones. Continuous change!

The housing development regulations are also somewhat different to those that are normally used in North American or European cities. In general, the regulations are more lenient and things are permitted that in our country would be unthinkable. For example, a plot of urban land can be divided up as much as you like, so that you can find plots of just a few square feet right in the city center where there is barely enough space for the owner to put a couple of vending machines. This small difference when it comes to dividing up land may seem trivial, but when you see there are five- or six-story buildings no more than 13 ft (4 m) wide, or cottages trapped between 50-story skyscrapers, you realize how much the implementation, or not, of a housing development regulation, however simple it may seem, can have a long-term effect. Besides that, there are also triangular, pentagonal, or amorphous plots which give rise to buildings with the most peculiar shapes. Utter chaos!

Of course, there is also the odd skyscraper zone, in the finest American style. In fact, Tokyo has more skyscrapers (buildings over 262 ft (80 m) high than any other city in the world. But in general, what dominates is chaos, disorder, decentralization, cities made up of "villages", the center of each of which is a

train station, and cities that go on forever and beyond forming gigantic megalopolises from which it's hard to escape. In Tokyo, a trend has also emerged of creating micro-cities dominated by an enormous skyscraper full of malls and offices, in turn surrounded by several medium-sized skyscrapers where people live. Two of the most popular micro-cities in Tokyo are Tokyo Midtown and Roppongi Hills.

Town planning in the West gives much more priority to the layout of a city being harmonious than it does in Japan, where the aim is for a structure to be useful and to create no conflict between land owners. To use engineering vocabulary, the Japanese plan their towns according to a bottom-up philosophy (start with the components and allow the overall picture to emerge), while in the West the philosophy is more top–down (start by planning the big picture and allow the details to emerge). Japanese cities change very fast. They mutate, grow, shrink. Residential zones become commercial ones and vice-versa. Housing is considered to be something temporary, so it's very rare for a person to live their entire life in the same house. Less strict regulations regarding plot size or the relative height of buildings to their neighbors, yet stricter regulations in areas such as earthquake proofing mean that Japanese cities ultimately evolve in a totally different way to what we are used to in the West. The result is cities without order, built according to the needs of the moment, cities in constant change, chaotic cities.

The architectural diversity in Japanese cities is such that after walking for just a few minutes you feel like you are in another, completely different city.

LANDSCAPES AND TOWN PLANNING

As well as chaos in the cities, disorder is also evident in small towns and villages in the appearance of the coast, the rivers, and even the woods. It's very difficult to find a place that hasn't been touched by the hand of man.

It turns out that Japan's domestic economy revolves around construction. In the 1990s, the average investment in construction in Japan was 18.2 percent of GDP, more than twice as much as in the United States, where it was 8.5 percent. The Japanese government spends around 9 percent of GDP on

(Left to right) Colorful advertisements cover most buildings in crowded areas.

public works, while the United States spends around 1 percent. There are 7 million people working for the government in public works, that is, 10 percent of the working population (data taken from *Dogs & Demons* by Alex Kerr).

There are political reasons behind so much money and so many resources being spent on public works. In many small villages and towns, enormous quantities of money are spent simply to demonstrate that money is being used for people's "benefit." Since there are so many people with jobs related to construction, as long as the government helps to stimulate the sector, everyone is happy. An ecosystem of government, construction companies, and realtors has been formed that is very difficult to change and is flooding Japan with cement.

More than 70 percent of the Japanese coast where there are no cliffs has been modified by construction companies, adding dams, which in theory offer protection against tsunamis and erosion. The Japanese coast could be beautiful, but in many places the only thing you see is concrete and tetrapods (concrete blocks with four legs). Some 55 percent of Japan's woods have been planted in the last 50 years. As trees are cut down, new ones are planted. The truth is, you can't really tell, but if you pay attention as you walk in the mountains, oftentimes you realize that the woods look like a collage. One of the problems with so much replanting is *kafunsho*, a pollen allergy that affects many Japanese (see page 49).

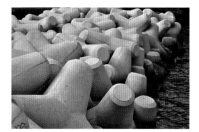

These concrete blocks, known as tetrapods, overrun the Japanese coast.

LIVING ON THE FLOOR

One of the first things you learn on arriving in Japan is that you always have to take your shoes off before entering a house. After spending some time in Japan, you realize that it's not just when you go into someone's home, it's also quite common in some restaurants or even in company offices. The floor is sacred in Japan and most of its architecture is influenced by this fact. Japanese lives revolve around the floor. Nowadays, when eating at home, more than 90 percent of Japanese sit on the floor at a table 12–16 inches (30–40 cm) high.

House floors tend to be made of wood or *tatami* matting and the Japanese normally lead their lives simply sitting on the floor. In Japanese architecture, the floor is much more important than the walls or the roof, whereas in the West the roof and walls usually take precedence. In fact, the dividing walls in Japanese homes are normally quite unimportant, or unnecessary. Sliding panels are often used and two rooms can be separated or joined straight away, creating a privacy problem in Japanese families. Spaces created by Japanese architecture are permeable and fluid and the distinction between the interior and exterior is often not clear.

All these elements make life on the floor easy. You can walk barefoot, sleep on a *tatami* on the floor, or sit on the floor under a *kotatsu*—a low wooden table frame covered by a *futon*, or heavy blanket, upon which a table top sits to keep warm during the cold winter.

Life in Japanese homes is centered on the floor, considered a sacred space in Japan.

In the West, what's important are the walls and roof. It's important to isolate the outside from the inside and we maintain the heat in the winter with central heating. In Japan, you hardly ever see central heating. On the other hand, the use of air-conditioning is very widespread, even more common than having a television. There weren't any brick buildings until the end of the nineteenth century and the concept of central heating was completely unknown. Today, it is still quite unusual.

To give you an understanding of just how important this idea of life on the floor is, the traditional and polite way of coming into a room without being rude is on your knees. You approach the room you want to enter, kneel down by the door, open it, make a bow, enter the room on your knees, and close the door. Traditionally, walking into a room is considered rude. This way of

The traditional way of sitting in Japan, with your bottom resting on your heels, is called seiza. If you are not used to sitting in this position, you get tired after a few minutes.

coming into a room can still be seen in traditional places, in tea ceremonies, or in *ochayas* where *geishas* work, and in luxury *ryokan* (traditional inns).

> "The construction and design of Japanese homes revolves around the floor. The floor is sacred in Japan and most of its architecture is influenced by this fact."

The average ceiling height of Japanese homes is very low. It is much lower than in Europe or the United States. The Japanese are quite short and, besides, living on the floor means that the kinds of chairs, beds, or tables we know in the West are not necessary. Leading a life on the floor means that everything is a lot smaller. Having a lower ceiling has more to do with the floor-dwelling lifestyle of the Japanese than with their height or some aesthetic reason.

In the West, we build things to be imposing, to impress, to give the feeling of being important. The offices of the most important executives and officials in the United States normally have higher ceilings than those of the rooms of the rest of the employees. However, the ceiling isn't important in Japan. The chairman's office ceiling is the same height as any other employee's office. What matters is the floor space and how it is distributed.

THE TATAMI

Tatamis are normally used to make the floor cooler and to protect against humidity. The first thing that is designed in a traditional Japanese house is the floor, and the standard unit size is the rectangular *tatami* (6 by 3 ft; 180 by 90 cm). Rooms with four and a half and six *tatamis* are the most common. By following this standard measurement, it creates patterns that are regular but at the same time not always very symmetrical due to the rectangular shape of the *tatami*. This standard measurement is so important that it is also used for doors and windows.

A traditional Japanese door is made up of two sliding panels, each one the size of a *tatami*. That is to say, the doors in traditional Japanese homes are 6 ft (180 cm) high. Many of us Westerners would have a hard time living in one of these houses. But the Japanese become used to living on the floor from the time they are children.

Living on the floor means not being seated on chairs. The Japanese like sitting on the floor. Even in houses of modern construction, the interiors are designed to make it easy to be barefoot and to sit on the floor at mealtimes. The television is practically at floor level and there are hardly any chairs in the house.

KEEPING WARM

In Europe, we have dry warm summers and cold damp winters. For our climate, it is better to live in brick houses and use heating. In Japan, the summers are warm and humid and the winters cold and dry. To adapt to this climate, it is better to live in wooden constructions.

> "The climate, culture, and traditions influence people's daily lives and consequently their architecture."

The tatami matting helps to cool down homes and other buildings in the summer.

(Above) In the center of the room you can see a kotatsu, where you sit and cover your legs to keep them warm in the winter.
(Below) As well as being mobile, the shoji panels let a little light through.

The traditional Japanese home does not retain heat as the walls are very thin and made of wood. To make them as cool as possible in the humid summers, the ground floor of traditional wooden houses is constructed so that it is raised slightly above ground level. In this way, air flows underneath and helps with the ventilation. In the West, walls and roofs are used to try to prevent the cold and heat from getting in. In Japan, the walls tend to be thin and aim to let the heat or cold in from outside.

In Japan, people try to heat themselves rather than their homes. This can still be seen today in certain traditions, such as having a really hot bath at the end of the day before going to sleep so as to keep warm during the night; eating spicy food; drinking warm *sake*; drinking tea or snuggling up beneath the cozy heat of a *kotatsu*. In even more traditional places, you can find *iroris*, which are holes in the center of a living room used as a fireplace and to cook (see page 51). Instead of trying to heat the home, everybody warms themselves.

This difference in the way of keeping the heat in and cooling homes is a consequence of how different the climate is in Japan, where summers are much more humid than in Europe or the United States. For example, in the warm, dry climate of the Mediterranean, there is little vegetation and stone is used for building. The buildings stand out in the landscape and there is an attempt to highlight the façade. You can see symmetry and a focus on frontage in those façades, two aesthetic characteristics that have been drilled into us since ancient Greece. In a climate with hot, humid summers, there is a lot more vegetation and the summer heat is much easier to bear in wooden houses adjoining this vegetation. The houses don't stand out in the landscape but blend in with it. The façade and symmetry cease to be important. What's important is to be in harmony with the environs, and the finishing touches, whether in the area that is most visible or at the back of the house.

Another of the advantages of wood is that many of the interior walls of houses are mobile. The interiors in Japan flow. They are changeable and can adapt according to the season or the needs of the moment. The sliding doors are known as *shoji*. The most traditional ones are made of semi-transparent paper, but in today's homes *shoji* made with plastic or even glass materials are also used.

FAÇADE VERSUS FINISHING TOUCHES

In Japan, homes are built and designed to make life easier and to be practical, with a focus on the interior. In the West, we often build things to be imposing, or to impress, for the façade to turn out pretty and be in harmony with the nearby constructions as a whole. Sometimes when you go in a room in a Western home, you were expecting a lot more, having seen a beautiful façade. In Japan, perhaps you see a house that seems shabby from the outside only to find that the interior is cozy and suggestive of being easy to live in.

In Western architecture, sharp contours and lines predominate. There is a play on light and darkness, symmetry, a holistic vision—generally a sense of a construction in its entirety—and high embellished ceilings, something we inherited from the Greco-Roman age. Whereas, in the Japanese world, they play with shadows. Both the façades and the interiors are normally asymmetrical. The Japanese have a horizontal, rather than a vertical way of looking at things, and everything is designed for life on the floor. There is great attention to detail, with a focus on the elements rather than on the whole. The Japanese house is camouflaged within its environs, with nature around it. The spaces inside Japanese homes are fluid and permeable. The distinction between the interior and the exterior is unclear.

Japanese homes are well finished, even in the parts that are not seen. For example, the walls that lead to the garden are as important as the façade that looks out onto the street. In Western architecture, on the other hand, there can be an enormous difference between the façade and the rear of a building or house. In the West, what's important is the façade. We like beautiful, majestic, symmetrical ones. In Japan, the important thing is the harmony between the interior and exterior, the finishing touches to the house, the elements rather than the whole.

Japanese buildings and houses are built paying attention to the slightest detail, even in the parts that are never going to be seen by people. Their construction centers on satisfying the needs of those who are going to live there, often focusing on the interior design and largely ignoring the exterior aspect. In Europe and the United States, it is often the other way around. A house seems majestic from the outside, but when you go in you realize that you really wouldn't like to live there. Oftentimes,

This apparently enormous room can easily be divided into four rooms by moving the shoji on the rails between the tatamis.

The important thing is not the façade but the interior. A comfortable life in the home is priority number one for the Japanese.

Wood continues to be one of the favorite materials in the construction of single family units in Japan.

Japanese style rooms have many moving parts that allow for different configurations.

the true needs of those who are going to live in the house or building are forgotten.

One of the things that might disappoint visitors to Japan is the façades of the streets, buildings, and houses in the big cities. The façades are dull, monotonous, and grayish, with small windows, and sometimes with no windows at all!

CONCLUSIONS

Japanese architecture and lifestyle have been heavily affected by foreign influence, but even so, subconsciously, many Japanese traditions remain intact. In many cases, the Japanese continue to use wood to build single family units and other materials are used for the interior. When designing, the Japanese continue to think not in terms of square feet or meters but in *tatamis*. Even if it's an apartment in a 40-story-high skyscraper, the interior is designed to make it easier to go about barefoot. Many concrete houses still have at least one room with *tatamis*, which is used to serve tea and relax in. The traditional *shoji* dividers are no longer seen so much, but the interiors are often designed with mobile walls that allow for the division of one room into two or three depending on the needs of the moment.

Tradition, history, culture, and the climate determine our day to day along with the best structure for our homes and our work and living spaces. As a result, this affects a country's architecture. In Japan, apart from the climate, another of the factors that has greatly influenced the way of life there are earthquakes, which make people not see buildings as something permanent but, rather, as something temporary and fleeting.

"Tadao Ando is one of the best-known contemporary Japanese architects among the international community. Tadao Ando was the architect of Japan's pavilion at the Seville World Fair in 1992. This was his first building outside Japan and the one with which he would begin to make an international impact."

DIFFERENCES BETWEEN EAST AND WEST

Japan	The West
Horizontal perspective, life on the floor	Vertical perspective, emphasis on walls and ceiling
Interior	Façade
Low ceilings	High ceilings
Integration of the interior and exterior	Separation of the interior and exterior
Attention to detail	Attention to the whole
Asymmetry, irregular contours	Symmetry, focus on frontage, sharp contours
Mobile partitions, fluid interiors	Fixed walls
Continue to make great use of wood	Brick and concrete

Tadao Ando is an expert in the use of exposed reinforced concrete in his buildings.

After understanding something of the history, traditions, and keys to Japanese society and business culture, let's now consider what life is like today in this country where, by the beginning of the 1970s, the Japanese had achieved a high degree of general well-being and had enough time to develop many cultural movements that have since influenced the rest of the world. Let's see what kind of life they lead in a land where there is hardly any unemployment, the education level is extremely high, and there is enough money for people not to have to worry too much about their future and to be able to devote themselves fully to their hobbies and interests.

LIFE OF AN OTAKU

Otaku is a Japanese word that has become international and is used to refer to people who are obsessive in their hobbies, especially hobbies connected with *anime* and *manga*.

THE ORIGIN OF THE WORD OTAKU

The word *otaku* has a curious origin. In Japanese, this term is used to refer to another person's house, but it's also a not very common second person honorific pronoun. Apparently, in the Japanese geek community, the *otaku* pronoun was often used to refer to fellow geeks when it wasn't really necessary to be so formal. Little by little, people outside geek communities noticed this phenomenon and started using the word *otaku* to refer to geeks. During the 1990s it became widespread in Japan, and at the end of the century it began to spread around the world, not only as a word but as a cultural movement.

WHAT IS AN OTAKU?

For the Japanese, an *otaku* is a person who spends much of his or her spare time shut away at home cultivating hobbies of the most diverse kinds. The most prevalent *otaku* in Japan are those interested in *manga*, video games, and *anime* or simply those addicted to the Internet. At first, in the 1990s, the word *otaku* was distinctly pejorative, implying that the person didn't have a real life beyond the Internet or his favorite comic books. But when it was exported overseas, it took on the meaning of "a fan of Japanese culture" and especially "a fan of *anime* and *manga*." The meaning it acquired overseas gave the word a slightly more positive connotation in Japan, and at present most people simply use it to joke with their friends, as in "You are an *otaku* of the music of the seventies," "You are a Ghibli *otaku*," "a Gundam *otaku*," "a computer *otaku*," and so on.

THE MOST COMMON AND WELL-DEFINED OTAKU TYPES IN JAPAN

Manga otaku: They don't only read *manga* (something most Japanese do without being *otaku*) but also collect every kind of material related to their favorite series.

Anime otaku: Similar to the preceding but focused more on collecting DVDs of their favorite *anime* series.

Figure otaku: They collect figurines based on series. There is a whole world of figure *otaku*. They have their own international conventions and stores. There are even entire department stores in Akihabara that sell figurines. The most popular figures are from the Gundam series.

Pasokon otaku: Obsessed with computers, they keep servers at home to host *otaku* communities and always have the latest thing, buying and selling in Akihabara stores. Many of them also like building robots and making electronic montages.

Wota: *Idol* otaku. They are fans of *idols*, both the *gravure* type (girls who pose in bikinis) and singers whose music, DVDs, and photo albums they collect.

Gemu otaku: Video game *otaku*. They own every game console on the market and usually focus on role-playing games for which they buy every single guide available in bookstores. There is a whole market of video game books in Japan aimed exclusively at them.

Densha otaku: Train *otaku* who collect figurines of all the trains in Japan and keep up to date with the help of hobbyist magazines that have the specs on the latest model locomotives and carriages.

Several types of otaku.

OTAKU

For the Japanese, an *otaku* is a person who spends much of his spare time shut away at home practicing his hobbies.

HIKIKOMORI

To refer to *otaku* in a negative sense—to those who really are obsessive and never go out so they can spend all their time at home with their hobbies—the new word *hikikomori* was coined. *Hikikomori* is considered an illness, and those who suffer from it shut themselves in at home to the point that they stop going to school or work and don't socialize at all. Many Japanese people are affected by this syndrome, and it's becoming a serious problem. Psychologists who study it point to the great social pressures on young people and their entry into the adult world as possible causes. Many young people feel unable to integrate into the system and they give up, confining themselves to worlds of fantasy that they can access by playing video games, reading *manga*, or surfing the Web.

Even without being *hikikomori*, the most extreme *otaku* don't socialize much. They are usually fans of *anime*, *manga*, and video games, and in general they lead a rather solitary life. They work *arubaito* (part-time jobs) to earn just enough to eat and buy the latest item in their favorite series. They spend weekends at home and are usually single. On the rare occasions they do go out, they go to conventions, events, or shopping in Akihabara.

> "Even without being *hikikomori*, the most extreme *otaku* don't socialize much. They are usually fans of *anime*, *manga*, and video games, and in general they lead a rather solitary life."

DIARY OF AN OTAKU

On weekdays: They go to work, probably a part-time job or temporary job at a store or a technology company. In the afternoon after work, they grab something quick for dinner at a restaurant, and go home to read *manga*, watch *anime*, or play on the Internet.
On weekends: They go to *otaku* events or for a walk around Akihabara (see page 156) to see the latest products.

THE MOST IMPORTANT OTAKU EVENTS

Tokyo Game Show: An annual event where new games and game consoles are launched. It's usually held in September or October at the Makuhari Messe Convention Complex. For more information, visit: http://tgs.cesa.or.jap or http://www.m-messe.co.jp/index_e.html
Comiket (Comic Market): This is the most important event of its kind in the world and is attended by the largest number of *otaku* every time it's held. It specializes in *manga* and takes place at Tokyo Big Sight in August.
Tokyo Anime Fair: An event specializing in *anime* that is also held at Tokyo Big Sight.
Wonder Festival: An event specializing in figurines that, like the previous ones, is also held at Tokyo Big Sight.

To learn the exact dates and see the building where the Comiket, the Tokyo Anime Fair, and the Wonder Festival are held, you can visit the Tokyo Big Sight convention center's official Web site: http://www.bigsight.jp/english/

LIFE OF A STUDENT

Teenagers in Japan are under a lot of pressure to prepare for college entrance examinations, a test that to some extent will determine the rest of their lives. Depending on the score they achieve on the exam, they will gain admission to a better or worse university, and when Japanese companies hire new employees, the name of the university where they studied is the most important factor. That's why kids are busy with after-school activities most of the time, even on vacation.

Besides taking math or science review, boys play sports like baseball or archery (*kyudo*; see page 33). Girls opt for more traditional activities like the tea ceremony or *ikebana*.

At all schools, uniforms are compulsory. In fact, this requirement has reached the point of being an obsession, to the extent that different schools compete to see who will have the most elegant uniform. Girls often wear their uniforms for pleasure on Sundays when they walk around Harajuku. And uniforms with a certain erotic styling are sold in adult stores in Akihabara.

DIARY OF A SCHOOLGIRL/BOY

On weekdays: Going to school, studying in the afternoon, going out with their friends for a while, watching television or reading *manga*.
On weekends: Saturdays are usually devoted to after-school activities and on Sundays to rest.

Schoolgirls eating onigiri (rice balls) near Harajuku Station after school.

Schoolgirls love to hang cute toys to their bags in order to differentiate their bags and themselves from their peers.

LIFE OF A CAREER WOMAN

Generally speaking, Japanese society is quite chauvinistic. Men control the country and the companies. In my company, for example, which has 1,000 employees, the 100 highest-ranking superiors are all men. By contrast, at the family level, the woman is the boss. Women control the home's economy, and they give their husbands an allowance for personal expenses. There has never been a strong feminist movement in Japan, and women are generally quite conformist. What has certainly changed in the last decades is that women have started working and building professional careers.

Women who have completed a university degree, found a good job, and attained a certain social status are known in Japan as "career woman." Until the end of the 1980s, most women went from studying to looking after the house. This tendency started to change in the 1990s, and nowadays the percentage of career woman is very high, especially in Tokyo and Osaka.

The lives of these women usually center on their job and on meeting their girlfriends for a coffee or to go shopping in Ginza or Shibuya (see pages 150 and 158) until they find the man they've been waiting for and get married. From that moment forward, they will refocus their lives on their family, leaving friends and work in the background. Normally, men over 30 years are paid enough money to support a family of four. Women's wages, however, are a lot lower and that's why, more often than not, they decide it's not worth it to keep working, and they devote themselves to the house and the children.

DIARY OF A CAREER WOMAN:

On weekdays: Work and meet their girlfriends for a coffee or dinner.
On weekends: Be with their boyfriend, go shopping with girlfriends, or go out partying and then to a karaoke club with friends.

Career women have more and more of a presence in Japan.

LIFE OF A SALARYMAN

The Japanese term "salaryman" literally means "salaried man." These are the typical Japanese employees in dark suits and ties who work for large corporations (Toyota, NTT, Dentsu, Nissan, Matsushita, Hitachi, and so on). When they finish college, the normal path is to join a major corporation, become a *shinnyushain* (see page 68), and then work for many years for the same corporation, very often until they retire, in what is considered a job for life. In the rigid structure of Japanese business, the only way to climb the corporate ladder is to spend many years at the same company. By the same token, if you change companies, you have to start out again at the bottom, which is why people don't change jobs often.

Salarymen wake up at around eight o'clock in the morning, have breakfast, put on their suits, take their briefcases, and get on the train for a commute of about an hour. They work, have lunch with their co-workers, and usually work overtime, arriving home very late at night. Often, before going home, they will go out for a drink with their workmates and pass the time at an *izakaya* (informal pub).

The prototypical salaryman is really standardized, and there are areas in Tokyo and Osaka where they flock together after their work day. Districts in Tokyo famous for this are Shinbashi (Yamanote line station near Shinagawa), Marunouchi, Roppongi, and Shinjuku (see page 154). If you want to see the ambiance created by gathering salarymen in Osaka, go to the Umeda or Namba districts any night during the week.

DIARY OF A SALARYMAN:

On weekdays: Work, go to an *izakaya* to drink, and sing at karaoke clubs.
On weekends: If they are married, they enjoy family life, and if they are not, they party at *izakayas* and karaoke clubs.

A good salaryman is always in a suit and is inseparable from his briefcase.

YAKUZA GANGS

In spite of being one of the world's safest places, Japan also has one of the largest criminal gangs in the world. The *yakuza* group began to form during the Edo Period (1603–1868) when many *samurai* were expelled by their feudal lords, who no longer needed them. These wandering, homeless warriors were known as *ronin*. Some of them did dirty work for people from the higher classes, and others simply became criminals. Over time, they organized themselves into *ronin* gangs that were charged with protecting small villages in return for food and accommodation, but later on they started extorting money from the villagers and asking for more things. Another problem that developed were battles between *ronin* gangs who wanted to control the same area. During the years that followed, new gangs organized themselves and looked for ways to make money. The *yakuza*, as we know them today, acquired real power from World War II onward when they gained control of prostitution, gambling houses, drugs, illegal commerce, etc. Furthermore, certain extreme right-wing branches of gangs started to operate and extort money within political groups.

The *yakuza* are organized in clans with a very rigid structure—as if the clans were companies—where they are all part of one "family." They also strictly apply the *senpai-kohai* apprenticeship system (see page 42) in order to train young gangsters, and above all they follow a code of honor. For example, if one of the members makes a serious mistake or commits some sort of treason, his little finger is cut off. If you see a Japanese man with his little finger amputated, he's very likely to belong or have belonged to a *yakuza* gang.

THE MOST IMPORTANT GANG

The largest *yakuza* gang is the Yamaguchi group, with 40,000 active members. They have the "honor" of being the largest gangster group in the world, not only because of their numbers but also because of their economic power. They manage various enterprises, from *pachinko* chains (see page 51) to Internet pornography, drug trafficking, and prostitution.

The members of yakuza clans usually wear tattoos to identify themselves with their group. This tradition began when the first yakuza members tattooed a ring around their arms every time they committed a crime. The more tattooed rings they had, the more powerful and dangerous they were supposed to be. Tattoos are not very common in Japan due to the bad reputation of the yakuza.

"The *yakuza* are organized in clans with a very rigid structure where they are all part of one "family." They also strictly apply the *senpai-kohai* apprenticeship system, and above all they follow a code of honor."

The *yakuza* are a serious problem in Japan, and they never cease extending their influence while keeping the police and politicians at bay, so they have their own space to do their dirty business.

SUBCULTURES AND URBAN TRIBES

GALS

Gals are girls who belong to one of the most influential urban tribes among Japanese youths since the mid-1990s. They are renowned for their attitude that breaks with the system and Japanese conservatism and for not caring about studies, their future, or marriage. Adults often disapprove of this tribe, but the truth is their fashion is triumphant, and the phenomenon is so big that there are several different subgroups or tendencies among the *gals*.

Gals have a whole world to move around in: stores specializing in the clothes they like, nightclubs with J-pop–techno–trance music, their private clubs where *gal*-only trips are organized, and even their own "*gal* code," a way of writing mobile phone messages in Japanese that is very hard to understand for anyone outside the group.

Gal fashion spread all over Japan during the 1990s and at the turn of the twenty-first century. The main spark for this surge was, among others, the singer Namie Amuro (see page 120), who in the 1990s began wearing high-heeled boots and sporting a dark tan and hair dyed blond. The Shibuya district is the center of this fashion, which has gained so much influence in the country that there are even several magazines specializing in *gal* fashion.

KOGAL

This is the basic *gals* type. The basic look of a *kogal* involves dyeing the hair gold and sporting tanned skin and white eye makeup. They also wear false eyelashes, high boots, miniskirts, etc. *Kogal* groups usually meet at Shibuya to have coffee and talk about

the latest hair styles, visit *purikura* centers (photo booths that produce stickers for mobile phones), attend fringe concerts, and so on. They are very materialistic, and one of the most important status symbols among groups of friends is the type of handbag they carry.

GANGURO

Ganguro look very much like *kogals* but are somewhat different in their tastes. The *ganguro* are a minority tribe with a look inspired by the very dark-tanned girls from California. They usually listen to R&B and American pop music, and they generally like American culture. This minority tribe basically gathers around Shibuya and Harajuku.

These days, you don't see as many *ganguro* as you did at the turn of the century. However, as their legacy they have left behind a style of dance called Para Para, which has become very popular among young people in Tokyo and Osaka. If you want to see the Para Para dance, I recommend you go to the Womb nightclub in Shibuya or Ageha Hall, the two largest nightclubs in Tokyo.

MAMBA OR YAMAMBA

The *yamamba* is a subcategory within the *ganguro*. The most extreme, they take fashion to the limit. They paint their faces black, wear shocking lipstick, and dye their hair white or in bright colors. Their clothes are plastic or latex. The male version of *yamamba* is known as *center-Gai*.

MEN-GAL

There are also men who dye their hair like *gals*, get a suntan at beauty parlors, and wear tight shirts, chains around their necks,

jeans, and pointy shoes. You often see them in Shibuya, normally not far from groups of *ganguro* or *kogals*.

ENJO KOSAI

Enjo kosai is a euphemism used in *gal* environments that might be translated as "compensated dating" but is actually the prostitution of young girls. This phenomenon appeared at the beginning of the 1990s when the Japanese economy entered a crisis and young girls no longer had their parents' money to satisfy their buying whims. *Gals* can practice prostitution via *enjo kosai* simply by registering on certain Web pages via their mobile phones. These services put them in touch with possible clients.

Youngsters from different groups chatting near Shibuya station.

ASPECTS OF OTAKU CULTURE

Otaku subculture has generated a number of phenomena that have spread far beyond the *otaku* themselves. Let's look at a couple of these phenomena. The first is the introduction of the word *moe*, used initially only by a small fringe group. The second is the creation of a whole movement, a new fashion, and a new business based on *meido kissas*.

MOE

Moe is the *otaku* word par excellence. Its exact meaning is difficult to explain. It's a kind of exclamation to declare one's passion/love for an *anime* or *manga* character considered adorable/pretty. You might use it, for example, when you see the drawing of a girl with big breasts and seductive eyes, by saying, "What a *moe* girl!" Another use of the word would be as a synonym for *otaku* or geek, as when we say, for instance, "You're a video *moe*," meaning, you're a video game geek. And the third way to use it would be as a synonym for "fetish," as in, for example, "You're a big-eye *moe*," meaning you have a thing or fetish for *anime* girls with big eyes.

The origin of the word isn't known for certain, but one of the most likely theories is that it came from such *anime* series as *Sailor Moon*, because the girls in them, like Hotaru Tomoe, were so adorable.

In 2005 there was a *dorama*—a *terebi dorama* (see page 128)—and a movie called *Densha Otoko*. The story was about an *otaku* who fell in love with a girl from a rich family. In the series, the hero often chats with his *otaku* buddies, and one of the most frequently used words is *moe*. Thanks to *Densha Otoko*, the word became popular. Today, it's commonly used in ordinary conversations as a synonym for beautiful or sexy.

MEIDO FASHION

The Japanese word *meido* comes from English *maid*. In *manga*, there are usually many female characters dressed in maid costumes, which fascinate the Japanese. As *mangaka* draw increasingly tight-fitting maid uniforms, the *meido* fashion is becoming one of the *otaku*'s favorite fetishes.

Among the most interesting phenomena produced by this fetish are *meido kissas*, coffee shops where young women dressed in maid costumes serve the coffee. These shops, or maid cafés, have been proliferating for almost a decade in the Akihabara district. The girls treat you as if you were the supreme chief of a *samurai* clan, using an extremely formal Japanese—that is, as if they were genuine maids. The *meido kissa* business has spread all over Japan, and it's now even being exported, mainly to large Asian cities such as Seoul, Taipei, and Hong Kong.

When you enter a *meido kissa*, you are greeted by several girls who bow to you and utter polite formulas like, "Welcome home, honorable man of the house." That is, they act in a way to flatter your nobility, treating you as if you were a rich man and the owner of a large mansion with lots of maids. Normally, you'll be well treated in any Japanese restaurant or coffee shop, but *meido kissas* take this to the extreme, as if the client was a genuine king.

This business/fashion originated in Akihabara, and that is also where new kinds of businesses based on the same idea are now appearing. For example, now there are not only *meido kissas* where girls serve boys, but also coffee shops for women where elegant men serve you, addressing you as "Queen" and the like. There are also hairdressers where girls dressed in maid costumes give you a haircut, and the latest trend is massage and aromatherapy parlors where, again, girls dressed as maids give you a massage.

If you want to go to a *meido* coffee shop when you visit Japan, it's not hard at all. You see them everywhere now that they're fashionable. Simply pay attention as you walk around any big city and you'll find one. However, as a general rule, you can't take photographs inside them.

The subculture around the *meido* phenomenon is taking many forms and generating new fashions, not only in Japan but also all over the world, mainly in *otaku* communities.

MOE

Moe is the *otaku* word par excellence. Its exact meaning is difficult to explain. It's a kind of exclamation to declare one's passion/love for an *anime* or *manga* character considered adorable.

The otaku subculture is a big influence on Japanese popular culture.

HIKIKOMORI

Hikikomori refers to the social isolation into which many young Japanese are plunged. Those suffering from this syndrome shut themselves away at home and spend their time watching television, playing video games, and surfing the Internet. They are usually teenagers who've been frightened by the degree of competitiveness they'll face in society when they finish their studies. They decide to shut themselves off and withdraw from society as soon as they leave high school, sometimes remaining at home for months or even years. Having a *hikikomori* in the family is frowned upon. It creates an embarrassing aura that leads the parents to try to hide the problem.

"Among the most interesting phenomena produced by this fetish are *meido kissas*, coffee shops where young girls dressed in maid costumes serve the coffee. These shops, or maid cafés, have been proliferating for almost a decade in the Akihabara district."

This phenomenon started in Japan but is apparently spreading to Korea where there is also a lot of competition to enter the best universities and then find a job that will define your life. Many studies by psychologists confirm that a main cause is the pressure created by a society defined by extreme capitalism and an extremely meritocratic education system.

The *hikikomori* problem is real but the media also exaggerates it. Psychologist Tamaki Saito once said there were more than a million cases, which set off alarm bells and gave the issue greater urgency, but he later admitted he had overstated the figures in order to draw attention to the problem and that, in fact, there were barely a few thousand cases.

VISUAL KEI

Visual kei is the name of a Japanese rock movement (see page 119) that became popular during the 1990s. Some people believe the founders of this movement were the members of the X Japan heavy metal band but it may be that they only lit the spark.

VISUAL KEI

The name of a Japanese rock movement that became popular during the1990s. It's characterized by the bands' visual style.

Visual kei bands are characterized by their use of over-the-top costumes and special effects onstage to maximize their impact on audiences at their concerts. Fans copy their idols' clothes, while at the same time the performers have evolved, following trends in pop culture. Lately, *visual kei*'s costumes have gotten very close to the clothes of characters in Japanese role-playing video games, and they sometimes merge with the *cosplay* world.

The *visual kei* phenomenon is still growing today, with hundreds of bands and tens of thousands of fans who imitate their style of dress, not only in Japan but in the whole world.

If you want to see the young people of this urban tribe in Tokyo, they usually congregate on the bridge over the railroad tracks at Harajuku Station on Sundays, a little after lunchtime.

Some visual kei followers, who, like their idols, put great effort into their appearance.

THE LOLITA COMPLEX

The term *lolita* refers to a fashion, a style, and a subculture influenced by costumes from the European Rococo period, with touches from Western punk and gothic subcultures. The term comes from the name of the character in Vladimir Nabokov's novel *Lolita*, which became a noun in English meaning "a precociously seductive girl." *Lolita* fashion began in the 1970s when some bands started wearing elaborate, frilly dresses and sporting eighteenth-century French hairdos. Girls following this fashion usually buy their clothes at stores specializing in Victorian-style apparel in Tokyo and Osaka. For accessories, they usually go to Sanrio (the Hello Kitty company) stores. As with *gals*, this urban tribe is divided into several subtribes.

GOTHIC LOLITA

This is the most famous style within the *lolita* subculture, and some people believe it came about as a response to *kogal* aesthetics. Gothic *lolita* outfits play with black and white, and makeup is also dark, distancing them from the more colorful *gals*. They also carry such accessories as crosses, patent leather handbags, parasols, and stuffed animals hanging from their waist or handbag. Their general appearance is rather sinister but with a touch of innocence. They usually listen to *visual kei* music, and they tend to mix with this movement's fan groups. Their influence is great enough for their style to have entered the *manga* and *anime* worlds, with characters considered gothic *lolita*. And their influence has even reached into movies: the protagonist in *Shimotsuma Monogatari* (Kamikaze Girls) is an obvious example.

SWEET LOLITA OR AMALOLI

Sweet *lolitas* dress in a style similar to gothic *lolitas* but go for a more childlike or "little girl" look, frequently taking inspiration from the way characters dress in *shojo manga* (*manga* for adolescent girls) and *anime*. They favor pastel colors, normally with many shades of pink, and they use softer makeup and aim to look as sweet as possible.

OTHER TENDENCIES

Classic lolita: They pursue a more "mature" style than gothic and sweet *lolita*, trying to appear more adult than they are.

Wa lolita: They mix Japanese traditional clothes (a *yukata* or a *kimono*, for example) with *lolita* elements.

Qi lolita: This style is similar to *wa lolita*, but instead of Japanese they use Chinese traditional clothes.

Erotic lolita: They go for a sexy look, wearing very short skirts and extremely high boots.

"Gothic *lolita* outfits play with black and white, and makeup is also dark, distancing them from the more colorful *gals*."

LOLITA

A fashion that has developed into a subculture influenced by costumes from the European Rococo period, with touches from Western punk and gothic subcultures.

Japanese girls with different lolita looks.

ROLE-PLAYING

The word *cosplay* comes from Japanese *kosupure,* which derives from the English words "costume" and "role-play."

The *cosplay* subculture is made up of people who like dressing up as characters from *manga, anime,* and video games or famous singers, superheroes, or movie monsters. They usually form communities and meet to talk about how they've improved their latest costume, what accessories and improvements they need for the group, and where to buy things to complement their costumes. It's a whole world, a hobby with its own customs. For instance, they will organize photo shoots during which *cosplayers* (those who practice *cosplay*) place themselves against a wall and *cameko* (amateur photographers who want to take pictures of them) form lines. The *cameko* wait their turn, and when this comes, they have a few minutes to photograph the *cosplayers* in different poses they've rehearsed for the occasion. Very often the *cameko* will print some of their best photographs and give them to *cosplayers* as gifts.

Cosplayers also organize competitions at conventions and at *cosplay* clubs in Akihabara. At the clubs, a *cosplayer* ranking is created, with the best in each group competing against each other, and ultimately there are rankings at the national level, which are published in specialty magazines.

Cosplayers gather at events like the Tokyo Game Show, the Comiket (the world's largest *manga* trade fair) and routinely by Harajuku Station in Tokyo on Saturdays and Sundays at noon.

Cosplay as a hobby has existed in Japan since the 1980s. It has gradually spread to elsewhere in Asia and is now becoming fully international. You will seldom see a *manga/anime* event or trade fair without a *cosplay* competition.

COSPLAY

The word *cosplay* originated from the contraction of "costume" and "role-play." It refers to the love of dressing up and acting like characters in *manga, anime,* and video games or famous singers, superheroes, or movie monsters.

"A *cosplayer* ranking is created at Japanese cosplay clubs: the best in each group compete against each other, and ultimately there are rankings at the national level, which are published in specialty magazines."

Cosplayers in action.

JAPANESE POPULAR CULTURE: A CHRONOLOGY

1947 ➡ Osamu Tezuka publishes his first *manga*

1949 ➡ Hibari Misora begins her professional artistic life

1950~1989 ➡ Success of the *enka* music genre

1950 ➡ **Rashomon** by Akira Kurosawa

1963 ➡ Astro Boy *anime* on TV

1965~1975 ➡ **Astro Boy generation**

ASTROBOY © 1951 by Tenzuka Prod.

1968 ➡ Beginning of Ashita no Joe

ASHITA NO JOE © 1968 Tetsuya Chiba, Asao Takamori, Kodansha LTD. Inc.

1970 ➡ Beginning of the publication of **Lone Wolf and Cub**

1973 ➡ First season of Kamen Rider

1975~1985 ➡ **Gundam/Mazinger (Tranzor Z) generation**

1975~present ➡ Beginning and evolution of J-rock

1982 ➡ **Waratte Iitomo** variety show hosted by Tamori

1983 ➡ **Captain Tsubasa** *anime*

1980 ➡ Seiko Matsuda becomes famous

1980~present ➡ *Lolita* and gothic *lolita* fashion

1981 ➡ Oretachi Hyokin **Zoku**, variety show hosted by Sanma Akashiya and Takeshi Kitano

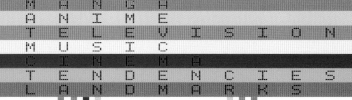

MANGA
ANIME
TELEVISION
MUSIC
CINEMA
TENDENCIES
LANDMARKS

1952 ➡ First edition of **Astro Boy** by Osamu Tezuka

1954 ➡ *Seven Samurai* by Akira Kurosawa.

SHICHININ NO SAMURAI (Seven Samurai) © 1954 TOHO CO., LTD.

1953 ➡ The NHK television channel starts broadcasting

1954 ➡ **Godzilla**

1955-1980 ➡ Jidaige-ki TV series and movies

1969 ➡ First film of the saga **Otoko wa tsurai yo**

1969 ➡ **The Drifters** begins

1970~1985 ➡ **Tokuhatsu** TV series and movies

1970 ➡ First stories of **Doraemon**

DORAEMON © 1969 Fujio F Fujiko/ SHOGAKUKIN Inc.

1976 ➡ First year the Comiket is held

1979 ➡ Beginning of the *anime* **Mobile Suit Gundam**

1980 ➡ **Kagemusha** by Akira Kurosawa

1981~present ➡ Heyday of J-pop.

1981 ➡ **Captain Tsubasa** (*Flash Kicker*) *manga*

CAPTAIN TSUBASA © 1981 Yoishi Takahashi/SHUIESHA Inc.

1984 ➡ **Dragon Ball** in *manga*

DRAGON BALL (manga) © 1984 BIRD STUDIO/SHUEISHA Inc.

1985~1995 ➡ **Dragon Ball generation**

DRAGON BALL (anime) © 1986 BIRD STUDIO/ SHUEISHA Inc./TOEI ANIMATION CO. LTD.

1985~present ➡ *Otaku* movement.

1985~present ➡ Japanese *anime* and movies go international

1987~2005 ➡ Heyday of *Visual Kei*

1988 ➡ Premiere and international success of animated feature film **Akira** by Katsuhiro Otomo

AKIRA (movie) © 1988 Katsuhiro Otomo/Akira Committee.

1989 ➡ Kawa no nagare no yo ni by Hibari Misora

1992 ➡ Beginning of Sailor Moon

1994 ➡ **Shonen Jump** sells more than 6 million copies in one week

1995 ➡ First album by Ayumi Hamasaki

1995~2000 ➡ **Pokémon** generation

POKÉMON (anime and merchandising) © 2008 Pokémon. © 1995–2008 Nintendo/ Creatures Inc./GAME FREAK Inc.

1998 ➡ First album by Hikaru Utada

1998 ➡ Beginning of **Vagabond** and **Love Hina**

1999 ➡ Beginning of the *manga* **Naruto**

2000~present ➡ **Naruto** generation

2000 ➡ Takeshi Kitano's **Battle Royale**

BATTLE ROYAL © 2002 Battle Royale Production Committee

2005 ➡ Densha Otoko phenomenon: feature film, *dorama*, *anime*, *manga*, and book

2006 ➡ Premiere of **Gedo Senki**, film by Hayao Miyazaki's son

2007 ➡ Kumi Koda, the best-selling J-pop star

2008 ➡ Premiere of Hollywood movie based on **Dragon Ball Z**

1986 ➡ Dragon Ball *anime*

1987 ➡ Beginning of serialization of **Ranma**

1988 ➡ Beginning of publication of Ah!! My Goddess

1990~2005 ➡ Heyday of *kogal* fashion

1990~present ➡ Spread of *cosplay*

1995 ➡ Neon Genesis Evangelion and Ghost in the Shell

1997 ➡ **Pokémon** *anime*

POKÉMON (anime and merchandising) © 2008 Pokémon. © 1995–2008 Nintendo/ Creatures Inc./GAME FREAK Inc.

1997 ➡ Beginning of the *manga* **One Piece**

1998 ➡ Premiere of **Ring** in Japan

2002 ➡ **Fuyu no sonata** arrives in Japan from Korea

2002 ➡ First album by Kumi Koda

2003 ➡ Ghibli's **Spirited Away** wins an Oscar

SEN TO CHIHIRO NO KAMIKAKUSHI © 2001 Tokuma Shoten, Studio Ghibli, Nippon Television Network, Dentsu, Tohokushinsha Film and Mitsubishi

2003 ➡ Sekai ni hitotsu dake no hana by SMAP

2009 ➡ Attack on Titan *manga* and *anime*

2016 ➡ Pen-Pine-apple-Apple-Pen a single by Pikotaro (Daimaou Kosaka) became popular worldwide

2016 ➡ **Kimi no na wa (Your Name)** by Makoto Shinkai internationally acclaimed *anime* movies

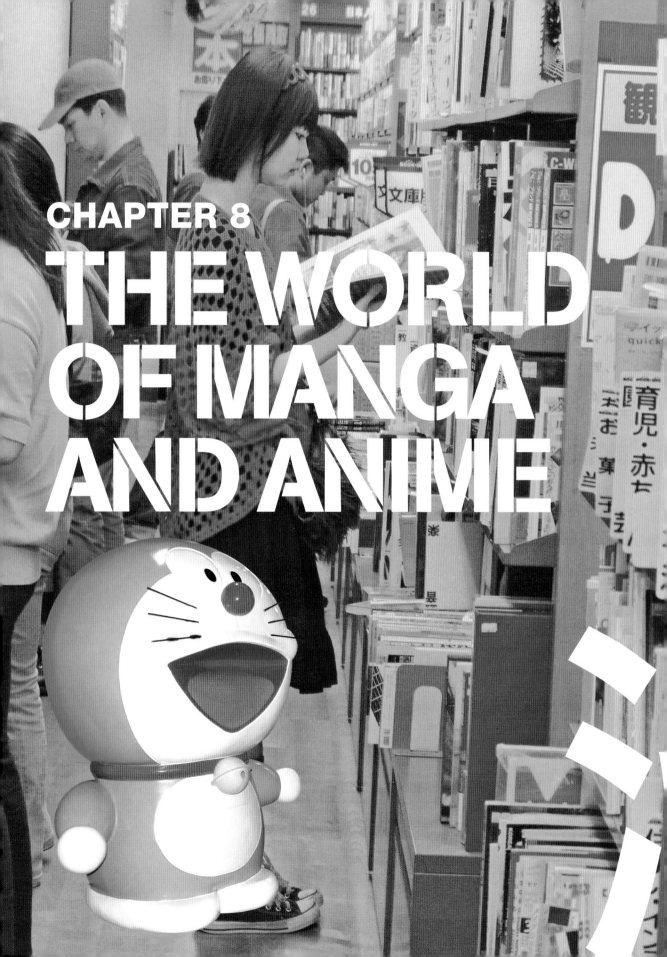

CHAPTER 8

THE WORLD OF MANGA AND ANIME

THE MANGA REVOLUTION

The impact *manga* has had in the West bears no comparison to its impact in Japan. The market is huge. To give you an idea, in the year 1996 the *manga* magazine *Shonen Jump* sold six million copies in just one week. That is more than all the comic books sold in the United States in a whole year.

The large supply means you can find *manga* on any subject you can imagine: adventure, *samurai*, cooking, history, music, *sushi*, basketball, board games, tennis, cars, etc. Readers of *manga* range from very young children to mature adults, passing by way of teenagers, and there are even *manga* targeted specifically to the elderly. *Manga* are sold everywhere: newspaper stands, bookstores, train stations, vending machines. And you can usually find free copies to read in coffee shops, hairdressing salons, and restaurants. *Manga* publications make up between 30 and 40 percent of the total sales of books and magazines in Japan. Consequently, the most important publishing companies are those that dominate the *manga* market. Among them, Shueisha, Shogakukan, and Kodansha stand out in particular.

Manga were not published in the West until the 1970s, but little by little they have spread to the most remote parts of the planet. *Dragon Ball*, *Doraemon*, *Sailor Moon*, and *Crayon Shinchan* are known by most young people all over the world.

> "*Manga* publications make up between 30 and 40 percent of the total sales of books and magazines in Japan."

MANGA

The word used to designate any Japanese comics.

Animated movies like *Akira* or *Ghost in the Shell* generated millions of dollars and helped stimulate the expansion of the Japanese *manga* and animation industry in the West. More recently, movies by Studio Ghibli have achieved great success among international critics and won the most prestigious movie awards.

Manga is the word used to designate any Japanese comics. It would be difficult to grasp contemporary Japanese society without studying the *manga* phenomenon, just as it would be hard to understand the degree to which *manga* is integrated into Japanese daily life and how it has helped Japan to spread its culture around the world. In this chapter we will analyze the connection between Japanese history and traditional arts with the development of *manga* and *anime* to the point where they have become global phenomena.

The publishing numbers generated by the manga market in Japan are dizzying.

THE ORIGINS OF MANGA

CHOJU-GIGA

Twelfth-century stories drawn on scrolls and using sequences of images and text to explain or recount events.

To understand the origins of the *manga* concept, we must go back to the twelfth century and the practice of drawing stories on scrolls—known as *choju-giga*—using sequences of images and text to explain or recount events. These scrolls already manifested in some ways features of modern *manga*. If you "read" the scroll from one side to the other, you grasp in a continuous way the flow of a story. (You can view original *choju-giga* at the National Museum. See the Ueno map, page 161.) The problem with the scrolls was that they could not be reproduced. They also cost a lot of money and only the wealthy had access to them. Much later, during the Edo Period, a new technique called *ukiyo-e* (see page 26) came into practice. With it, you could reproduce the same image multiple times. One of the best artists using this technique was Hokusai, who published a book of sketches called *Hokusai Manga* in 1814. This was the first time the word *manga* was used to refer to something comparable to present-day Japanese *manga*, although there were other artists doing similar things but calling them by different names. For example, a trend among *ukiyo-e* artists was *shunga*, whose main subject was eroticism. *Shunga* has influenced Japanese artists up to the present day, culminating in the erotic-pornographic *manga* genre known as *hentai*.

THE WORD "MANGA"

Manga in Japanese is written 漫画, where the first character means "involuntary" or "rambling" and the second means "drawing" or "strokes." The original meaning Hokusai intended would be something like "involuntary/rambling/random/whimsical strokes/drawings/sketches." He probably never imagined the word would become an international synonym for Japanese comics.

Hokusai's term *manga* continued to be used for this kind of creative work, where a series of connected images followed each other in sequence and were characterized by strong facial expressiveness verging on caricature. With advances in printing and the arrival of foreign comics, its use spread. *Manga* were published mainly in short strips in newspapers before the war. These strips looked very much like today's Western comics but still hadn't achieved the appearance and essence of present-day *manga*, which would be established by Osamu Tezuka.

Shunga is the origin of present-day hentai.

Example of a forerunner of Japanese manga.

"In 1814, the master artist Hokusai published a book of sketches called *Hokusai Manga*. This was the first time the word *manga* was used to designate something comparable to present-day *manga*."

An example of a choju-giga scroll.

Two pages from "Hokusai Manga" considered the first work to be called manga.

OSAMU TEZUKA: THE FATHER OF MANGA

But how was the *manga* we know today really born? The legend goes that when Osamu Tezuka was studying medicine in 1945, he saw a movie poster advertising a Japanese animated cartoon called *Momotarou*, which was highly influenced by the style of Walt Disney. He was so affected by it, he decided to devote his life to drawing comics, a resolve that might have been considered sheer madness in those days. He wanted to create stories that would move people as much as movies did. He wanted to make people cry, smile, and think with his comic vignettes. That was the decisive moment, but his ability to create a new genre didn't come about by divine inspiration. As a child, Tezuka had grown up in a family that was very modern for the times. His father was a great reader of comics. He ordered them from the United States and he even tried his hand at drawing some, while Tezuka's mother would read the American comics to their son. Later, Tezuka became interested in theater and the movies, too, which his parents also had a lot to do with.

Many people consider Tezuka not only the greatest master of *manga* but something like the god of comic books. Some even thought he deserved the Nobel Prize for Literature. That might be going too far, but nobody can deny that comics in Japan would never have become what they are today without Osamu Tezuka.

MODERN MANGA

Osamu Tezuka was inspired by Disney's animation, which he combined with centuries of Japanese artistic tradition while adding his own innovations to create a completely new genre. *Manga* is halfway between a movie and a novel. It has a strong expressive power, and its length allows authors greater depth in developing characters than American or European comics do.

Tezuka finished his first work in 1947 and very quickly sold 400,000 copies. He had created a new art form that combined the movement, vitality, and realism of movies with the text and drawings of comic books. Contemporary *manga* was born. Influenced by Tezuka's work, many artists copying his style started to create *manga*, and *manga* began flooding bookstores, newspaper stands, and libraries all over the country.

LANDMARK WORKS

Osamu Tezuka wrote many *manga* that are now included today on the lists of Japan's literary masterpieces. One of his most outstanding works is *Buddha*, with thousands of pages of adventures and philosophy, where we read about man's weaknesses and the power of self-sacrifice and perseverance—two essential values in Japanese society that derive from *bushido* (see page 15) and, as we have seen, determine the lives of the Japanese, who give their all for their jobs. Others are *The Phoenix*, with more than 3,000 pages of Japanese history and myths; and *Metropolis* and *Astro Boy*, which concern the degree of society's maturity and the possibilities, as well as the dangers, inherent in technology. For Tezuka, any living being is extremely important and must be respected to the utmost, an idea very much in keeping with Shinto (see page 18).

Tezuka, like many of the first *mangaka*, lived the war in the flesh and in all his work. Regardless of genre, there is always a touch of criticism for humanity's immaturity.

TEZUKA'S LEGACY

He died at the early age of 60 but left a legacy of more than 150,000 pages and 60 animated movies. By a rough estimate, Tezuka produced an average of 10 pages a day. He was a virtual machine for creating stories, drawing, writing, and exploring his imagination. He gave everything for his work, which was his passion, with perseverance and absolute commitment. He not only wrote and drew, he also worked tirelessly to spread the culture of *manga*, preaching that it was an art in its own right.

"Comics in Japan would never have become what they are today without Osamu Tezuka."

OSAMU TEZUKA

He was the artist who established the bases for modern *manga*. He combined the movement, vitality, and realism of movies with the text and drawings of comic books, creating a dynamic and attractive form for treating a variety of subjects.

Osamu Tezuka's Atom has become one of the icons of Japanese pop culture.

The author of this book at the celebration of the twentieth anniversary of the beginning of "Dragon Ball."

"*Manga* foster the values of friendship, perseverance, and achievement, values that originated in *bushido* and helped Japan quickly and successfully emerge from the postwar recession."

MANGA'S GOLDEN AGE

From Tezuka's time to ours, just over 70 years have gone by, enough for *manga* to have become the most powerful comic industry in the world and for Japanese animation to be watched not only on televisions all over the planet but on the big screen, where it has won a privileged place.

GEKIGA

During the 1960s and 1970s, *manga* reached its teenager stage, creating specialized genres to satisfy the desires of several sectors of the population and developing new genres, among them *gekiga*. *Gekiga* is a genre aimed at an adult audience that was quite critical of Japan's problems at the time. The authors developed their own style, with very elaborate backgrounds, simple characters, and mostly traditional subject matter, but always under Tezuka's obvious influence. The magazine *Garo* became the greatest exponent of *gekiga*, which was considered both an underground movement and a very potent genre of *manga*, so much so that it even influenced Tezuka, who started drawing more serious works on serious topics, such as *The Phoenix* or *Adolf*.

ACTION SHONEN

The 1970s and 1980s were the superhero years, with *manga* aimed at young people—action *shonen*—helping new generations to dream. But the superheroes in action *shonen* were not American-style immortal heroes. They were heroes who sacrificed everything for their passion since they were children, becoming increasingly better at what they did and constantly outdoing themselves, growing, aging and knowing that one day they would die. There were even cases where the hero did die in the *manga*, causing huge upset among

the series' fans. This happened with *Ashita no Joe*. Many people objected and fans demonstrated outside the publishing company.

The common message in most popular *manga* is, if you work hard, you can achieve anything. This is valid both for children and adults, and it might be the reason why *manga* are read by everyone from the youngest to the oldest. According to the editor of magazine *Shonen Jump*, Hiroki Goto, *manga* foster the values of friendship, perseverance, and achievement, values that originated in *bushido* (see page 15) and helped Japan quickly and successfully emerge from postwar recession.

SHONEN AND SHOJO

Among *manga*, there are many genres but the most successful are *shonen* and *shojo*, which mean "boy" and "girl" respectively. *Shonen manga* are aimed at teenage boys, while *shojo manga* are aimed at the young female sector.

The *shonen* series are the ones that have achieved the most international fame. You have probably heard of *Bleach*, *Naruto*, *Dragon Ball* and *Fullmetal Alchemist*, all well-known *shonen* series that were also produced or are being produced as *anime* series. The subject matter in *shonen* series varies widely, from superheroes to the most conventional high school students recounting their adventures. Generally speaking, the main characters are young men with whom teenagers can identify.

In contrast, *shojo* are aimed at teenage girls and have less varied subject matter. They are almost always romantic stories with female protagonists. After *shonen*, this is the genre that sells best. *Sailor Moon* and *Card Captor Sakura* are perhaps the best-known *shojo* series internationally.

GEKIGA

A *manga* genre aimed at an adult audience that was quite critical of Japan's problems in the postwar period.

In manga, heroes are usually naïve and pure at heart. Enemies are evil at first but very often end up revealing their good side.

MANGA TODAY

Manga is just another element in the daily life of the Japanese. People read them as if they were newspapers. They buy 200–300 yen *mangazasshi* (weekly *manga* magazines) on a regular basis, read them, and then leave them in trains or on benches so that the next person to come along can read them. Reading *manga* is not considered special. It's something people do naturally, just as they read books, magazines, or newspapers in the United States. If someone recommends a title, you don't know whether it's a book or a *manga* until you buy it. As with all Japanese cultural expressions, the group of obsessive fans called *otaku* (see page 92) see *manga* as a way of life. Some *otaku* even make their own *manga*, and there are magazines created by fans called *dojinshi* that are commercialized in places like Akihabara or at events like the Comiket (see page 93).

WHERE DO YOU READ MANGA?

Manga are usually read in the train on your way to work; in establishments called *manga kissas* where you pay by the hour and can choose the *manga* you want to read from shelves full of them; in *konbinis* (24-hour convenience stores), where reading *manga* for free while you're standing there is not frowned upon; in specialized bookstores; in public libraries, etc.

MANGA CHARACTERISTICS

The Japanese are very good at incorporating things from overseas, adding their part, creating an improved version, and then selling it again to the rest of the world, for example, the transistor radio, curry, cars, etc. As regards comics, they took the basic idea from American comics, they Japanized it, and they created something completely new, known as *manga*. Its length is far greater than the typical 32 pages in a comic book, and there are dozens of genres beyond superheroes and adventures. *Manga* achieves an expressive power similar to novels or movies. In fact, Japan is one of the countries with the fewest movie theaters in the world because the *manga* industry is much more powerful than the film industry.

A SOCIAL PHENOMENON

The last two decades have seen the development of a new trend—making television series and movies out of *manga*. For example, *Nana* started off as a *manga* and now there is a book, an animation series, a movie, and video games. With *Densha*

Otoko, the movie was the original medium, and now there is a television series, an animation series, video games, books, and, of course, several *manga*, to the point where it has become a viral phenomenon in Japanese society at all levels. In 2005, *Densha Otoko* popularized a new Japanese word–*moe*–that is used to underscore the obsessive feeling you have with the beauty of a person or animation character (see page 98). There are T-shirts with the word *moe* on them for sale in Akihabara, just to give you an idea of the power *manga* has in Japan.

The life of Japanese people is quite controlled, both at work and in school. They must follow rules at all times and show their respect to people according to their place in the hierarchy, age, etc. They live under a certain degree of repression, and perhaps this is what stimulates their creative power as well as their urge to let the reins of their imagination go by reading *manga*. In the global capitalist society that the world is becoming, *manga* fits in perfectly, helping children and adults dream and encouraging them to try to make their dreams come true.

The golden age of *manga* peaked halfway through the 1990s and since then sales have dropped dramatically. In 2008, sales weren't even half of what they were a decade earlier. The reason is that people are finding other ways to escape, such as the Internet, video games, or mobile phone services. In the 1990s, you could see an average of 10 people per car reading *manga* in the train. Nowadays, there may be about 20 people per car surfing the Internet with their mobile phones, three people playing on their portable game consoles, and one person reading *manga*. The rest read books or newspapers, or sleep.

Other modes of entertainment have eaten up part of the market at the expense of companies with interests in *manga-nime*, who seem to have found the solution to the fall in sales in the export of *manga* culture to other countries. While the *manga* market is declining in Japan, it's growing in Korea, China, and the United States–where it has already become a multi-million-dollar business–and Europe, where the growth trend that began in the 1990s continues. That said, during the last decade, the new *Attack on Titan* is selling so well that it is giving new hope to the industry in Japan. Also, classics like *One Piece*, *Hunter x Hunter*, and *Detective Conan* sell millions of copies per year.

In Japan, manga is considered just another form of culture and is read by everyone, young and old alike.

MANGAKA

A *mangaka* is a manga artist, and he or she always lives under great pressure, particularly the ones who publish in weekly *mangazasshi*, because they must produce about 20 pages every week. Normally, the publisher and the *mangaka* form an inseparable duo and work night and day to meet their deadline. In the *mangaka*'s studio, there are usually several assistants to help draw backgrounds and other details. They almost always remain anonymous and very often work as trainees. For young artists, this is a good way to enter the profession, since the art of *manga* has to be learned under the tutelage of a *sensei* (teacher) and through constant repetition and ceaseless practice until the students outdo their teachers. Another way to start is to join a *manga* school, where they teach you how to draw and tell stories. The most famous *manga* school in the world is run by Kazuo Koie, author of *Lone Wolf and Cub*. The entrance tests for his school are very rigorous.

With *manga* and *mangaka*, authors and stories go hand-in-hand. If an author stops drawing or dies, his *manga* disappears, apart from very few exceptions, such as *Doraemon*. By contrast, in American comics successful titles like *Superman*, *Batman*, *Spiderman*, and X-Men are controlled by the publishing companies/ producers and never by their authors, and as long as the title is profitable the story will never end.

People reading at a konbini outlet.

MANGAKA

A *mangaka* is a *manga* artist. He or she usually works with a team of assistants who help meet deadlines.

PUBLISHING CYCLES AND FORMATS

A *mangaka* who wants to make a living with his drawings usually starts by sending stories to *mangazasshi* publishers. If the publishers decide to publish a story of his, it will appear in one of their weekly magazines. In every *mangazasshi* there is an opinion card to be filled out by readers, who send it to the publishing company for a popularity ranking. Publishers listen to their readers attentively, and if readers say something is good publishers will continue asking the *mangaka* for more material. If the series ends up being very successful, it's published in *tankobon* (compiled volume) format. And if it becomes a "hit," it's published in other formats, such as *bunkobon* (paperback format) or collector's format, or is made into an *anime*. This was the course followed by Akira Toriyama, for example. He sent some stories to *Weekly Shonen Jump* that readers didn't like very much, until he came up with *Dr. Slump*, which gave him his first success. Later on, with *Dragon Ball*, he broke all records, and today he has sold more than 150 million volumes in Japan alone—more than one volume per inhabitant!

FORMATS

Mangazasshi: Thick magazines printed on cheap paper that contain approximately 20 stories of 20–30 pages each. Their low prices help them to be consumed as if they were newspapers. The difference is that for *mangazasshi* there is a second-hand market because people discard them and others with little money pick them up and resell them. The most popular *mangazasshi* is *Weekly Shonen Jump*.

Tankobon: Compiled volumes of only one series in about 200 pages. This is the real meat of the business, where publishing companies make money.

Bunkobon: Similar to *tankobon* but smaller. They are usually the paperback version. Only the most successful series come out in *bunkobon*.

Other formats: There are other *manga* formats for special editions and collector's editions, as well as really inexpensive volumes sold in 24-hour convenience stores.

Examples of mangazasshi, which are published weekly and contain many stories.

Tankobon, a compiled volume format.

Bunkobon, a paperback format.

JAPANESE ANIME

Anime is an adaptation of the English word animation and is used worldwide to refer to animated cartoons produced by Japanese artists. The art of Japanese animation goes back to the turn of the twentieth century. However, it began to grow in earnest thanks to the *anime* production studio founded in the 1950s by Osamu Tezuka, who tried to imitate Walt Disney but with a much lower budget and using animators who had no real experience.

THE BIRTH OF A NEW INDUSTRY

During the 1960s and especially the 1970s, a whole animation industry came into being, thanks to the success of *manga*. These two industries always go hand in hand. In the 1970s, animation series with gigantic robots for heroes came into fashion. *Gundam*, *Macross*, and *Mazinger Z* are some of the most famous productions. In the 1980s, many more genres appeared, and almost all best-selling *manga* were adapted into animation series.

A GLOBAL PHENOMENON

Toward the end of the 1980s, *anime* became a global phenomenon that gained in strength with the arrival of the Internet in the 1990s. The most successful animation series are those that have been adapted from *shonen manga* for teenagers, such as *Dragon Ball*, *Naruto*, and *One Piece*, and series aimed at children, like *Doraemon*.

ANIME IN THE MOVIES

Besides series, the *anime* industry also produces movies. Studio Ghibli is perhaps the Japanese animation studio best known worldwide. Founded in the 1980s, it specialized in film production. Its most famous movie is *Spirited Away*, which won awards at the Oscars and the Berlinale competing against movies with real live actors. The main creator in Studio Ghibli is Hayao Miyazaki, considered one of the most important artists in the country. In 2005, I had the honor of meeting the president of Ghibli, Toshio Suzuki, and his words summing up the company's philosophy are engraved in my mind: "Hayao Miyazaki takes care of creating movies that will make both children and adults dream, and I take care of getting those movies to make money."

Besides Ghibli productions, other movies such as *Akira*, *Neon Genesis Evangelion*, and *Ghost in the Shell* also achieved international success in the 1980s and 1990s, and influenced and inspired people all over the world. For example, director Quentin Tarantino likes *anime* so much, particularly animation made by Studio Production I.G., creators of *Ghost in the Shell*, that he ended up working with them to create *anime* scenes for his movie *Kill Bill*. Furthermore, movies by Makoto Shinkai, such as *Your Name* or *The Garden of Words*, are achieving international recognition.

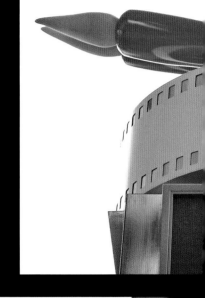

"Hayao Miyazaki takes care of creating movies that will make both children and adults dream, and I take care of getting these movies to make money." —Toshio Suzuki

The figure of Joe from "Tomorrow's Joe," probably the most successful manga at the end of the 1960s and beginning of the 1970s. It's considered a classic.

北自由通路

KYOTO
塚治虫ワールド

destrian Walkway

Astro Boy, the hero created by Osamu Tezuka, is considered one of the country's symbols.

Images from the Ghibli Museum.

CHAPTER 9
MODERN JAPANESE MUSIC

Two Japanese women wearing the traditional kimono and playing the koto. This is a string instrument that arrived from China more than 1,500 years ago.

The taiko drum is one of the most common percussion instruments in Japanese traditional music.

A BRIEF HISTORY OF JAPANESE MUSIC

The Japanese word for music is 音楽 *ongaku*. It combines the *kanji* for 音 (sound) with the *kanji* for 楽 (comfort, pleasure, music). In Japan there are thousands of bands. The country is also the empire of Sony, one of the world's largest record companies, creator of the Walkman and, together with Philips, creator of the compact disc. However, Japanese musicians and singers don't usually achieve worldwide fame. Why not? Let's take a look at the origins of Japanese music in order to understand the main characteristics and peculiarities of the music culture in this country.

THE FIRST STYLES

If we go back to the seventh century, we find *gagaku*, one of the earliest styles of Japanese music for which there is documentary evidence. It actually came from China and Korea. During the following centuries, it underwent transformation but today there are still performances at the imperial court. The main instruments in *gagaku* all derive from the lute. String instruments played an essential role in the development of Japanese traditional music.

MUSIC IN THE SCENIC ARTS

In *Noh*, *kabuki*, and *bunraku* traditional theater (see page 29), music is one the most important elements in the performance. Traditional instruments like the three-stringed *shamisen*, *taiko* drum, and *shakuhachi* flute were used, and those forms of theater influenced the evolution of musical styles. Today, these instruments are still used in theater as well as in traditional

music performances, at Shinto and Buddhist festivals, and in establishments where *geisha* entertain. Contemporary musicians looking to innovate also incorporate some of these instruments to add a traditional touch to their compositions. With the arrival of the Meiji Restoration at the end of the nineteenth century, Western music was introduced rather successfully, and it began to influence Japanese artists.

ONGAKU

The Japanese word for music is 音楽 *ongaku*. It combines the *kanji* 音 (sound) with the *kanji* 楽 (comfort, pleasure, music).

The shamisen is a traditional three-stringed Japanese instrument, which is plucked.

Misora Hibari, an enka singer, was the best-known public figure in Japan during the postwar decades.

ENKA BALLADS

Enka constitutes a genre of Japanese popular ballad that could be considered the greatest popular exemplar of Japanese traditional music, although it arose only in the nineteenth century. When we listen to *enka*, we penetrate the heart of Japan. Frequently labeled Japan's national music, it came into being with the arrival of Western instruments and their use in playing compositions based on the pentatonic scale.

Generally speaking, *enka* music is melodramatic, sad, and nostalgic. The lyrics usually revolve around the loneliness and yearning the hero feels during lengthy stays far from his or her loved ones. Another recurrent theme is hopeless or unrequited love. The ballads reveal traditional notions held by Japanese men and women in secret, and they exemplify the Japanese concept of romance. Contemporary *enka* music is very similar to 1950s *enka*. It's a genre that doesn't change much, and that helps it transport the Japanese to other periods through music.

THE STRUCTURE OF ENKA MUSIC

Enka music is highly repetitive and is based on patterns that have been used for decades with little variation. These patterns are nothing other than *kata*, repetitions used for practice and to improve a person's ability in an art. *Kabuki*, the tea ceremony, and flower arrangement also rely on *kata* as the center of their creation. Since *enka* doesn't change, they say that even listen-

"*Enka* music is melodramatic, sad, and nostalgic."

ing to a modern song you will find yourself transported to the past. However, since the song is new, the feeling is nostalgic and comforting at the same time, because you have the sense that time doesn't go by.

ENKA

Japanese traditional music, born of Western influence, with a melancholy feel and a highly repetitive structure.

MISORA HIBARI: THE ENKA QUEEN

Misora Hibari is considered by many people as the queen of *enka* music and the most important Japanese music artist of all time. She started her singing career in the 1940s when she was only seven years old. In addition to being a singer, she was also an actress and appeared in more than 70 films from 1949 to the end of the 1980s. Thanks to her twin abilities, she became the first great celebrity in the postwar years. During her lifetime (she died at 52), she launched more than 1,000 songs, many of which would become authentic classics, for example, "Kawa no nagare no yo ni," considered by many to be the best Japanese song ever written.

JAPANESE MUSIC TODAY

In Japan there are thousands of karaoke clubs, and people love to go there to sing and spend time with their friends. Generally, karaoke clubs consist of entire buildings with private rooms that are rented by the hour so you can have as much privacy as you wish.

More than once, I've been surprised at how well some of my Japanese friends sing; they sound like professionals. But when they tell me they've been going to karaoke clubs two or three times a week for 20 years, it's not surprising.

"Many amateur bands practice on weekends in Tokyo's Yoyogi Park."

HOW TO ACHIEVE FAME

There are more and more ways to become famous through music. Some singers and bands become famous by creating music for video games; for others, coming up with a tune for a TV commercial suffices, and some become stars from the soundtrack for a *dorama* or an *anime* series.

Composing music for a furniture store commercial may seem insignificant, but the truth is that given the number of people watching television in Japan, advertisements can have a huge impact. Surveys say that 97 percent of the population of 127 million watch television at least once a day. Another way to gain stardom in music is by becoming an idol from appearing on television or being a fashion model. Once someone has achieved celebrity by either of these two routes, producers jump into action and help the idols create their first record.

MUSIC IN VIDEO GAMES

The world of video games is so important that many musicians become famous making music only for this format. Such is the case of Koji Kondo, Nintendo's main composer, and Nobuo Uematsu, Squaresoft's main composer. Higher profile artists like Utada Hikaru have used video games to spread their music or extend their audience, composing songs for games or for video game commercials on television.

Playing the guitar in Yoyogi Park on a Sunday is a popular pasttime.

Practice time for a drummer in a J-pop band.

Exile is probably the best-known male pop dance band in Japan.

J-POP

J-pop is the abbreviation for "Japanese pop," coined by J-WAVE radio in the early 1990s. It refers to Japanese popular music and covers all musical creation not considered *enka* or traditional. At first, J-pop was the universal term used to distinguish any new Japanese song from imported music. But, little by little, coinages like J-rock, J-ska, J-soul, J-rap, and Visual Kei were created to designate different music styles of Japanese artists.

Today's J-pop style arose at the end of the 1970s from an earlier genre called *kayokyu*, literally Western music, that had, for its part, evolved after World War II with the arrival of jazz in Japan and the introduction of a number of instruments hardly used by Japanese musicians up until then.

THE SECRET OF SUCCESS

J-pop songs, being generally easy to sing, and the popularization of karaoke at about the same time gave the genre a boost. Japanese people love karaoke and love to imitate their idols.

Thanks to the spread of karaoke clubs and the arrival of CDs and the Walkman, catchy J-pop music enjoyed greater and greater popularity. The boom in bands of the 1980s and 1990s made the genre famous even outside Japan.

Music stores in Japan commonly classify music in the following categories: J-pop, *enka*, classical music, and English/international.

"In Japan, the term J-pop is used to distinguish modern music styles from classical music and traditional *enka*."

J-POP

J-pop is a term that groups together many different music genres, but it essentially refers to Japanese popular music.

X Japan

J-pop idols start trends among young Japanese people.

POPULAR SINGERS AND GROUPS

Hikaru Utada Daughter of an *enka* singer and raised in Tokyo and New York, Hikaru Utada is one of Japan's most internationally known artists. Many of her songs are in English. She holds the record for solo album sales in Japan and is one of the country's one hundred wealthiest people. She has sung the main themes of some of the most popular video games and acclaimed movies.

Dreams Come True This duet comprises Masato Nakamura and Miwa Yoshida. Nakamura was the composer of the music for the video game *Sonic the Hedgehog* for Sega Megadrive. Miwa Yoshida is the singer, and together they make music with a romantic undertone that is very successful among Japanese schoolgirls.

Ayumi Hamasaki A soloist, Ayumi Hamasaki has sold the most records in all of Japan's history. She was born in 1978, and by 2005 she had already sold almost 50 million records. Ayumi worked as an actress in minor television series because she wasn't tall enough to be a model, until a talent scout discovered her singing at a karaoke club in Shibuya, one of the places most frequented by young Tokyo girls.

From the very beginning, Ayumi showed enormous talent, coupled with a somewhat rebellious attitude. When she was 21, she had her first number one hit on the Japanese charts with "A Song for XX." From then on, it was all smash hits, big concerts, music for video games, television programs, being the face of important commercial firms, modeling for magazines, and fame in China and Korea. In short, she is an idol and trendsetter with a strong influence on young Japanese people.

Seiko Matsuda Born in 1962, she wore the popularity crown from the 1980s to the end of the 1990s when Ayumi Hamasaki replaced her. She is still considered one of the most influential J-pop singers in history. In fact, you could say her music defined what is today considered J-pop. In 2006, Sony launched a collection of no fewer than 55 CDs comprising all her records.

Namie Amuro Born in 1977 in Okinawa, the islands south of Japan, Namie Amuro achieved fame in 1995. From then on, her music was a big success, surpassed only by the music of stars like Ayumi Hamasaki and Hikaru Utada. Starting in 2000, her style began to change, shifting from J-pop to R&B. Her dark skin induced many young women fans to want to imitate her, and suntan salons came into fashion. Little by little, and due also to the influence of American singers, the urban tribe of *gals* came into being (see page 96), characterized by their tanned skins, extravagant hairdos, and platform shoes, which Namie Amuro had worn in the early days of her career.

Morning Musume We mustn't forget Morning Musume, a group in which the singers are never the same but change constantly. As one becomes famous, he or she abandons the group, and the opening they leave is always filled by new hopefuls discovered by the producer's talent scouts.

"Ayumi Hamasaki is the solo artist who has the sold the most records ever in Japan."

Ayumi Hamasaki

Perfume This Japanese pop group comprises three singers from Hiroshima. They started in 2000 and reached global fame after signing a contract with Universal Music Group in 2012. Their style is difficult to classify as they have evolved different styles over the years, combining Shibuya-kei with electronic dance music, thus creating their own unique type of music.

Orange Range This is a pop-rock group made up of five boys from Okinawa. Their music mixes many styles, and one of their singles was chosen as the official song for the 2006 World Cup in Germany. Many of their songs have become famous in Japan from being used in television commercials.

Kumi Koda Born in 1982, she's ready to snatch the crown away from veterans Ayumi Hamasaki and Hikaru Utada and, to a certain extent, she already has. She was chosen as the best pop artist in 2006 and 2007. Her image is slightly more radical than Ayumi or Hikaru's, because she tries to project the image of a strong and domineering woman, something rather unusual in Japan, where traditionally women choose an image that is *kawaii,* "cute" or "pretty."

Kumi Koda

Namie Amuro

The band AKB48 from the Akihabara otaku area became one of the most popular groups by 2010.

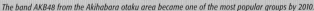

Ai Otsuka She became famous not long ago and lately has bolstered her fame hosting television shows. One of her best-known records is *Love Jam*, which was popularized partly thanks to its controversial cover featuring a photo of herself with jam smeared on her face.

L'Arc-en-Ciel This is a male pop-rock band, considered by HMV as one of the 100 best Japanese bands of all time. They achieved international fame thanks to the fact that their music appears in many *anime* series.

SMAP A band composed of five men, it is probably the most famous male group in Japan. Besides performing music, they appear as actors in movies and *dorama* and on television, where they even have their own show. Their song "Sekai ni hitotsu dake no hana" is one of the most popular songs in Japanese karaoke clubs.

X Japan This heavy metal group gained great popularity in the 1990s. Their success continued until the group broke up and all of its members struck out on their own as solo artists. In 2007,

they announced a comeback after more than 10 years not playing together. X Japan is often credited with inspiring *visual kei* (see page 99).

GLAY This is another pop-rock band. Its members have known each other since they were students at the same high school in Hokkaido. They are one of the best-known bands in Asia.

AKB48 AKB48, a girl group, is the modern version of Morning Musume. Founded in 2005 in Akihabara, AKB48 was for many years the top J-pop idol group in Japan. The group started with 48 members but grew to include more than 100 singers and dancers, who were split into different teams. The band was active from 1988 until 2016. Its breakup in 2016 hit the headlines for weeks.

Nogizaka 46 Nogizaka 46 is another female J-pop idol group, which was created in 2011 to compete with AKB48. Considered more "elegant and refined" than its rival, Nogizaka 46 has become one of the hottest and most popular girl groups in Japan, generating the most sales among girl groups.

CHAPTER 10
MOVIES AND TELEVISION

HOWL'S MOVING CASTLE

大

画

ぱちんこ
仮面ライダー
ショッカー全滅大作戦

!! KYORAKU

Akira Kurosawa's movies brought Japanese cinema to the international scene. "Seven Samura" and "Sanjuro" were two of his most successful movies.

JAPANESE CINEMA

The movie and television industry in Japan is the second most lucrative in the world, right after the United States. It's a huge industry where everything intermingles, and if a story is successful it is quickly adapted from *manga* into an animation series, then a television series with live actors, or it can even make it to the big screen.

THE FIFTIES:
BIRTH OF JAPANESE CINEMA

The separate worlds of *manga*, *anime*, television, and movies have been evolving together since the postwar period. The 1950s saw the arrival of television in Japan as well as the birth of the *manga* and *anime* industries. It was also the beginning of the internationalization of more sophisticated Japanese movies, of which Akira Kurosawa was the greatest exponent.

THE SIXTIES AND SEVENTIES:
POPULARIZATION

In the 1960s and 1970s, the first *doramas* and long *anime* series appeared on television. *Manga* reached maturity during the same period, giving rise to all the genres that would keep on developing in subsequent decades.

THE EIGHTIES AND NINETIES:
INTERNATIONALIZATION

Beginning in the 1980s and 1990s, movies, *anime*, and *manga* achieved international fame. In the case of *anime* and *manga*, international diffusion on a large scale was partly due to Akira Toriyama, Katsuhiro Otomo, and Studio Ghibli, and later on to the success of *Evangelion*, *One Piece*, and *Naruto*. In the world of cinema, Takeshi Kitano and, above all, Hideo Nakata's movie *Ring* again drew Western attention to Japanese movies, especially in the genre of psychological horror. Hollywood began adapting more and more Japanese movies, which as remakes found their place on Western movie listings.

"Akira Kurosawa marked the beginning of Japanese movies achieving international impact in the 1950s. His first movies to win wide acclaim were *Rashomon* and *Seven Samurai*."

The march toward the success of Japanese audiovisual productions began with Akira Kurosawa and his black-and-white film *Rashomon,* which won the Oscar for Best Foreign Film in 1951.

THE TWENTY-FIRST CENTURY

The next milestone was Studio Ghibli's animation movie *Spirited Away*, which captivated the most demanding movie critics and won numerous awards, including an Oscar for Best Animated Feature, placing Japanese creators on the international scene. Another milestone was Yojiro Takita's *Departures*, winner of the Oscar for Best Foreign Film and many other awards in 2008.

Today, Japanese animation artists are world leaders in this domain and no one can outdo them in creating animation. In movies with live actors, too, Japanese directors have their own clearly defined style, which is starting to influence other productions. Quentin Tarantino, for instance, confesses to being a fervent admirer of Japanese movies.

Japanese movies tend to have a slow rhythm but they hook the audience with their atmosphere, which makes you think, and with their long silences suffused with meaning, scores using traditional instruments, and a suite of lesser narrative devices that add up to a distinctive Japanese style.

For example, the 2010 movie *Norwegian Wood*, based on Haruki Murakami's best-selling novel, communicates profoundly to viewers about the Japanese heart and way of feeling the emotions of love and affection. Another internationally acclaimed Japanese director is Hirokazu Koreeda, thanks mainly to his movie *Shoplifters*.

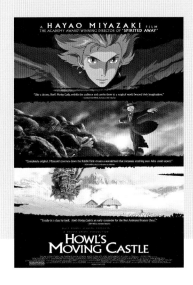

Takeshi Kitano's "Kikujiro" is a moving film about friendship and family.

A statue of Tora-san, a beloved and charismatic fictional character from Japanese cinema.

THE CLASSICS

AKIRA KUROSAWA

Akira Kurosawa marked the beginning of Japanese movies achieving international impact in the 1950s. His first movies to win wide acclaim were *Rashomon* and *Seven Samurai*. Another leading director of this period was Yasujiro Ozu, who created and directed *Tokyo Story* in 1953, a melodramatic movie with certain stylistic touches directly imported from American movies.

KAIJU: MONSTERS MADE IN JAPAN

Godzilla was released in 1954. It was the first movie featuring the monster that would gradually become one of Japan's most recognizable international symbols. Godzilla is a mutant monster, the result of some failed experiments with hydrogen bombs—recalling the Hiroshima and Nagasaki catastrophes—that yearns to destroy. Halfway through the 1960s, rival studios created Gamera to compete with Godzilla's popularity. Gamera is a gigantic biped turtle with great destructive power thanks to its mighty flame-throwing breath. The passion for gigantic mutant creatures (*kaiju* in Japanese) kept growing, with the appearance of many more series and movies with new gigantic monsters in the leading roles. The ceaseless production of this kind of movie ended in a new genre known as *kaiju*, although *kaiju* is really a subgenre of *tokuhatsu*, as we will see in the *dorama* section at the end of this chapter.

JIDAIGEKI: SAMURAI IN THEIR ELEMENT

Another important genre among Japanese movies is *jidaigeki*— period movies. These historical movies are usually set in the Edo Period (1603–1868) and have *samurai* as protagonists. *Seven Samurai* by Akira Kurosawa and *Zatoichi* by Takeshi Kitano are the most notable examples. There are hundreds of *jidaigeki* movies, but most of them never get seen outside Japan.

THE TORA-SAN PHENOMENON

The 1970s marked the beginning of a series of films called *Otoko wa tsurai yo* (It's Tough Being a Man), which holds the

KAIJU MOVIES

The prototypical Japanese movie genre, devoted to gigantic monsters like Godzilla and Gamera.

"A very important genre among Japanese movies is *jidaigeki*. These historical movies are set in the Edo Period and their heroes are most often *samurai*."

Guinness record for the longest film series in history, with 48 feature films. The first episode in the series was released in 1969 and the last one in 1995. The hero in all of them is Tora-san, a businessman who is always looking for love but never achieves his aim in any of the movies. Tora-san is one of the most charismatic and best-known fictional characters in Japan.

INTERNATIONALIZATION OF ANIME

The 1980s saw the beginning of the internationalization of *anime* movies with features like *Akira* by Katsuhiro Otomo and *Nausicaä of the Valley of Wind* by the master Hayao Miyazaki.

THE POWER OF TAKESHI KITANO AND TAKASHI MIIKE

In the 1990s, Takeshi Kitano became famous worldwide with several movies that won awards at international festivals. Another Japanese director, Takashi Miike, also began to be known overseas, thanks to movies like *Audition* and *Dead or Alive*.

CONQUERING AMERICA

Beginning in the year 2000, a new wave of Hollywood remakes started with horror movies like *The Ring* and *Dark Water*. Takeshi Kitano has kept making successful movies, and Hayao Miyazaki achieved international success with *Spirited Away* and subsequent *anime* features, such as *Howl's Moving Castle*, a drama/fantasy.

TELEVISION

Since the early years of television, Japan has always been at the forefront of the industry. In 1960, Japan already had five channels and it was the third country in the world to enjoy color television. TV rapidly became a mass phenomenon, and today surveys say that 97 percent of Japanese watch television at least once a day. NHK is the national television company, with several channels. Also prominent are Fuji TV, Nippon TV, TV Asahi, and TBS. The world of television is huge in Japan. There is a whole agglomeration of producers, model agencies, actor agencies, and even agencies that organize life for those who are on television.

TYPES OF GEINOJIN

People who are famous thanks to the small screen are known as *geinojin*.

Aidoru (Idol): *Idols* are young women who are either beautiful or have some outstanding attribute and who become famous when they appear scantily clad in magazines. Those with charm end up being on shows simply to display their beauty and offer a comment now and then.

Geinin (Comedians): Comedians usually work in pairs known as *manzai* and do short performances as guests on programs. Those who make it big may end up landing their own show. Takeshi Kitano, for example, started as a *geinin* working with a partner in the purest *manzai* style and ended up hosting his own program and directing movies.

Haiu-joyu (Actor/Actress): Actors on Japanese television series, known as *dorama*, may also achieve quite a lot of fame, often surpassing movies actors.

Tarento (Talent): These are celebrities without having any outstanding ability who appear on television. They are neither singers, comedians, nor actors, but personalities who usually appear as guests on talk, interview, game, or similar shows. Normally, *tarento* possess a well-defined personality and some mannerism they use whenever they're on television, for example, a particular way of saying goodbye or laughing that makes them unique and easily remembered by the general public.

Kashu (Singer): The most famous singers not only sing on television but also host programs. The members of the SMAP band (see page 122) are the most prolific at this. They appear in several programs, series, and commercials, and even have their own show.

Anaunsaa (Host): These are newscasters or television hosts who become famous. The best known end up working for many shows, with their faces on television all the time. Mino Monta is one of the TV hosts with the most on-screen hours. In 2006, there were times when he was on live TV more than 20 hours a week!

Seiyu (Voice Actor): They are voice actors in movies and *anime* series. It's not hard to find them making guests appearances on TV shows since they have hordes of admirers.

(see page 122)

The name given to people who become famous thanks to television.

Fuji TV is one of the most emblematic studios in Japan.

In 1960, there were five TV channels broadcasting in Japan. Today, more than 30 million Japanese people own a mobile phone fitted with a digital TV receiver.

THE FIRST TELEVISION PHENOMENA

One of the first television shows to achieve national prominence was *Hachiji da yo, Zenin shugo*. Its main attraction was a group of comedians called The Drifters. It began to be televised in the 1960s and didn't end until 1985. A comedy variety show, it was the most watched program of the 1970s and is still considered the most watched in the history of Japanese television. In the 1980s, its success started to decline with the arrival of *Oretachi Hyokin Zoku*, starring Sanma Akashiya and Takeshi Kitano, both of whom had an innovative style of humor that made people forget about the classic Drifters.

SANMA AKASHIYA

Sanma Akashiya continued his career as the star of his own interview show called *Sanma no manma*, which in 2010 celebrated its twenty-third year on the air. For the occasion, Takeshi Kitano appeared on the show. Together with Takeshi Kitano and Tamori, Sanma Akashiya is considered one of the three greatest showmen on Japanese television.

TAKESHI KITANO

Takeshi Kitano achieved international fame when he starred in movies like *Zatoichi* and *Battle Royale*, which were shown in many movie theaters around the world. However, he had already created an international phenomenon with *Operation! Takeshi's Castle*, known in the United States as *MXC* (*Most Extreme Elimination Challenge*). In the show, the aim of the contestants was to survive all the challenges and defeat Takeshi Kitano. The winner received a prize of one million yen. Nowadays, Takeshi Kitano is still one of the most recognized faces in the country. He is on several television shows every week and directs movies from his own studio in Tokyo.

"Besides the national television company NHK, the most important networks are Fuji TV, Nippon TV, TV Asahi, and TBS."

TAMORI

The third big name in Japanese television is Tamori, famous since the 1970s and easily recognizable by the sunglasses he always wears on TV. His top program is *Waratte Iitomo*, which has been on the air since 1982. This program, filmed in Studio Alta in Shinjuku, is shown live on a giant screen outside the building and can be watched from the street. The Studio Alta screen has become one of the most famous rendezvous points in Tokyo. You see it as soon as you set foot outside the East Exit of Shinjuku (JR). If you get there by the subway, it's Exit 13B. Studio Alta is easy to recognize because it has the large screen, and the rendezvous point is right below it. When you consider that Shinjuku Station has almost 100 exits, the reason it's such a good meeting place is obvious.

WATCHING TV IN JAPAN

If you travel to Japan, watching television for a while can be entertaining even if you don't understand the language. You'll see commercials that sometimes verge on the absurd and would appear ridiculous if they were broadcast on a Western channel. You'll watch comedy shows where you'll appreciate how one of the ways to get Japanese people to laugh is to make fun of someone. And you'll see a high percentage of programs devoted just to showing people eating and giving their opinions on the food.

"Densha Otoko" is one of the best-known Japanese doramas overseas.

Several TV programs are filmed in Studio Alta. The most famous is "Waratte Iitomo," which has been running for more than 20 years.

DORAMA TV SERIES

In Japanese, the word *dorama* is used to designate any kind of television series in general, be it romance, comedy, or any other genre. Successful television series usually have a greater impact than good Japanese or foreign movies, and they often provide a wonderful opportunity for actors and actresses to go from obscurity to absolute stardom.

> "Korea has ended up developing its own *dorama* style, and now it is exporting *doramas* to Japan where they enjoy greater success than in their country of origin."

SUBJECT MATTER IN DORAMAS

Japanese *doramas* usually take on burning issues in modern Japanese life in order to deeply touch the audience. Many of them revolve around the life of a family, the problems of each one of its members, the problems the father has managing his company, the daughter and her boyfriends, the son who gets into trouble with gangs, and so on. But the most successful ones are undoubtedly romantic *doramas*, which are normally about a pure, ideal, platonic love that cannot be fulfilled due to some obstacle.

TOKUHATSU SUPERHERO

One of the *dorama* genres best known overseas is *tokuhatsu*. Its golden age was in the 1960s and 1970s. *Tokuhatsu* are *doramas* or movies with certain "special effects," and, generally speaking, in those decades, were productions where the heroes wore bright superhero suits. *Ultraman*, *Power Rangers*, and *Kamen Rider* are some of the most successful *tokuhatsu doramas* of that period. With the arrival of computer-generated special effects, the genre lost steam, but today there are still reruns, new movies, and video games based on them.

DORAMAS OVERSEAS

Some of the most successful *dorama* are usually exported to Korea or Taiwan. In Korea's case, something curious has happened, for Korea ended up developing its own *dorama* style and now is exporting to Japan, where the shows enjoy greater success than in their country of origin. *Fuyu no sonata*, (Winter Sonata) created in South Korea, became Japan's most-watched *dorama* in the last decade when NHK, the Japanese national television station, brought it to Japan. Its main actor, Bae Yong-joon, became one of the most popular celebrities in Japan, much more so than in his native country. This is a shining example of the level of success a television series can achieve in Japan. But *dorama* haven't only traveled to Korea, Taiwan, and Asia in general. Thanks to the Internet, series such as *Densha Otoko* or *Nodame cantabile* became vehicles for the Japanese *dorama* phenomenon to spread all over the world.

DORAMA

In Japanese, the word *dorama* is used to designate any kind of television series, be it romance, comedy, or any other genre.

"Kamen Rider" was one of the first superheroes in the tokuhatsu genre.

A Kamen Rider pachinko machine advertisement.

In Chapters 8–10 we only scratched the surface of Japanese pop culture but have tried to emphasize how intertwined movies, manga, anime, music, and television, etc. are in Japan. In this last photograph, you can see the superheroes in a tokuhatsu series, a J-pop singer (Kumi Koda) and a manga character teaming up to advertize a pachinko parlor.

DIAGRAM OF A CULTURAL PHENOMENON IN JAPAN BASED ON THE ACTUAL CASE OF DENSHA OTOKO

In the last three chapters we have seen how *manga*, movies, *anime*, and music are all interconnected. The industry makes the most of its success in any one of these media and adapts it to the other media. The way a phenomenon begins can vary greatly. Often an *anime* is made from a successful *manga*, and then come the movies and the video games. Other times, the process begins with the *anime* or video game. Sometimes it starts off with a toy or figurine that is especially successful among children and teenagers. An *anime* series is then based on the toy, followed by the *manga*, video games, and all kinds of other things. Below is a diagram of how *Densha Otoko* became a worldwide Japanese pop culture phenomenon from a series of messages on the largest Internet forum in Japan, 2-channel.

IT BEGINS ON THE INTERNET

An anonymous person writes the story on 2-channel, the largest Internet forum in Japan.

DORAMA

Word of it gets around, and Fuji TV decides to create a *dorama* based on the 2-channel story.

VIDEO GAMES

Video games are created by groups of fans of 2-channel.

WORLDWIDE PHENOMENON

Fans subtitle the *dorama* in English and distribute it over the Internet so that it becomes a worldwide *otaku* phenomenon.

NOVELS

Several light novels—a very conversational style of Japanese novel—are published, developing and extending the story in the *dorama*.

THE MOVIE

A movie based on the original story and having a very similar plot to the *dorama* is made.

THEATER

A theatrical production based on the movie.

MUSIC

A J-pop song by Orange Range that is used in the movie becomes a nationwide hit.

ANIME

Anime series based on the *manga*.

MANGA

Manga based on the *dorama* and the light novels.

MERCHANDISING

Card games and general merchandising based on the *manga* and the *dorama*.

MOE

The word *moe* used by the *dorama* characters becomes part of the Japanese language and Japanese aesthetics (see page 98). The characters in the images at left exemplify the *moe* aesthetic.

Crypton Future Media/CC BY-NC

COSPLAY

Many people do *cosplay* of the main characters at events.

FIGURINES

Figurines based on the characters in the *manga*.

CHAPTER 11
VIDEO GAMES

The Pokémon Center in Yokohama. There are eleven such shops around Japan.

JAPANESE VIDEO GAMES

At the beginning of the 1990s, more than 50 percent of the video games sold in the world were made in Japan. Over time, Japanese video game producers have lost quite a lot of market share although Japan is still the biggest producer of video games.

The Japanese are very good at developing and manufacturing hardware but not so good when it comes to software, a sector in which generally speaking the Americans outdo them. Big software companies such as Microsoft, Sun Microsystem, and Oracle are American, while Japan is notable for its multinationals which are specialists in creating hardware, such as Sony, Toshiba, and Sharp. But it is not easy to name Japanese companies dedicated to developing software that stands out globally. The exception is in the development of video games, which although software driven are something that the Japanese are extremely good at and have been leaders in for several decades.

Even here, when it comes to developing video games for computers, they are also outdone by the Americans. They are undisputed leaders when they are the ones that design both the hardware and the software, as is the case with Nintendo, Sony Computer Entertainment, and Sega (until they stopped developing hardware).

Why? I'm not sure, but maybe it's a consequence of the Japanese nature and of the development methodology that is implemented in Japanese companies. In general, Japanese companies tend to take few risks. They take decisions after weighing up all the possible consequences and don't carry out changes until they are absolutely sure. This is an excellent philosophy when it comes to manufacturing hardware in which the development of each product can go on for several years and in which each new version of the product uses parts of the previous ones. For example, inside today's televisions there are chips that are the result of the evolution of an idea that has been growing and evolving within a company for decades. The television as a product is slowly improving bit by bit. This methodology of continuous improvement is known as *kaizen* (see page 64) and one

> "A video game development company without an engine to work with is like a photographer without a camera.... The better the engine, the higher the maximum theoretical quality of the video games created by it."

of the companies that best applies it is Toyota, whose production system is studied by business owners all over the world.

However, in the software industry, you need to be more agile when dealing with change. It is an industry that can change in a matter of months, especially since the emergence of the Internet. American, European, and also most recently Israeli companies, are much more skillful at facing up to change and developing new software as trends change. Do you know of a big Japanese software company, with the exception of video games? Do you know of a big Japanese Internet company?

What is special about the development of video games that allows them to adapt to Japanese companies' way of operating even though they are still software? Video game programming is quite compatible with the Japanese mentality. To develop games you need an engine, the development of which can go on for many years and be used as the basis for creating tens of video games. A video game development company without an engine to work with is like a photographer without a camera. The engine is the fundamental tool with which to create new games, in the same way that the camera is the photographer's tool for creating art. The better the camera, the higher the maximum theoretical quality of the photos the artist can take. The better the engine, the higher the maximum theoretical quality of the video games created by it.

None of Japan's video game companies have any trouble applying "continuous revision" (*kaizen*) to improve their engine or engines, and continue improving the tool which allows them to build their games. For example, Nintendo has a big advantage over its competition. As one of the companies that has spent the

(Left) The Pokémon phenomenon is huge in Japan.
(Below) If you love retrogaming, Japan is filled with places to buy second-hand games, such as in Akihabara or Den Den Town.

most time in the industry, it has internal development tools and engines whose foundations have been settling for over 20 years. It is unlikely that a new European company could compete at the same level.

Another example is Square Enix, whose engines to create RPG-type games have also been in development for more than 20 years and without a shadow of a doubt are the best in the industry. In Square Enix, the main task in creating a new game is not really to create new software. It is not a task for programmers or engineers. Creating video games is increasingly an artist's job. Some call it "the eighth art." Movie and photography directors work part-time creating games; musicians who previously created soundtracks for movies now do it for games; and most importantly, thousands of cartoonists who at another time would have devoted themselves to drawing *manga*, these days make video games. Even Akira Toriyama, the creator of *Dragon Ball*, has for the last few years worked mainly on the design of the characters in Square Enix's *Dragon Quest* franchise games.

To sum up, to be good at creating video games, it is important to have solid foundations, a good engine, and a piece of software whose programming is the responsibility of engineers, but whose development is quite stable and malleable in comparison with other areas of the software industry, such as the web. Once you have an engine on which to build games, what's really important when it comes to creating a good game is to write a good script, plan, and design and plot all the other artistic elements that together will create a unique experience for the gamer. Combining all these elements skillfully is not easy, but Japan has some of the best artists with the capability of doing it. Among many others, these include Hideo Kojima, the Steven Spielberg of video games, and Shigeru Miyamoto, the Alfred Hitchcock of video games. I'll talk about them in greater detail later on in this chapter.

Another of Japan's advantages when it comes to creating new video game franchises is its power in the animations industry, where many synergies can be found. There are many video games created from an *anime* series or *manga*, and at the same time many *manga* and *anime* that emerge after the success of

"When I arrived in Japan, I considered myself to be quite good at gaming after years of training during my time as a student. I stopped thinking that when a 56-year-old Japanese woman kindergarten teacher beat me ten times in a row at Street Fighter."

a video game. It is a safer, simpler, less laborious, and less risky path than thinking up a new game from scratch. The characters are already designed, part of the music and the plotline can be reused and, what's more, if the *anime* has been successful, part of the sales of the video game are guaranteed, thus reducing the risk of failure, which the Japanese are so averse to.

In this chapter we will see in more depth how the video game industry was born in Japan, how some of the sector's best known franchises were created, the achievements of some of the key characters, and in general how the Japanese coexist with video games.

When I arrived in Japan, I considered myself to be quite good at gaming after years of training during my time as a student. I stopped thinking that when a 56-year-old Japanese female kindergarten teacher beat me ten times in a row at *Street Fighter*. All my preconceived ideas came tumbling down. Games here are not the preserve of children and adolescents. I started to see all of Japanese society as first-class players.

NINTENDO

Nintendo was founded in 1889 by Fusajiro Yamauchi. The company started out doing something very different to video games—devoting itself to designing, manufacturing, and selling *hanafuda* cards. *Hanafuda* cards had some success from the beginning and Fusajiro Yamauchi took on more people to mass produce them. For over 50 years, Nintendo grew bit by bit working exclusively on card production.

MAKER OF HANAFUDA "FLOWER CARDS"

Hanafuda (花札) literally means "flower cards," and you can play a series of card games with them that originated in Japan.

In the seventeenth century, when Japan was still open to foreign influence, the Portuguese introduced Western decks of cards. But with the beginning of the Edo period (1603–1868), foreign card decks were banned. Even though they were banned, the cards had already become so popular that people started to create other card games and new decks, some with as many as 100 cards. Amongst all these new card decks, the one that had the most success was the *hanafuda* with 48 cards, the same as almost all Western decks, but the strange thing is that they aren't numbered. It's a completely visual deck where each card has the picture of a flower or tree.

As with a Spanish deck, a multitude of games can be played with a *hanafuda* deck. Nintendo, besides manufacturing the *hanafuda* cards also created many games based on the deck, which have been quite successful. These days, people still play with *hanafuda* in South Korea, Hawaii, and Japan.

YUNPEI YOKOI

After World War II, times were hard for Nintendo. *Hanafuda* card sales were much less than they had been up until the war. The board of directors decided to try to expand their business by entering other sectors. They created a subsidiary company that was dedicated to the taxi business and even built several "love hotels." Nonetheless, the company didn't manage to get back on its feet until Yunpei Yokoi started to work at Nintendo.

Yunpei Yokoi is possibly one of the people Nintendo fans love the most. He studied engineering and after graduating started working in 1965 as a maintenance engineer in one of Nintendo's *hanafuda* factories. During his early years at Nintendo, it would appear he had quite a lot of free time but that time was not wasted.

In 1970, Hiroshi Yamauchi, the president of Nintendo, visited the factory where Yunpei was working. The latter proudly showed the president some of the toys he had created during his spare time. The president's attention was grabbed by a mechanical hand. He liked it so much he ordered Yunpei to leave his maintenance job so he could develop the mechanical hand concept and convert it into a commercial product. Yunpei set to it and a few months later Nintendo launched the Ultra Hand on the market. It sold over a million units during the Christmas season, a

Nintendo started as a company more than a century ago manufacturing cards.

These are cards released much later using videogame characters like Mario, Luigi, and Yoshi from Super Mario Bros.

Donkey Kong was one of Nintendo's first successes.

The Switch console is yet another example of how Nintendo always reinvents the industry.

great success. Yunpei carried on thinking up toys. He created the Ultra Machine, which was like the Ultra Hand but threw baseball balls. He also created the Love Tester, which was an electronic device that measured a couple's compatibility. Thanks to Yunpei, during the 1970s Nintendo became a successful company in the toy market as well as in the card deck market.

The story goes that at the end of the 1970s, Yunpei was traveling on the bullet train. He was sitting next to a bored-looking salaryman who was playing with numbers using a Sharp LCD calculator. It occurred to Yunpei that at Nintendo they could use the technology employed in calculators to create video games. The idea was to use technology that was established, cheap, and easy to get hold of, but instead of making boring calculators they would sell portable video game machines. And that is how the famous Game & Watch, which triumphed in the 1980s selling millions of units, was born.

The portable Game & Watch devices introduced many new ideas which are still being used after more than 20 years. For example, the d-pad or four-way control stick to control the movement of characters within a game or the double screen is still used in today's Nintendo 3DS.

The most popular version of Game & Watch was "Donkey Kong." The person entrusted with designing the software for Donkey Kong was the young Shigeru Miyamoto under the supervision of Yunpei Yokoi. Later on, Shigeru Miyamoto would also become a key figure at Nintendo, creating franchises like Mario or Zelda. Many of you will be asking yourselves why the game Donkey Kong has that name when the main character is a monkey. It turns out that when Shigeru Miyamoto and Yunpei

Yokoi talked on the telephone with Nintendo America, they were misheard. Shigeru and Yunpei said that the name of the game was Monkey Kong, but in the United States they "heard" Donkey Kong! They soon realized their mistake, but it seems that in the United States they liked "Donkey Kong" more because it was catchier and that's the way it stayed.

Yunpei Yokoi was also the creator and principal designer of the Game Boy, the most successful video console in history up to now. He also took part in the development of the NES and was the head producer of the Fire Emblem, Super Mario Land, and Metroid franchises, among many others.

Among so much success there was also a much talked-about failure, the Virtual Boy, for which Yunpei Yokoi was the main person in charge. The original idea, the project management, and the first games for the device were all his responsibility. It was the first portable 3D video game console in history and didn't achieve the hoped for success. Maybe it was ahead of its time.

Tensions within the company after the failure of Virtual Boy made Yokoi leave Nintendo in 1996, shortly after the launch of the Game Boy Pocket, which he had also designed. But Yokoi

The iconic Game Boy (above) sold nearly 119 million units. New Nintendo releases of games like "Legend of Zelda: Ocarina of Time" (below) are always announced everywhere. This particular advertisement features Matsumoto Jun from Arashi.

According to a survey carried out around the world, Mario is better known these days than Mickey Mouse.

In the words of Shigeru Miyamoto:
"What is important is that the people I work with are also recognized and that the Nintendo brand goes forward and keeps on being strong and popular. If there are people who believe the Nintendo brand is on the same level as the Disney brand, that is something very flattering and it makes me happy to hear it." (Copyright New York Times, extract from an interview)

Shigeru Miyamoto started working at Nintendo under the supervision of Yunpei Yokoi. One of his first tasks was to design casings for Nintendo's first video game consoles, but he soon demonstrated his genius and originality creating some of the industry's most recognizable video games and characters.

He has worked directly on the production of over 70 video games, among them "Mario Kart," "Zelda," and "Super Mario." Although he is nearly 60 years old and one of the richest men in Japan, he's just another worker within the company. Right now he is in charge of supervising the work of over 400 people and they say that he even takes an interest in temporary workers. He lives in Kyoto with his wife and two children and cycles to work. Nothing special at first sight but for the fact that when he gets home he finds his children playing video games that he has created, that Nintendo has created.

Miyamoto might be responsible for the consumption of more billions of hours of human leisure time than any other person in the world. In an interview in *Time 100*, he was voted the most influential person in the world. There are very few people in the video game industry who have managed to stay at the top for so long.

THE FUTURE OF NINTENDO

The greatest legacy that Yunpei Yokoi left behind at Nintendo, much more than even his successes like Game Boy or Super Mario Land, was his philosophy when it comes to developing new products. Using the newest and most expensive technology is not necessary. In fact, using something too new may become a hindrance when it's time to create a good product since nobody knows what problems there could be with this new technology. It is better to use proven technology.

But apart from using tried and tested cheap technology, you need to think differently. You have to find a revolutionary new way of using this technology. Oftentimes, the industry insists on using technology in the same old way, but in reality the possibilities are infinite. The only limit is the inventor's imagination. In the words of Yokoi: "Lateral thinking based on mature technology" (枯れた技術の水平思考). This is one of the fundamental pillars that has guided Nintendo to where it is now. For example, the Nintendo Wii is the least technologically advanced video game console on the market but its revolutionary way of using this technology is what has made it the seventh-generation king.

Nintendo is the world's oldest producer of video games and has managed to survive all the changes in market trends up to now. It sold 520 million video game consoles and over 3,350 million video games between its early days and 2010. To get an idea of the immensity of those figures, it means almost one Nintendo video game for each two inhabitants of planet Earth.

wasn't at all discouraged. His passion for creating ever better hardware for playing video games led him to create his own company called Koto. After a joint development agreement with Bandai, Yokoi and his new team started to develop a new portable video game console that would be called the WonderSwan. Unfortunately, Yokoi never saw the WonderSwan finished; he died in a traffic accident in 1997 at the age of 56. WonderSwan was sold in Japan from 1999 and was moderately successful. It is still a cult video game console among the keenest gamers.

SHIGERU MIYAMOTO

I'm sure my dear mother knows that Walt Disney created Mickey Mouse but I'm equally sure she doesn't know that Shigeru Miyamoto created Mario. In the United States, individuals are often as well known or better known than companies: Microsoft—Bill Gates; Apple—Steve Jobs; Oracle—Larry Ellison. These well-known people act as brand images for American companies. In Japan, individuals generally prefer to remain anonymous. Can you name the president of Toshiba? The president of Sharp? The president of Sony? The president of Nintendo? The Japanese try not to stand out, preferring to give centerstage and the credit to the company.

Hiroshi Yamauchi, the richest man in Japan, president of Nintendo until 2002, and Shigeru Miyamoto, the person responsible for the majority of the great games created by Nintendo, are two of the key people who have made Nintendo what it is today. Despite this, they are totally unknown outside video game circles. What everyone does recognize are the franchises and characters that they have created. According to a survey carried out with children in over 100 countries, Mario is better known than Mickey Mouse!

SQUARE ENIX

Square Enix is the world's biggest company specialized in role-play production. It was created in 2003 when Enix bought over Square. Both had been rival companies for decades but finally ended up joining amicably. Square dominated the world scene with the "Final Fantasy" saga and Enix led the local RPG games market with the "Dragon Quest" saga.

Square Enix makes great use of its franchises and ideas and creates authentic fantasy worlds, not only within video games but also through the use of other media like *manga* or cinema. A recent example is "Fullmetal Alchemist" where they started out with the *manga*, saw that it was successful and proceeded to adapt it to an *anime* series. The *anime* series also worked out and from there they produced several video games and even novels and a movie. They test ideas in one medium, and if they work they exploit them through all the means at their disposal.

In 2005, Square Enix bought over Taito, another of the giants in the world of video games, creator of legends like "Space Invaders," "Bust a Move," "Lufia," and "Bubble Bobble." Since then Square Enix has been one of the world's biggest producers of video games and will continue making more and more instalments of "Final Fantasy" and "Dragon Quest."

"ALL YOUR BASE ARE BELONG TO US"

"All your base are belong to us" is a meme known to nearly all the world's gamers. It is an example of Japanglish—Japanese-to-English translation done by some Japanese person with no real knowledge of English.

The English version of the spaceship game "Zero Wing," published by Taito (which now belongs to Square Enix) in 1989, was very badly translated. One of the most famous translation errors was "All your base are belong to us," a phrase that for some reason has become fashionable among geeks. The phrase has been used by DJs around the world, in other video games, in *manga*, in webpage, and even in several movies.

HIRONOBU SAKAGUCHI

Hironobu Sakaguchi was the creator of the first "Final Fantasy" and the majority of its sequels. Square became a major company thanks largely to "Final Fantasy" and Hironobu Sakaguchi soon went from being a mere employee to the president of Square in the United States. In 2004, he decided to leave Square Enix, where he had worked practically his entire life, to found and run his own video game development studio, where he still creates RPGs for all platform types, from XBOX to iPhone.

COMPOSER NOBUO UEMATSU

Nobuo Uematsu is the best-known music composer in the video game industry. He began working at Square at almost the same time as Hironobu Sakaguchi and one of his first jobs was the music for the first "Final Fantasy." The "Final Fantasy" music was so well liked that from then on he has been in charge of the music for all the sequels and in general for nearly all of Square's games, and later Square Enix's. His music, which is quite orchestral, has been used at concerts worldwide, from the Tokyo to Berlin Philharmonic. In 2004, he also left Square Enix. He now has his own production studio where he continues to compose music for games for Square Enix and also for his lifelong colleague Hironobu Sakaguchi's independent studio.

One of the earliest shooting games, "Space Invaders," was created by Tomohiro Nishikado and has become a pop culture icon.

Taito Station game centers are still popular and are thriving in the Tokyo area.

CATS : ALL YOUR BASE ARE BE
TO US.

"All your base are belong to us" is a Japanese translation error that has become one of the most famous geek memes in the history of video games.

SEGA

Sega, founded by Americans in 1951 in Tokyo, started out making slot machines and photo booths. The business worked quite well and the company grew, especially in the United States. In the late 1970s and early 1980s they began to have financial problems.

Sega decided to focus on the video game market, where they had some experience designing gambling and arcade games and developed their first video game console, the SG-1000. It helped them to keep their heads above the water, but they had to deal with intense competition from Nintendo, who in 1985 controlled over 90 percent of the video game market in Japan.

It wasn't until 1989 that Sega became a real threat to Nintendo. In that year, Sega launched the Sega Megadrive, a 16-bit video game console at practically the same price as Nintendo's 8-bit NES. At the end of 1989, Sega became the world's second biggest video game company. The company is responsible for having created some classics that have gone down in video game history as being revolutionary at the time and for being much copied by their competitors, such as "Virtua Fighter," "Shenmue," "House of the Dead," and "Phantasy Star."

(Above) *Sega is always present at the Tokyo Game Show, an annual video game expo/ convention held in September in Chiba.*
(Below) *Sega World Game Centers boast an array of arcade games and UFO catchers. The largest is in Shinjuku.*

Sega's last video game console was the Dreamcast. They couldn't continue in the difficult world of video game console manufacturing where the competition was increasingly ferocious in the late 1990s and at the turn of the century. Sega continues to develop hardware for arcade games but centers its business on developing and distributing video games for third parties. A series of mergers and acquisitions with other Japanese companies, mostly toy companies, over the last few years have led to the company now being called Sega Sammy Holdings.

YUJI NAKA

Yuji Naka is one of the key figures in Sega's success. He was the principal programmer of the first Sonic and after that became the main designer and head of the development team of all the Sonic sequels.

We all know Sonic the Hedgehog, SEGA's official mascot. What is not so well known is that before Sonic, until 1991, the mascot was Alex Kidd. Sonic was created in order to compete with Nintendo's Mario. A mascot capable of starring in games that could sell millions of copies was needed and they managed it.

During the development of the first Sonic, Yuji Naka focused on the game's programming and his colleague Naoto Oshima was responsible for designing and animating Sonic. As well as being involved in practically all the versions of Sonic, he has also been the producer of games like "Virtua Striker 3" and "Phantasy Star Online."

YU SUZUKI

Before entering the world of video games, Yu Suzuki tried studying to be a dentist but it didn't work out for him. He also tried his hand in the music world playing the guitar. He had no "luck" earning a living with the guitar either, but today still carries on playing with a small local band.

Finally, he decided to study computer science engineering at the University of Okayama and graduated with honors. Straight after finishing his studies in 1983, he began to work as a programmer at Sega, where he started out as an assistant programming games for Sega arcade games and later for the SG-1000.

He is the creator of some of Sega's most popular arcade games, such as "Out Run," "Virtua Fighter" and "Virtua Cop." "Virtua Fighter" was the first 3D combat game in the history of video games. The masterpiece his fans love the most is "Shenmue," considered one of the best games in history upon its release for Dreamcast in 1999. "Shenmue" was innovative due both to the way it gave freedom to the player and its interactive environment. It is considered the first game of its genre.

SONY INTERACTIVE ENTERTAINMENT

One of the first Sony PlayStation prototypes was developed in collaboration with Nintendo in 1991. It worked with Super Nintendo cartridges and also with CD-ROM. The idea was to be compatible with Nintendo, the leaders at that time, and at the same time introduce games onto the market with more CD-based multimedia content. But without warning, Nintendo decided to break the agreement with Sony at the last moment, severing all relations with them.

The story goes that after the collaboration with Nintendo was broken off, there was a lot of debate within Sony. Most executives voted to leave the video game industry and concentrate on other things. But Ken Kutaragi, who would shortly afterwards become the father of the Sony PlayStation that we all know, con-

Sony Interactive Entertainment has become one of the most profitable subsidiaries of Sony Corp, with the release of the PS Vita (above, below left, below right), the Playstation 4 (below center), and popular games like "Overwatch," "Dissidia Final Fantasy," and "Final Fantasy XV" (below).

(Left, right and below left) *The Playstation consoles in all their permutations.*
(Below right) *The Sony Interactive Entertainment headquarters.*

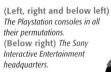

(Above) *Ken Kutaragi at the Game Developer Choice Awards with his Lifetime Achievement Award for his three decades of contributions to the gaming industry.* (Right) *A piece of history showing how Sony and Nintendo collaborated in the video game industry.*

character, believing in his ideas and carrying them through even if the company does not agree with them, and always wanting to be one step ahead as regards technology.

In the 1980s, Ken Kutaragi saw how his daughter enjoyed playing on a Nintendo video game console every day. Kutaragi thought video games were the future of the electronic consumer industry, something that at the time was far from sure.

He went to speak to Nintendo directly, without asking for permission from any of his superiors at Sony. Within a few months, he managed to close a deal with Nintendo through which Sony would develop the sound processor for the next Super Nintendo. Kutaragi worked in secret for months. The result was the SPC700 sound processor, used by the Super Nintendo and considered at that time the best sound processor in the video game console world. In the end, Kutaragi's bosses found out he had been working secretly and had developed a chip for Nintendo and they were on the verge of kicking him out of the company. Things were finally straightened out when he was bailed out by one of his bosses and great friend, Norio Ohga, who would go on to become president of Sony in 1988 and hold the post until 1999.

With knowledge gained by his work with Nintendo, but this time not cooperating with them, Kutaragi decided to use Sony's resources to create a video game console—the PlayStation. The success of the Sony video game console led Sony executives to reconsider Kutaragi's past rebelliousness and assign him the position of Sony Computer Entertainment president, and in time the vice presidency of Sony Corporation, working hand in hand with Norio Ohga, his close friend and president of Sony.

They were good times for Kutaragi for a little over a decade until the sales of the PlayStation 3 failed to be as good as expected. His reputation in the company took a nosedive and he decided to leave and start again from scratch, albeit with some help from Sony. Thus was born Cellius, a company presided over by Kutaragi and founded with capital mainly provided by Sony and also by Bandai-Namco. For the moment, there are several engineers working in the basement of a modest building in the suburbs of the Tokyo neighborhood of Shibuya.

vinced Norio Ohga, the president of Sony, that they couldn't sit back and do nothing after having been humiliated by Nintendo. Norio Ohga was also quite angry at what had happened with Nintendo. They finally decided to invest all possible resources in entering and revolutionizing the entertainment world on their own, a decision that would change the company's direction forever. To achieve this, in 1993 they founded a new subsidiary, Sony Computer Entertainment, which would take over all the operations related to the video game business line within Sony. Soon after, in 1994, the Sony PlayStation went on sale.

The PlayStation achieved massive success during the second half of the decade, becoming the first video game console in history to reach 100 million units sold and completely changing the video game industry scene. Its successor, the PlayStation 2, is now the best-selling video game console in history.

Soon Sony Computer Entertainment became a multinational with headquarters in several continents, and through its development studios created some globally successful video game franchises, such as "Gran Turismo" or "Little Big Planet."

The Sony Corporation is at present facing a lot of difficulties in competing globally. The multinational stays afloat in part thanks to the success of the PlayStation and its successors. PlayStation is Sony's best-known trademark worldwide, ahead of Walkman, Vaio, and Bravia.

KEN KUTARAGI

As a child Ken Kutaragi liked taking toys apart and seeing how they worked inside instead of playing with them. His innate curiosity led him to the study of electronic engineering at the University of Tokyo, and straight after graduating he started work as an engineer at Sony. During the 1970s, he devoted himself to experimenting with processor designs and enjoyed putting together devices with LCD screens.

As well as being an excellent engineer, Ken Kutaragi has a reputation for being quite ambitious and for having a strong

The versatile Nintendo Switch can be used both as a home console and as a tablet computer.

KONAMI

In 1969, Kagemasa Kouzuki founded Konami as a small jukebox rental and repair service in Osaka. The business succeeded and they started to create their own jukeboxes and also slot machines. With the experience gained here, in 1981 they produced their first amusement arcade games with original games they had also developed. The classic "Frogger" and "Super Cobra" are among the first games Konami released in 1981.

During the 1980s, Konami became a multinational and began to develop video games for all sorts of platforms. Kagemasa Kouzuki not only founded the company but also made Konami into one of the world's biggest developers and distributors of video games. In recent years, the Konami CEO has been changed several times.

Video games are Konami's main business. They are the creators of classics like "Castlevania," "Contra," "Dance Dance Revolution," and "Kirby," among others. But as well as video games, they have carried on making slot machines and *pachinko* machines (see page 51) and have tried their hand at other businesses, such as *tokuhatsu* movie production (see page 128) and gymnasiums. Yes, Konami has a gymnasium chain although it only operates locally, mostly in Tokyo.

Game Center CX is a Japanese TV show dedicated only to playing video games.

With the purchase of Hudson Soft, another big Japanese games distributor, in 2001, Konami became one of the ten biggest game distributor-developers in the world. Hudson Soft is known for the creation, in collaboration with NEC, of the TurboGrafx video game console and for counting among its employees a hero of any self-respecting video game fan— Takahashi Meijin.

TAKAHASHI MEIJIN

Takahashi Meijin (高橋名人) is a legend in the Japanese video game world. He is the spiritual and artistic leader of the video game company Hudson Soft, where he has worked since practically the beginning of his career.

Takahashi Meijin is famous because he is capable of pressing the control button on a video game console 16 times a second! He is also famous because a pixelated version of his outline is the hero of the games in the "Adventure Island" series.

His fame as a gamer reached its pinnacle when he faced off against Mouri Meijin on a television program that was broadcast live nationwide. It was a "Star Soldier" duel. At the start of the program, they showed images of both of the men training. In one of the scenes, Takahashi Meijin was seen chopping a watermelon in half with one finger. It turned out Takahashi Meijin's fingers are fast and strong and he is capable of pressing the buttons on a video game console 16 times a second.

Takahashi Meijin is one of the most popular figures in the video game industry in Japan.

KONAMI CODE

In the mid-1980s, Konami was developing a game called "Gradius" for Nintendo's new video game console. The chief programmer of "Gradius" added a secret code to the game to make it easier for him to test it. The secret code consisted of pressing ←, ←, →, →, ↑, ↑, ↓↓, B, A. On finishing the sequence, the programmers of "Gradius" got loads of extra items and lives, which helped them test the game more quickly.

The story goes that they forgot to wipe the code when the video game was launched on the market. Others say they left it there on purpose because the game was too difficult. For some strange reason, the code became so popular that it started to be added to many more Konami games. With time, it was also added to other companies' games and nowadays it has even been added to webpages on the Internet. Try typing in the code on Facebook!

HIDEO KOJIMA

Hideo Kojima is currently one of the most successful game producers in Japan. He is very young in comparison with some of the industry's "dinosaurs," such as Shigeru Miyamoto. In fact, Hideo Kojima is a fan of "Super Mario Bros" and regards Shigeru Miyamoto as his master and a great inspiration to keep on developing better and better games.

Hideo Kojima started his career writing stories and novels but he never managed to get anyone to publish them. However, he didn't give up. His next step was to try to produce and direct movies but that didn't work out either. Maybe he didn't get to be a novelist but what he learned during those first two stages of his working life came in really handy for him in his subsequent life as a games creator. The background and script of Kojima's games tend to be crafted in great detail. In fact, there are books and *manga* based on some of his games, and their settings make you feel as if you were in a movie.

His first game came out on sale in 1987 and was called "Metal Gear." After two decades, with over 20 different sequels and versions, the "Metal Gear" video game series became one of Konami's greatest sources of income. Kojima is regarded as one of the most innovative creators of video games in history.

Hideo Kojima became vice president of Konami but left his full-time position at Konami to create his own studio, Kojima Productions. He is still a member of the Konami board and at Kojima Productions they work hand in hand with Konami to develop and distribute video games around the world.

CHAPTER 12
VISITING TOKYO

東

TOKYO'S VARIOUS DISTRICTS

After six years living in Tokyo, the city never stops surprising me. I'm getting used to some things but I'm still discovering details I didn't notice during my first walks around. Together with the other cities in the Greater Tokyo Area, Tokyo forms the largest megalopolis in the world, with a population of over 35 million. It's like a country squeezed between Mount Fuji and the sea. Tokyo has a curious structure. It's a city without a center, formed of multiple nerve centers concentrated around train stations. The bigger the station, the more important the district or area surrounding it. In this chapter we'll look at some of the capital city's most characteristic districts, which nobody traveling to Japan should miss.

ROPPONGI

Roppongi is one the areas that has undergone the greatest re-development during the two decades in Tokyo. The two futuristic micro-cities, Tokyo Midtown and Roppongi Hills, are the twin nerve centers of the district.

ROPPONGI HILLS AREA

Roppongi Hills is a futuristic microcity that was inaugurated in 2003. The complex includes more than 800 apartments, the of-fices of Yahoo Japan, Livedoor, Rakuten, Konami, Goldman Sachs, and Google, a cinemaplex, a hotel, gourmet restaurants and cafés, a museum, a television studio, gardens, a gym, shops, and several department stores. Everything you need is compressed into sev-eral towers, the main one being Mori Tower, with 54 stories. The rent for a 1,000 sq ft (93 sq m) apartment in Roppongi Hills is about $12,000 a month. Its construction was groundbreaking, and it revived financial activity in Roppongi, which had been limping along since the bubble burst at the beginning of the 1990s.

I have marked the best exits (1 and 2 at Roppongi Station, Hibiya Line) to get to Roppongi Hills. However, you can also get there by the Oedo Line and use the Roppongi crossing (number 7) to orient yourself. If you are interested in architecture, you might enjoy yourself for several hours. If not, a one-hour walk should be enough to capture the essence of the complex. If you go up to the observation deck or the museum, add an extra hour for your visit.

THE GIANT SPIDER (1 ON THE MAP)

A sculpture by Louise Bourgeois outside the main entrance to Mori Tower. Take a good look at the detail of the spider's eggs.

ENTRANCE TO THE MUSEUM (2 ON THE MAP)

On the top floors of Mori Tower are a museum and an observa-tion deck. If the weather is clear, you can see Mount Fuji.

CINEMA COMPLEX (3 ON THE MAP)

One of the biggest movie theater complexes in Tokyo. It is managed by Virgin.

TV ASAHI AND DORAEMON STORE (4 ON THE MAP)

The Asahi television studios are next to Mori Tower. Inside the building is a store full of Doraemon merchandise.

BARS AND CLUBS AREA (5 ON THE MAP)

The area with some of the best clubs and bars in Tokyo. Ideal for your first beer of the evening.

GARDEN (6 ON THE MAP)

It's particularly beautiful when they light it up at night, especially at Christmastime.

ROPPONGI CROSSING (7 ON THE MAP)

The center of activity in the district. Around the crossing are quite a number of cafés and nightclubs.

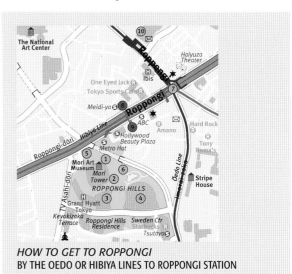

HOW TO GET TO ROPPONGI
BY THE OEDO OR HIBIYA LINES TO ROPPONGI STATION

MAP

1. The Giant Spider
2. Entrance to the Museum
3. Cinema Complex
4. TV Asahi and Doraemon Store
5. Bars and Clubs area
6. Garden
7. Roppongi Crossing
8. Hibiya Line, Roppongi Station, Exit 2
9. Hibiya Line, Roppongi Station, Exit 1
10. Tokyo Midtown: see facing page.

TOKYO MIDTOWN AREA

Tokyo Midtown is the name of another of Tokyo's futuristic mico-cities. Its construction cost $3 billion and it opened its doors in March 2007. It is in direct competition with Roppongi Hills, which lies only 500 yards (460 meters) away, and it exceeds Roppongi Hills in height; the main building in Tokyo Midtown is the tallest in the city. It also managed to get several renowned companies, such as Konami and Yahoo Japan, to move some of their offices from Roppongi Hills to the newer facilities in Tokyo Midtown. The rent for office space is cheaper and the rent for a 1,000 sq ft (93 sq m) apartment in Tokyo Midtown is about $6,000 a month. Tokyo Midtown Hibiya is opened in 2018.

MAIN ENTRANCE (1 ON THE MAP)

From this entrance you have the best view of the complex and direct access to the luxury shopping mall that occupies the first five floors of several buildings in the complex.

SUNTORY MUSEUM OF ART (2 ON THE MAP)

A museum with temporary exhibitions of elegant "lifestyle art."

HINOKICHO PARK (3 ON THE MAP)

My favorite part of the complex. A very quiet and relaxing park that lets you forget you are right in the middle of the city.

OEDO LINE, ROPPONGI STATION, EXIT 7 (4 ON THE MAP)

This is the best way to get there by subway.

21-21 DESIGN SIGHT (5 ON THE MAP)

A small building in the park area. It houses design exhibitions and was designed by Taku Sato and Issey Miyake.

CHIYODA LINE, NOGIZAKA STATION, EXIT 3 (6 ON THE MAP)

If the Chiyoda Line is more convenient for you, this is the closest exit. It's five minutes away by foot.

ROPPONGI HILLS (7 ON THE MAP)

See the description on the previous page.

NATIONAL ART CENTER (8 ON THE MAP)

One of the best museums in Japan. Don't miss it if you like museums. It usually houses traveling exhibitions of works from some of the most prominent museums in the world. (www.nact.jp/english/exhibitions/index.html)

ROPPONGI'S MAIN CROSSING (9 ON THE MAP)

Considered the center of activity and a point of reference in the Roppongi area.

The garden is my favorite spot when I visit Midtown.

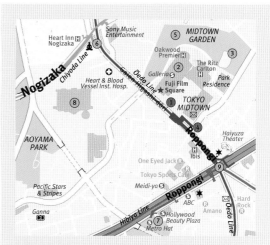

HOW TO GET TO MIDTOWN
BY THE CHIYODA LINE ON THE TOKYO SUBWAY TO NOGIZAKA STATION, OR BY THE OEDO OR HIBIYA LINES TO ROPPONGI STATION

MAP

1. Main entrance	6. Chiyoda Line, Nogizaka Station, Exit 3
2. Suntory Museum of Art	
3. Hinokicho Park	7. Roppongi Hills
4. Oedo Line, Roppongi Station, Exit 7	8. National Art Center
5. Design Sight	9. Roppongi Crossing

The National Art Center building is worth a visit just for the beauty of its design, both inside and outside.

MEGALOPOLIS WALKING TOURS

Tokyo is a huge city. You can travel for an hour on the train and see nothing but houses. Sometimes you can't help feeling it's too much. The structure of Japanese cities is quite different from what we are used to in the West. There is usually no main center. Instead the city is structured around train stations, which make for multiple subcenters. Each district is like a small town whose office buildings, restaurants, and businesses are clustered near the station. As you move away, you enter the residential areas, until you reach the next station.

To capture the essence of the metropolis, you need to move around and visit some of the main stations—the diffuse nerve centers in the city.

FIRST DAY

In the morning, take the Yamanote Line to Shinjuku. Walk to the Tocho Building (Tokyo City Hall) and ride up to see panoramic views of the city. Go back to the east side of the station and look for somewhere to eat. In the afternoon, take the Oedo Line to Roppongi. There you can visit Roppongi Hills and Tokyo Midtown.

"The structure of Japanese cities is quite different from what we are used to in the West. There is usually no main center and the city is structured around train stations."

SECOND DAY

In the morning, go to Odaiba, the island full of futuristic buildings. Return by way of Ginza for lunch and then stroll in the area around the main crossing. Another option is to walk from Ginza to Tokyo Station and there take the train to Shibuya for a wander and dinner. To crown your day, you can look for a karaoke building—there are dozens of them—and rent a room to try out the way Japanese people have fun. There are usually songs in English.

If you have an extra day, a very rewarding day trip would be to go to Yokohama. There are several trains departing from Shibuya and Shinjuku, and the trip takes about one hour. The most interesting areas in Yokohama are Chinatown and the harbor. If you're interested in architecture, don't miss this visit.

Tocho Building (Tokyo City Hall).

The Jump Shop in Odaiba.

Getting "lost" in the back streets can be fun.

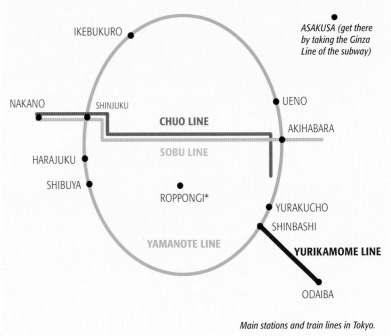

Main stations and train lines in Tokyo.

CULTURAL WALKING TOURS

Tokyo is a city with hundreds of museums, cultural centers, concert halls, and opera houses that offer events and performances of the highest quality. Many of the world's most famous singers consider Tokyo, Paris, London, and New York the four places to begin their world tours. As to monuments, in Tokyo you won't find spectacular temples like in Kyoto or Nara. As much as 90 percent of Tokyo was destroyed during World War II and there were hardly any buildings left standing. The Asakusa area is perhaps the only one that retains a certain traditional spirit.

Something to bear in mind when you do this walk is that temples, museums, and other public buildings in Japan usually close at five o'clock in the afternoon.

FIRST DAY

In the morning, start at Ginza and walk toward the fish market. Eat *sushi* in some restaurant near the fish market and then take a leisurely walk around Hamarikyu Gardens, where you can enjoy green tea in the park's teahouse. Go to the jetty—the last ferry departs at around 3.30 pm—and board a ferry bound for Asakusa. There you can stroll along the shopping area, visit the temple grounds, and look for a good restaurant for dinner.

SECOND DAY

Travel on the Yamanote Line to Ueno Station. Walk around the park and visit the National Museum, where in just a few hours you can learn a lot about Japan's history and culture, from its very beginning to the present. For lunch, leave Ueno Park and look for a restaurant in the Ameyoko area, southeast of the park near the train tracks.

"Temples, museums, and other public buildings in Japan usually close at five o'clock in the afternoon."

In the afternoon take the Yamanote Line to Yoyogi Station. Go for a walk around Yoyogi Park and visit the grounds of the Meiji Jingu, the imperial family's official shrine. For dinner, you can head down to Shibuya and take in the nightlife.

Hamarikyu Gardens is an ideal place to relax and enjoy a cup of green tea.

GADGET WALKING TOURS

If you like gadgets, computers, video games, or cameras, this is definitely the place for you. Tokyo has the most electronics stores of any city in the world. Besides Akihabara, there are a number of other areas in the city where you can check out the latest in Japanese technology.

FIRST DAY

Go directly to Odaiba Island and the National Museum of Emerging Science and Innovation, where you'll see the humanoid robot Asimo in action. Afterward, Panasonic's nearby

exhibition hall is worth a visit. End the day going up to the "ball" in the Fuji TV building.

SECOND DAY

In the morning, go to the Sony Building in Ginza, then walk to Yurakucho Station on the Yamanote Line and visit the Bic Camera mega department store. After lunch, take the Yamanote Line to Akihabara and spend the afternoon rummaging through the stores in that district. If you like electronic devices, don't miss Radio Center next to Akihabara Station.

Big electronics stores like Bic Camera, Yodobashi Camera, and Labi are worth visiting for their huge array of electronic devices.

Shibuya is one of Tokyo's liveliest areas and a main center for trends and fashions.

SHIBUYA

Together with Shinjuku, Shibuya is one of the liveliest places in Japan. It's one of the main centers for trends and fashions in Asia, where many of the urban tribes we discussed in Chapter 7 live. It's also the city's most fashionable district, where young people like to walk around, shop, have dinner, go to karaoke clubs, and dance.

Shibuya's street plan is complicated and it's easy to get lost even if you have a map. If you don't want to stray too far from the station, the general rule is to avoid walking beyond the point where neon lights and signs become scarce. As long as you can see neon lights around you, you'll be close to the station. Another tip is that Shibuya Station is located at the lowest spot in the district, so if you choose a descending street you will almost always end up at the station.

THE SHIBUYA DOG (1 ON THE MAP)

When you get to Shibuya Station by the Yamanote Line, your best option is to leave by the special Hachiko Exit. You'll see tons of Japanese in a small plaza and, if you look carefully, you'll notice an area where the crowd is even denser. Get closer and you'll find the small statue of a dog. This is Hachiko, the most famous dog in Japan, the pet of Tokyo University teacher Eisaburo Ueno. They say Hachiko went every day to wait for Mr Ueno at the end of his workday. Even after his master's death in 1925, he kept going to wait for him faithfully for 11 years. The dog inspired such great admiration among the Japanese that they made a movie about him, and they even decided to erect a statue in his honor right where Hachiko waited for his master every day. This spot, just next to Shibuya Station, is the most popular rendezvous point in Tokyo. It's easy to locate and the special exit in Shibuya Station makes it simple. You can't possibly get lost, so it's the ideal place to meet someone.

SHIBUYA CROSSING (2 ON THE MAP)

Next to Hachiko you'll see the pedestrian crossing used by the largest number of people a day in the world. It's amazing to watch the crowds of people crossing, almost every day and at any time of day, under the several huge television screens that are constantly flashing advertisements. One of the places to view the crossing is from the Starbucks inside the building with the largest advertisement screen.

109 (3 ON THE MAP)

After the crossing, turn onto the street on the left and you'll find yourself opposite 109, Asia's most famous department store, which sells women's and girls' clothing. Korean and Chinese women travel to Tokyo specifically to shop at 109. Have a look inside for the busy shopping ambience.

CENTER GAI (4 ON THE MAP)

Center Gai is the pedestrian street that begins on the other side of Shibuya Crossing. It's the liveliest street in the area, full of video game centers, clothing stores, and restaurants and is especially worth a look on weekends or on any weekday after sunset. Young Tokyo dwellers who want to go out with friends go here.

LOVE HOTEL AREA (5 ON THE MAP)

In the alleys behind 109 you will find a love hotel area. If you're there with your partner, you can take the opportunity to go in and see one of the most curious institutions in this country. But simply walking around and checking out the façades is great fun.

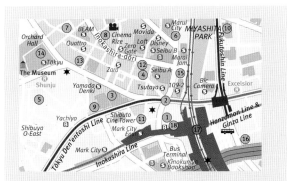

HOW TO GET TO SHIBUYA
BY THE JR YAMANOTE LINE OR BY THE SUBWAY HANZOMON OR GINZA LINES TO SHIBUYA STATION

MAP
1. The Shibuya Dog
2. Shibuya Crossing
3. 109
4. Center Gai
5. Love hotel area
6. A 10-minute walk heading north will take you to Harajuku.
7. Mandarake manga store
8, 9, 10, 12. Game centers
11. Pachinko area
13. Biggest H&M mall in Japan
14. Bunkamura cultural center: hosts internationally acclaimed art exhibits and theater
15. Restaurant area
16. Panoramic view from a pedestrian footbridge
17. Shibuya Station
18. Okamoto Taro painting

Fountain at the end of the Icho-namiki, a street famous for its gingko trees.

Aoyama shopping areas.

Gingko trees in autumn.

AOYAMA

Aoyama means "blue mountain"(青: blue, 山: mountain). The district was named after Aoyama Tadanari, a *samurai* retained by the Tokugawa shogunate who lived here in a large mansion. Today, Aoyama is one of the most expensive residential areas in Tokyo. Located between the Imperial Palace on the west and Harajuku-Omotesando on the east, it's filled with many small streets of little houses as well as large green spaces. It's pretty and quiet, and many of Japan's most famous writers, such as Haruki Murakami, and other artists have chosen to live here.

Although the district is mainly residential, the streets near Omotesando also have lots of trendy shops selling mainly high-end global brands, together with tiny clothing stores and chic boutiques. Aoyama is also popular because of its restaurants and delicious food. I can say without hesitation that you can choose almost at random any restaurant in the area and the food will surprise you. Bordering Aoyama Avenue are the headquarters of many international businesses, such as Honda Motor, Sony Computer Entertainment, Itochu, and Louis Vuitton Japan.

But what I like the most about Aoyama are the green areas of Aoyama Cemetery and Meiji Jingu Gaien. Aoyama Cemetery, Japan's first municipal cemetery, opened in 1872 and is especially beautiful during the sakura blossom season (end of March and beginning of April). The Meiji Jingu Gaien area is filled with sports facilities, green spaces, and museums. My favorite part is the avenue you take to enter the area from the direction of Aoyama 1-Chome Station. It is referred to as Icho-namiki, which means "street of the gingkos" (銀杏: gingko tree; 並木: roadside tree, row of trees). The street is filled with ginkgo trees on both sides and it's overwhelmingly beautiful in autumn (especially the end of November), when the leaves of the ginkgos are dyed with yellow. Walking through the yellow ginkgos from Aoyama 1-Chome Station to the center of Meiji Jingu Gaien is something you will probably never forget.

OKAMOTO TARO MUSEUM (9 ON THE MAP)

Taro Okamoto is one of the most important Japanese artists of the last century. He was a painter, sculptor, and writer. His masterpiece was the *Tower of the Sun*, which he designed for the 1970 Osaka Expo. Taro Okamoto studied in France and traveled around Europe when he was young. He later recognized that he was greatly influenced by Picasso, André Breton, Antonio Gaudí, and Miró. For years he also traveled to little villages around Japan to learn about Japanese legends, superstitions, and mythological monsters. He mixed all that in his head and created his own style, which included funny and the same time mysterious

faces. Many of today's Japanese artists have been influenced by Taro Okamoto. For example, some of Hayao Miyazaki's characters have faces that suggest his inspiration.

Okamoto lived in Aoyama for 50 years, until he died at age 84. The house where he lived is now the Taro Okamoto Memorial Museum Aoyama. The house is preserved as it was when Okamoto lived there and the museum displays one of the world's most complete collections of his art.

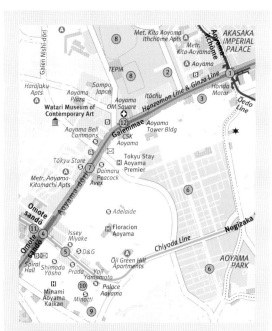

HOW TO GET TO AOYAMA
BY THE GINZA LINE, HANZOMON LINE & TOEI OEDO LINE TO AOYAMA 1-CHOME STATION; BY THE GINZA LINE, CHIYODA LINE & HANZOMON LINE TO OMOTESANDO STATION; AND BY THE GINZA LINE TO GAIEN MAE STATION

MAP
1. Aoyama 1-Chome Station
2. Icho-namiki street and Meiji Jingu Gaien area
3. Sony Computer Entertainment headquarters
4. Aoyama-Omotesando crossing
5. Aoyama shopping street
6. Aoyama Cemetery
7. Aoyama-dori (shopping avenue)
8. Baseball and rugby stadiums
9. Okamoto Taro Museum
10. Aoyama residential area
11. Omotesando Station
12. Gaien Mae Station

HARAJUKU AND OMOTESANDO

Harajuku, north of Shibuya, has been gaining in importance ever since the station was opened in 1964 to serve as a transportation hub for the Olympic Stadium, and now the Harajuku, Yoyogi, and Omotesando area is one of the most vibrant in the city. If crowds don't bother you, the weekend is the best time to enjoy its cosmopolitan atmosphere.

A simple stroll on Harajuku's streets on a Sunday will bring constant surprises, even if all you do is check out how people look. For Harajuku is a gathering place for such urban tribes as the *ganguros*, *kogals*, and *gothic lolitas* that we discussed in Chapter 7.

Ideally, you should divide your visit in two parts. For example, in the morning I would suggest a quiet stroll around the Meiji Jingu Shrine and in Yoyogi Park. Then, after lunch, sample the streets in Harajuku, beginning with Takeshita Dori and ending with Omotesando Avenue.

TAKESHITA DORI (1 ON THE MAP)
This is Harajuku's main commercial street and a must if you travel to Japan for the ambience. It's full of small clothing stores of all kinds. There are many shops selling *gothic lolita* and *visual kei* clothes and collectors' items as well as clothing in general, accessories, vinyls, etc. Young Japanese go shopping here because prices are generally low. I highly recommend the crepes sold on a corner halfway down the street.

COSPLAY BRIDGE (2 ON THE MAP)
Right between Harajuku Station and the entrance to the Meiji Jingu Shrine there is a bridge that spans the Yamanote Line train tracks. This bridge has become one of the favorite gathering places for all kinds of *cosplayers*. They usually meet there on Sundays starting around eleven o'clock in the morning, and you can see anything from video game *cosplay* to the most bizarre *gothic lolita* outfits.

If you want to astonish people with your photographs when you return from your trip to Japan, you really should drop by on Sunday.

MEIJI JINGU (3 ON THE MAP)
One of Tokyo's most important Shinto shrines, devoted to the emperor and visited ceremonially by Japan's prime minister every year. It's not exceptionally beautiful, but seeing a temple surrounded by lush woods right in the middle of the metropolis has a certain power. If you go there on Sunday morning, you are very likely to witness a Shinto wedding ceremony.

YOYOGI PARK (4 ON THE MAP)
Yoyogi is the most active park in Tokyo. On Sundays, many people gather here to practice their favorite hobbies, among them acting, sparring with swords, bongo drumming, juggling, playing in a band, etc.

OMOTESANDO HILLS (5 ON THE MAP)
The most expensive shopping mall in the country. Almost all merchandise is either luxurious or exclusive. Even if you have no intention of buying anything, it's worth going in to see the interior's very original design, which gives you easy access to several floors without climbing stairs. Moreover, its Zen public address system provides different sounds and music as you enter different areas within the building.

KIDDYLAND (8 ON THE MAP)
In Omotesando, one of the most interesting stores from an economic point of view is Kiddyland. It's something like a toy store but where you'll find all sorts of geeky or *otaku* stuff: *anime* series T-shirts, Ghibli stuffed animals, robots that you assemble at home, etc. If your inner child is strong within you, it's a place you have to see.

Meiji Jingu shrine is entered through a large torii gate.

Omotesando Hills, the most expensive shopping mall in Japan.

"Harajuku is the fashion district where most of Japan's young urban tribes circulate."

OMOTESANDO (9 ON THE MAP)

Omotesando Avenue is near Takeshita Dori but has a totally different ambience. Omotesando stands out because of its glamour, pricey boutiques, and upmarket department stores, and it features people with lots of purchasing power walking around in their most exclusive outfits.

Harajuku Station seen from a nearby bridge.

Out-of-the-box design of the Audi building in Harajuku.

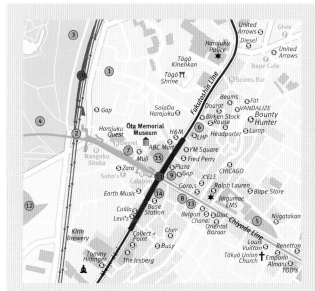

HOW TO GET TO HARAJUKU

BY THE JR YAMANOTE LINE TO HARAJUKU STATION OR
BY THE SUBWAY CHIYODA LINE TO MEIJI-JINGUMAE STATION

MAP

1. Takeshita Dori
2. Cosplay bridge
3. Meiji Jingu Shrine
4. Yoyogi Park
5. Omotesando Hills
6. KDDI Building
7. SoftBank Mobile cell phone store
8. Kiddyland
9. Omotesando
10. Harajuku Station
11. Meiji-Jingumae Station
12. Olympic Stadium
13. MOMA shop
14. Uniqlo T-shirt shop
15. La Foret Department Store and Museum

SHINJUKU

If we were to compare New York City to Tokyo, Shinjuku would be Manhattan. It's the district with the most skyscrapers and neon signage in the city. It's a must if you want to feel transported to the setting of a Ridley Scott movie or to one of the cities in *Ghost in the Shell*. Shinjuku often appears in movies, *manga*, and *anime*. Some examples are *Lost in Translation*, *Death Note*, *Tokyo Tribe*, *Wasabi*, and *Tokyo Drift*.

One of the most impressive things in Shinjuku is its train station, which is the largest and busiest in the world. An average of three million people use it every day, and it has more than 200 exits.

SHOPPING DISTRICT (2 ON THE MAP)
At the South and East Exits, there are several department stores selling all sorts of goods: clothes, second-hand video games, electronics, books, etc. It's fun to walk around the wide streets full of neon signs that you see when you leave by the East Exit. You will also see one of Japan's most famous rendezvous points, Studio Alta.

SKYSCRAPER AREA (1 ON THE MAP)
The area to the west is filled with the skyscrapers of major corporations. You'll see armies of Japanese in spotless dark suits and ties carrying briefcases and walking hurriedly, like ants. One of the most interesting buildings is Tokyo City Hall (also known as Tokyo Metropolitan Government Building, or Tocho Building), easily recognizable because it is one of the tallest and it splits into two towers. Visiting the City Hall observation deck is free, and from there you can enjoy views of most of Tokyo. If you're lucky and it's a clear day, you'll be able to see Mount Fuji. Near City Hall is the Park Hyatt, a three-tower building famous as the hotel where most of the sequences for the movie *Lost in Translation* were shot.

"Shinjuku is the Tokyo district with the most skyscrapers and neon signage. It's a must if you want to feel transported to the setting of a Ridley Scott movie or to one of the cities in *Ghost in the Shell*."

BARS, PACHINKO PARLORS, BROTHELS, AND LOVE HOTELS (4 ON THE MAP)
Kabuki-cho is an area in the northeast of Shinjuku that has a very lively nightlife. It's full of *pachinko* parlors, nightclubs with girls who serve you drinks while they sit and talk with you, and premises of dubious repute usually controlled by *yakuza*. If you want to observe the nightlife and see how the Japanese have fun, take a walk around. Toward the edges of Kabuki-cho you'll find the love hotel area. Love hotels are specifically designed for sex. They rent rooms for two or three hours, although an eight-hour option is also available if you want to spend the night.

YAKITORI STREET (3 ON THE MAP)
The "yakitori street" is a place with seedy bars where they serve *yakitori*—equivalent to our kebabs– and the only thing that varies from one bar to the next is the ingredients they use. For instance, there are kebabs made of liver, chicken skin, chicken cartilage, Japanese mushrooms, etc. The best way to get there is by taking Shinjuku Station's East Exit and crossing under the train tracks. You'll recognize the street at once from its gloomy atmosphere in the purest *Blade Runner* style.

SHINJUKU GYOEN (5 ON THE MAP)
Shinjuku Gyoen is a park that mixes both Japanese and European styles. The best time to visit it is during the *sakura* season when the cherry trees are in bloom.

Shinjuku Station is the busiest in the world with over three million people passing through it every day.

Shinjuku Gyoen park during the sakura blossom season attracts enormous crowds.

Shinjuku is full of attractive neon signs.

Food in Shinjuku is cheap and good.

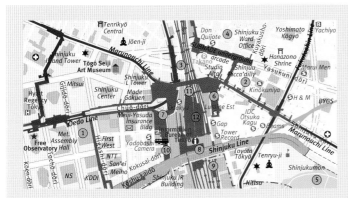

HOW TO GET TO SHINJUKU
BY THE CHUO OR YAMANOTE LINES TO SHINJUKU STATION

MAP

1. Skyscraper district
2. Shopping district
3. Yakitori street
4. Bar area
5. Shinjuku Gyoen park
6. East Exit
7. West Exit
8. South Exit
9. New South Exit
10. Odakyu Lines
11. Subway lines
12. Shinjuku Station

Idols being photographed are a common sight in Akihabara.

Akihabara's main avenue, where the largest electronics department stores are concentrated.

Akihabara's main avenue on a Sunday.

AKIHABARA

Tokyo's ultimate *otaku* district is Akihabara, famous for its electronics centers, computers, *manga*, *anime*, and figurines. This is the district with the most electronics stores in the world. Hundreds of stores are concentrated in small alleys and side streets and in buildings full of neon signs, where they sell everything from the latest products on the market to second-or-more-hand 50-year-old radios.

Akihabara is one of Japan's symbols of prosperity. It is a place where new electronic products are put to test and where, very often, even American companies test market public acceptance of their early prototypes.

My advice is that you go straight to the stores you're most interested in, because if you don't time will fly and you may not see what you came for. As it happens, stores in Japan usually occupy entire buildings, so wherever you go you can lose yourself for hours on end. For example, in Akihabara there are 10-story department stores devoted exclusively to *manga*, others full of cameras, and others with erotic DVDs. These stores are highly specialized and you can find virtually anything in them.

If you want to buy an electronic device, Akihabara is one of the cheapest sources. However, my advice is that the only things worth buying here are cameras because they usually come with an international warranty, can be connected to our power supply, come with a manual, and almost always have English menus

> "Tokyo's ultimate *otaku* district is Akihabara, famous for its electronics centers, computers, *manga*, *anime*, and figurines."

as an option. Moreover, there is a considerable price difference between cameras in Akihabara and in the United States. As for computers, flat screen TVs, or video game consoles, I would advise you not to buy because the price difference is minimal and, in the case of computers, they might even be more expensive and there might be language problems as well. For example, laptops are usually sold exclusively with a Japanese keyboard, video game consoles can be used only with games bought in Japan, and manuals often come only in Japanese.

As soon as you exit the station, you'll see lots of neon signs as well as the seedy part of the station building, with many small stores right next to it. This shopping complex is known as Radio Center. First, go into Radio Center where you'll see tiny stores selling light bulbs, walkmans from the 1980s, humanoid robots, and all sorts of electronic stuff. It has a certain charm, with filthy corridors and hanging wires everywhere, recreating a cyberpunk atmosphere. When you leave Radio Center, you'll see an avenue packed with buildings full of things to discover. From this point on, choose your destination according to your tastes.

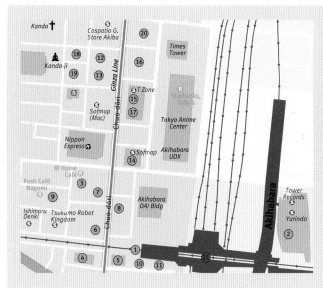

HOW TO GET TO AKIHABARA
BY JR YAMANOTE LINE TO AKIHABARA STATION, AKIHABARA
ELECTRIC TOWN EXIT

MAP

1. Radio Center
2. Yodobashi Camera
3. Super Potato
4. Laox
5. Laox and Sega
6. Club Sega and Softmap
7. Gera Gera and Ramen Internet cafés
8. Akihabara Asobit: figurines, idols, and video games
9. Computers, second-hand, etc.
10. Kotobukiya, Kaiyodo, VOLKS
11. Sato Musen: electronics and video games
12. Gee Store cosplay costume stores and meido kissas
13. Gachapon Kaikan
14. Taito
15. Don Quixote
16. Tsukumo
17. Animate and Comic Toranoana
18. Tsukumo Robot Kingdom (Robot-Herokan), photograph of KHR-1
19. Second-hand computing
20. Rare Godzilla figurines, spline.tv/ goleen_age/
21. Akihabara Station

SEGA GAME CENTERS (5 AND 6 ON THE MAP)

If you like video arcades, there are a couple of Sega buildings full of them in Akihabara. In the most curious ones, you can play the drums, the guitar, or the *taiko* (Japanese traditional drum). Besides these, you'll find all kinds of machines, from the newest on the market to classic coin-operated arcade games like "Street Fighter II."

YODOBASHI CAMERA (2 ON THE MAP)

The largest department store in the world. It's a huge building, where you can spend a whole day looking at computers, cameras, flat screen TVs, the latest generation sound systems, etc.

SUPER POTATO (3 ON THE MAP)

Second-hand retro games store. If you are old school and are into platform games and immediate entertainment video games, Super Potato is your paradise. Two floors full of games from the 1980s and 1990s, second-hand video consoles, and strange machines you may have never seen before.

SECOND-HAND STREET MARKET AREA (9 ON THE MAP)

If you leave the main avenue, in the side streets and alleys of Akihabara you'll find many small shops where they sell all sorts of second-hand goods.You can find anything here, from plug adaptors to Internet servers. The storefronts merge with one another and the shopkeepers display their wares in boxes out on the sidewalk as if they were greengrocers.

SOFMAP (6 ON THE MAP)

Sofmap is Japan's largest chain of second-hand stores selling computers and video game consoles. If you're looking for inexpensive games or some used computer device, this is your place. Before paying, make sure the games you buy will work in an American machine.

LAOX (4 AND 5 ON THE MAP)

This is another big Japanese home electronics chain with several department stores. The Laox in Akihabara is one of the few places where you can find several models of laptops with an English keyboard.

TSUKUMO (16 ON THE MAP)

A big store specializing in computers. From normal and inexpensive computers to powerful servers that you can probably only find here.

ANIMATE (17 ON THE MAP)

Animate is Akihabara's biggest *manga* and *anime* store. An entire building full of *manga*, figurines of *manganime* characters, movies in DVD, complete boxed sets of *anime* series, posters, and a long list of products. The dream store for anyone interested in *manganime*.

COMIC TORANOANA (17 ON THE MAP)

Toranoana is another big *manganime* store and it's right next to Animate. Here you will find more material related to its subculture, such as Japanese fanzines, information on Tokyo clubs for *anime* series, etc.

FIGURE SHOPS

There are lots of shops specializing in figurines and general merchandise. You can find figures from Godzilla and Batman to Naruto and Son Goku, as well as many others.

MEIDO KISSAS

Meido kissas are a special type of coffee shop where young women dressed in maid costumes serve coffee. The *meido kissas* fashion originated in this district and has spread beyond the borders of Japan. If you want to go to a *meido* coffee shop when you're in Akihabara, it's not hard to do; there are tons of them. Just keep an eye out for the striking signs on the street.

This is how Ginza streets look on Sunday.

GINZA

This is the pricey, upscale district where wealthy people go on Sundays to shop for clothes and accessories. Ginza has spotless streets, luxury buildings with small boutiques, and large department stores selling clothes, jewelry, and luxury goods. It's also famous for its coffee shops and *sushi* restaurants.

Ginza 銀座 means literally "silver mint." At the beginning of the Edo Period, in 1612, one of the most important mints in the country was established in this district. Since then it has always been considered the money and glamor center of Tokyo.

The best days to visit Ginza are Saturday and Sunday when the main streets are closed to traffic until five o'clock in the afternoon. Ginza also has a vibrant nightlife. Below are some of the interesting places to see:

NISSAN GALLERY (1 ON THE MAP)
On the main crossing in Ginza, Nissan has a small showroom where they display some of their latest futuristic prototypes. Even a five-minute stop is worthwhile.

POKÉMON CENTER
(6 ON THE MAP—BEHIND THE APPLE STORE)
If you have a passion for Pokémon video games, visiting this store is a must. Here you'll find all kinds of stuffed animals, video games, and even Pokémon kitchen utensils. The cash registers are in the shape of Pokéballs.

SONY BUILDING (7 ON THE MAP)
Those with a passion for technology will enjoy the Sony Building. You can see not only products that are already on the market but also prototypes of future products, and there are explanations for such things as how their new flat screens work. The four bathrooms in the building are completely automated: the toilet flushes by itself and even the soap automatically drops onto your hands when you go to wash them.

APPLE STORE (6 ON THE MAP)
Another four-story building that technology buffs shouldn't miss. They have all the Apple products on the market, a repair area, a room where you can surf the Internet for free, a conference room where talks are given all day long, etc. The exterior of the building is beautiful, especially in the sunlight.

LEGO STORE (5 ON THE MAP)
Did you love Lego when you were a kid? Are you still playing with Lego Mindstorms? In Ginza there's a store full of Lego!

SUSHI RESTAURANTS
(2 ON THE MAP AND IN 3, THE FISH MARKET)
Ginza is full of expensive restaurants. If you want to eat well for a reasonable price, I'd recommend walking a little ways toward the Tsukiji area where there are dozens of excellent *sushi* restaurants all around, especially in the Tsukiji Outer Market where there are dozens of food stalls and restaurants.

HAMARIKYU GARDENS (4 ON THE MAP)
Hamarikyu Gardens, near the *sushi* restaurant area, is one of the most tranquil spots in Tokyo. Surrounded by tall skyscrapers and the waters of Tokyo Bay, Hamarikyu Gardens manages to create a Zen atmosphere where you can enjoy a quiet walk among the trees pruned Japanese-style, ponds, and a traditional teahouse. In the teahouse, you can taste *matcha*, the green tea used in the famous tea ceremony. From the park, a ferry will take you to the Asakusa district or Odaiba.

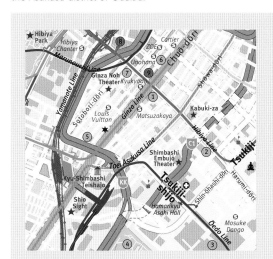

HOW TO GET TO GINZA
BY THE GINZA SUBWAY LINE TO GINZA STATION OR BY THE JR YAMANOTE LINE TO YURAKUCHO STATION

MAP
1. Nissan Gallery
2. Sushi restaurants
3. Fish Market
4. Hamarikyu Gardens
5. Lego Store
6. Apple Store
7. Sony Building
8. Yurakucho Station
9. Ginza Station

Seafood restaurants and stalls selling fresh produce at Tsukiji Outer Market.

TSUKIJI AND TOYOSU

On October 6, 2018, Tokyo's famous 83-year-old Tsukiji Fish Market, the largest wholesale fish and seafood market in the world and one of the Tokyo's most popular destinations for international visitors, closed its doors, marking the end of an era. Tsukiji was part of a larger market, the Tokyo Central Wholesale Market, which included other produce as well as fish. Located beside Tokyo Bay near Ginza and Shiodome, Tsukiji was best known for its tuna auctions, where huge tuna, some weighing more than 600 lb (27 kg), were lined up, ready to be bought. For visitors willing to arrive at 5 am, the bidding was a once-in-a-lifetime spectacle!

TSUKIJI OUTER MARKET (2 ON THE MAP)
Even without the famous tuna auctions, the Outer Market at Tsukiji survives and is just as intriguing. It houses dozens of food stalls and restaurants crammed along narrow lanes, many specializing in *sushi*. It is definitely worth visiting for the freshest fish and seafood in town although the restaurants and fish shops can be very crowded on weekends.

Tsukiji Outer Market is located a short walk from either Tsukiji Shijo Station on the Oedo Line or Tsukiji Station on the Hibaya Line. The closest JR station is Shimbashi. From here, a walk to the market will take about 20 minutes.

TOYOSU FISH MARKET
Located 1.2 miles (2 km) east of Tsukiji on the Toyosu waterfront, the Toyosu Fish Market opened its doors to the public on October 13, 2018. Set in a spanking new, purpose-built facility comprising three interconnected buildings, it is a far cry from the charm and chaos of Tsukiji, but with 600 fish merchants in action it is still a sight to behold. Dedicated viewing platforms behind glass allow visitors to more easily see the workings of the market, which is liveliest at about 8 am. The tuna auctions will open to the public in 2019 and start at 4.30 am. Access to the market and the auctions is free and no reservations are required. There are around 40 food stalls, carried over from Tsukiji, located on the rooftop.

The closest subway station to Toyosu Fish Market is Shijomae Station on the Yurikamome Line (the station connects directly to the market). It's also two stops from Toyosu Station, which can also be accessed via the Yurakucho Line.

Cutting up a big tuna after it has been purchased at a morning auction.

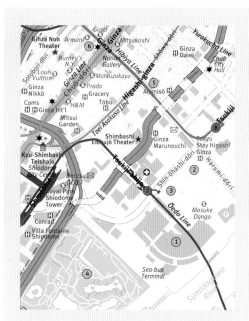

HOW TO GET TO TSUKIJI
BY THE OEDO SUBWAY LINE TO TSUKIJI SHIJO STATION
OR BY THE HIBIYA SUBWAY LINE TO TSUKIJI STATION

MAP

1. Old Tsukiji Fish Market
2. Tsukiji Outer Market
3. Good sushi and fish restaurants
4. Hamarikyu Gardens
5. Kabuki Theater (Kabuki-za)
6. Ginza
7. Tsukiji Shijo Station
8. Tsukiji Station

The Asakusa Temple is one of the most spectacular in the country.

ASAKUSA

Asakusa is Tokyo's most traditional district. It has a spectacular Buddhist temple with several pagodas, a street full of shops where you can find all sorts of traditional souvenirs, and lots of quality restaurants with reasonable prices.

In olden times, Asakusa was Tokyo's entertainment center, but this began to shift after World War II, with Shinjuku superseding it, closely followed by Shibuya.

> "Asakusa is Tokyo's most traditional district, with temples, pagodas, the Kaminari Gate, and souvenirs."

KAMINARI GATE (1 ON THE MAP)
You should start your walk at the Kaminari Gate, a meeting place for many Japanese as well as a favorite place to take the typical tourist photographs. It's notable for its two traditional guardians and a big red lantern in the middle.

SHOPPING AREA (2 ON THE MAP)
At the Kaminari Gate, you'll find a street full of small souvenir shops. This is one of the best places in Japan to buy souvenirs, so make the most of this opportunity.

ASAKUSA TEMPLE (SENSO-JI) (3 ON THE MAP)
At the end of the shopping area is Asakusa Temple. It stands out partly because of the height of one of its structures but mainly because of the festivals celebrated on the surrounding streets on weekends and special holidays.

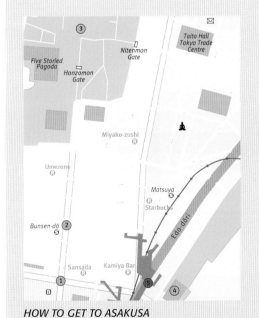

HOW TO GET TO ASAKUSA
THE EASIEST WAY IS BY THE TOKYO SUBWAY GINZA LINE (YELLOW). ANOTHER OPTION IS BY FERRY, FOR EXAMPLE FROM HAMARIKYU PARK (see section on Ginza).

MAP
1. Kaminari Gate
2. Shopping area (Bunsen-do)
3. Asakusa Temple
4. Ferry jetty on the bay
5. Asakusa Station

The National Museum seen from the Ueno gardens.

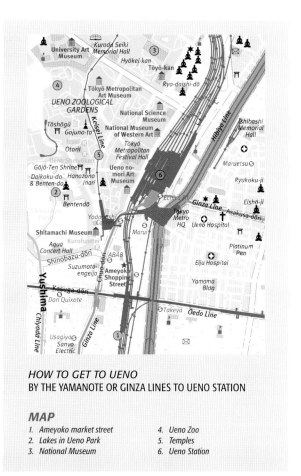

HOW TO GET TO UENO
BY THE YAMANOTE OR GINZA LINES TO UENO STATION

MAP

1. Ameyoko market street
2. Lakes in Ueno Park
3. National Museum
4. Ueno Zoo
5. Temples
6. Ueno Station

"Ueno is a beautiful park with lots of museums and a zoo. It's a must visit during the cherry tree flowering season or when traditional festival days are celebrated."

UENO

Ueno is another traditional area in Tokyo. It has one of the largest parks in the city, with seven museums, several temples, and the city zoo. It's a beautiful place and a must visit during the cherry tree flowering season at the beginning of May or when traditional festival days are celebrated.

UENO ZOO (4 ON THE MAP)

The Ueno Zoo is famous for its panda bears and the number of people who visit it every weekend. It's not essential to visit, but if you love animals or you have time to spare then seeing a few panda bears in Tokyo is not a bad idea.

NATIONAL MUSEUM (3 ON THE MAP)

The National Museum at the north end of the park is an ideal place to get a feel for the history of Japan. Admission is cheap and an assortment of objects, works of art, armor, and *samurai katana* make it the most appealing museum in the park. At the back of the museum is a small traditional garden worth viewing.

LAKE AND TEMPLES (2 AND 5 ON THE MAP)

Walking around the southern part of Ueno Park, you will come across many small Shinto shrines, stalls selling various food, and a lake famous among Tokyo residents for the swan-shaped boats that are available for rent.

AMEYOKO MARKET STREET (1 ON THE MAP)

Leaving the park by the south end, if you go to the shopping area outside the Yamanote Line, you will find the market street called Ameyoko, famous for its traditional stores and a typical outdoor market selling spices, fish, vegetables, and second-hand clothes, with all sorts of bargains.

Ameyoko Street is one of the most traditional shopping streets in Tokyo.

The man-made island of Odaiba exudes a characteristic air of modernity.

ODAIBA

Odaiba is a small island in Tokyo Bay where people often go for day trips. Visiting isn't a must, but if you are in Japan for more than two weeks it could be a good option. Most buildings on the island are of fairly recent construction. There are many museums, research laboratories, etc. In short, it has a very modern and hi-tech feel about it, similar to visiting a city of the future. It's also the legendary island where the MXC show was filmed.

FUTURISTIC TRAIN

The Yurikamome Line is one the principal connections between the center of Tokyo and Odaiba. Neither a train nor a monorail, it's actually a hybrid that runs on something like rubber adapter wheels that couple to the sides of a concrete structure elevated above ground level. It doesn't require a driver and is controlled by computers, monitored remotely by human beings. For the passengers, the advantage of not having a driver is that you can sit in the first car and enjoy amazing views that make you feel transported to Gotham City or New Port. The line starts at Shinbashi, a station you can get to by Tokyo's Yamanote Line.

MUSEUM OF EMERGING SCIENCE AND INNOVATION (5 ON THE MAP)

If you like science, visit the National Museum of Emerging Science and Innovation where you can watch the famous humanoid Asimo in action. As well, you'll find many other robots, explanations of how new superconductor trains work, the secrets of the Internet, and so on.

FUJI TV BUILDING, DRAGON BALL AND ONE PIECE MUSEUM (1 ON THE MAP)

One of the most spectacular buildings in Japan is the Fuji TV building, which houses the legendary television channel that once broadcast the *Dragon Ball* series and now has the very successful *One Piece*. The building is easy to recognize, thanks to a sort of embedded huge sphere. In areas that are open to the general public, you can have your photo taken with the Fuji TV mascot or go up to the observation deck on the 24th floor and view Tokyo from Odaiba. There is also a museum/shop with merchandising from animation series that were among Fuji TV's biggest television hits. If they are not broadcasting at the time of your visit, you can also visit the set of Mezamashi TV.

Just opposite the Fuji TV building are a couple of buildings with stores for shopping. The most interesting are Sony, which occupies several floors, and the Osamu Tezuka Store, with all kinds of products based on the series by the man known as the creator of modern *manga*.

SEGA PARK (3 ON THE MAP)

Right next to the Tezuka Manga Museum building is another building housing Sega Park. It's a huge game center with the company's latest video arcade games.

PANORAMIC VIEW OF TOKYO BAY (4 ON THE MAP)

A good place to take your typical tourist photos. From here, you'll notice that Japan owns a copy of the Statue of Liberty, behind which you'll see Tokyo Tower, a copy of France's Eiffel Tower.

TOKYO BIG SIGHT (6 ON THE MAP)

Shown in the photo above right, this is one of the most important convention centers in Tokyo. It hosts trade fairs and events, one of the biggest being Comiket, the world's largest gathering of *manga* authors and fans. Check their Web page, http://www.bigsight.jp/english/, before traveling to Japan, in case your visit coincides with any event you might want to attend.

HOW TO GET TO ODAIBA
BY THE YURIKAMOME LINE TO DAIBA STATION

MAP
1. Fuji TV Building
2. Shopping mall
3. Sega Park
4. Panoramic view
5. Museum of Emerging Science and Innovation
6. Tokyo Big Sight
7. Daiba Station

Scenes from Akihabara, the ultimate otaku district.

OTAKU WALKING TOURS

If you identified with the *otaku* when you read Chapter 7, or if you enjoyed reading about the history of *manga* in Chapter 8, Tokyo is your city. As soon as you arrive at the airport, you get the first hints of this, for several huge signs with *anime* characters are there to welcome you to the country.

In previous sections, we reviewed some of Tokyo's most important areas. Now let's see how to plan a visit so you don't miss the city's main *otaku* highlights. You'll need at least two days.

FIRST DAY

In the morning, start off in Akihabara and visit the stores that interest you the most. Have a quick lunch in any restaurant in the area then take the Chuo Line to Nakano Station. Once there, leave the station by the North Exit and walk down Nakano Broadway, an entertaining street full of stores with a treasure at the end: the famous Mandarake store, considered the largest *manga* store in the world. On its several floors you'll encounter every type of *manga*, *anime* DVD, figurine, video game, etc., both new and used. It's a must for all enthusiasts of *manganime*. However, you'd better not dawdle, because they close at eight o'clock at night.

After your stroll down Nakano Broadway and your visit to Mandarake, I would recommend dinner at one of the most famous *ramen* restaurants in Tokyo. It's called Aoba and it's located on a street that crosses Nakano Broadway. It's a bit out of the way but if you ask any sales clerk in any of the stores around, they will certainly be able to give you directions.

To conclude the day, before returning to your hotel, linger a while in Shinjuku, look for a game center, and enjoy taking in the spectacular skills of the Japanese when they play video games.

SECOND DAY

Get up very early in the morning and go to Odaiba. There, visit the Fuji TV building and its *anime* merchandise stores. Don't forget to stop by the Osamu Tezuka store in the facing building as well. To finish, go into the Sega Park to check out the latest Japanese video games. By mid-afternoon, head back to the center of Tokyo and stop at Ikebukuro Station (north of Shinjuku) on the Yamanote Line. In Ikebukuro, you'll find Animate, one of largest *anime* stores in the city.

EXTRA DAY

Visit the Ghibli Museum (go to Mitaka Station on the Chuo Line, a bit farther than Nakano). Try going on a weekday at around 10 am because later in the day it might be full and you won't be able to get in without a reservation. You can have lunch near Mitaka Station and head back in the afternoon, stopping in Harajuku for a relaxed walk and to shop at the Kiddyland store.

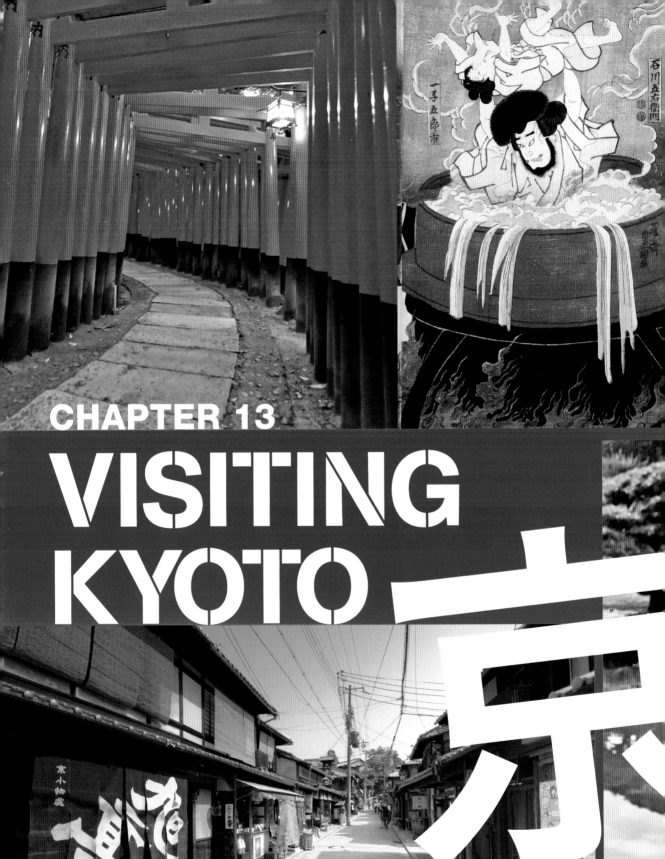

CHAPTER 13

VISITING KYOTO

京

KYOTO'S VARIOUS DISTRICTS

The Kansai region, whose main cities are Osaka, Kyoto, and Kobe, is the second most populous area in Japan after Kanto (Tokyo, Yokohama, and surroundings). Even though it is one of the densest and largest urban zones in the world, it is much easier to visit than Tokyo. To give you an idea of the distances and sizes in this area, it takes less time to go from Kyoto to Osaka than between stations in the east and west of Tokyo.

The best thing to do is to stay for a few days in a hotel in Kyoto, which is more or less halfway towards most of the places of interest in Kansai.

PLANNING YOUR STAY IN KYOTO

3-day plan: I would allot one day to walking around the temples in the east of Kyoto and another to seeing the Kinkaku-ji and the Ryoan-ji, which are in the western zone. I would spend a full evening on either the first or second day strolling through the Gion neighborhood. On the third day, I would visit Nara.

5-day plan: I would spend another day in Kyoto visiting Fushimi-Inari Taisha and the Kyoto Imperial Palace or Nijo Castle. On the fifth day, I would go to see Osaka Castle and to walking around Dotonbori in Osaka.

Tip: If you can, try to visit Kyoto and Nara during the week because the weekends are crawling with tourists. If you go mid-week, you are only likely to come across children and pensioners on day trips.

Accommodation: My recommendation is to look for a hotel or traditional *ryokan* near Kyoto Station where there are a lot to choose from. This is also the best connected zone both with the rest of the city and with Nara and Osaka.

Don't forget: The temples normally close at five in the evening and open at eight or nine in the morning.

KYOTO INTRODUCTION

Kyoto was the second capital of Japan after Nara. In fact, Kyoto in Japanese is written 京都, with the first character meaning "capital" or "place where the Emperor resides" and the second character meaning "metropolis" or "capital." When the capital city was moved to Tokyo at the end of the nineteenth century, they considered changing Kyoto's name since it had lost its capital status, but in the end they decided against it.

Today, Kyoto is one of the most beautiful cities you can visit in Japan and is regarded as the country's most important cultural center. In Kyoto, a great number of temples are conserved, thanks largely to the fact the city wasn't a bombing target during World War II. There are over 2,500 historic places, what with temples, gardens, castles and palaces; 17 of them are listed as World Heritage Sites by UNESCO.

Kyoto is a much smaller and more manageable city than Tokyo. The atmosphere is much more intimate and you sense a certain village air and a more open attitude among the people. The street planning in Kyoto was done during a time of great Chinese influence in Japan, giving it a symmetrical grid pattern look, something which is not often seen in other Japanese cities.

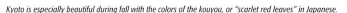

Kyoto is especially beautiful during fall with the colors of the kouyou, or "scarlet red leaves" in Japanese.

Explore hidden areas of Kyoto on a rickshaw ride with a knowledgeable guide.

The best time to catch a glimpse of an apprentice geisha on the streets of Gion is in the early evening.

The Imperial Palace was located in the center of the city, and an avenue began at the south gate and ended at an enormous gate called Rashomon. The Imperial Palace still stands today and may be visited, but the Rashomon Gate was destroyed. What remains of the Rashomon Gate are legends. It is said that a demon lived in the gate, which was used to abandon unwanted babies. Ryunosuke Akutagawa wrote a tale about the gate and Akira Kurosawa made the film *Rashomon* based on this tale.

> "Kyoto has the country's highest concentration of places of interest"

The grid pattern street layout makes walking around Kyoto, and even traveling by bus, easy and user-friendly for visitors. The city map may be visualized as a large rectangle trapped between mountains. Kyoto is in a wide valley open to the south. The summers are very warm and the winters very cold. The largest quantity of temples are found in the eastern mountains. The most famous of them is Kiyomizu-dera, which has impressive views from the mountainside.

MY PERSONAL EXPERIENCE AND TIPS

In Kyoto, you can find practically everything that seeing films or photos has led you to expect of Japan. There is still something left of the spirit of medieval Japan.

The first time I visited Kyoto I went to the most touristy places, the most famous temples, which the guidebooks say you shouldn't miss. We had a good time, but the truth is, the best memory I have of that first visit is not of a famous temple.

The best thing was when we got lost on purpose and went into one of those small, virtually unknown temples, the kind that don't appear in the guidebooks. We spent three unforgettable hours there, strolling through the surrounding woods and having tea in one of the temple buildings. I still remember those three hours vividly. I felt like the star of a *samurai* novel exploring the mountains of eastern Kyoto.

My advice is, lose yourself for a while. Go into an area that isn't recommended in any of the guidebooks, including this one, and visit small little-known temples. Oftentimes, the temples that in theory hold little historical interest are the most peaceful and the ones you can enjoy the most.

CENTRAL KYOTO

GION (1 ON THE MAP)

Gion is one of the best neighborhoods in the city to get a taste of ancient Japan. Many examples of traditional Japanese architecture have been conserved here. It is also famous for being the area of the country in which the most *geisha* still work. When night falls, you can sometimes see *geisha* and *maiko* (apprentices) walking in its narrow streets. As well as being the *geisha* neighborhood, it is also one of the liveliest areas when night falls.

In Gion, many houses, called *machiya*, have been conserved following traditional building standards. The style of the *machiya*, which are built with wood, comes from the Heian period (794–1185). One of the main characteristics that enables you to recognize a *machiya*, apart from the wood, is its shape. They have small discreet façades but are elongated and stretch back into the block, hiding gardens in their interior.

If you visit the city in April, don't miss the Miyako Odori event. This is a show at the Kaburen-jo Theater featuring *geisha*

Tradition is the word that defines Kyoto.

Attending the Miyako Odori show in Gion is the perfect way to appreciate the art of the geisha and geiko.

and *geiko* from the Gion neighborhood. This is a tradition that started in 1872 as a means of promoting Kyoto's prosperity after its slight decline on losing capital city status in 1869.

How to get to Gion: From Kyoto Station, take the Karasuma subway line to Shijo/Karasuma. Change to the Hankyu-Kyoto Line and take it to Kawaramachi Station.

Recommended time for the visit: A full evening to walk around, have a cup of tea, eat dinner and soak in the atmosphere.

How to get to the Kaburen-jo Theater (to attend the Miyako Odori): Walk 5 minutes in a southerly direction from Kawaramachi Station.

Miyako Odori ticket prices: There are four performances every day during April: 12.30 am and 2, 3.30 and 4.50 pm. Tickets cost from 2,000 yen up to 4,500 yen depending on the seat. There are normally seats to spare, but if you prefer reserve your seats in advance by calling 075-541-3391 from Japan, +8175-541-3391 from abroad or booking online at www.http://miyako-odori.jp/english/

NIJO CASTLE (2 ON THE MAP)

Nijo-jo is an enormous castle situated right in the city center. Construction of it was begun in 1601 by Tokugawa Ieyasu, one of the most important historical characters in the history of Japan (see pages 10–11).

I don't consider it a must see, but since it's in the city center you can visit it if you have a couple of hours on your hands.

How to get there: Take the Karasuma subway line from Kyoto Station to Karasuma-Oike Station. Change to the Tozai Line and go to Nijojo-mae Station. It's a 20-minute journey.

Recommended time for the visit: Two hours.

> "Nijo-jo is an enormous castle situated right in the city center."

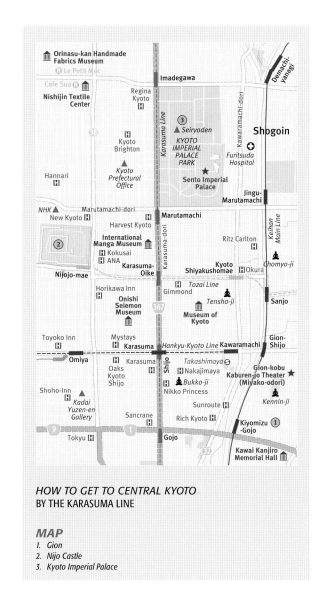

HOW TO GET TO CENTRAL KYOTO BY THE KARASUMA LINE

MAP
1. Gion
2. Nijo Castle
3. Kyoto Imperial Palace

Entrance to the Nijo-jo Castle in central Kyoto.

When you encounter a pond in Japan, such as this one at the Ginkakuji, look at the reflections and marvel at how the pond and the garden were created with the intention to create beauty.

KYOTO IMPERIAL PALACE (3 ON THE MAP)

Kyoto's Imperial Palace was the emperor's residence until 1869 when his place of residence changed to Tokyo. Unlike Tokyo's Imperial Palace, where the visit is restricted to some of its gardens, Kyoto's Imperial Palace is open to the public.

Apart from seeing the gardens, one of the most interesting parts of the visit is being able to see the Seiryoden, the building in which the emperor led his private life, and access to which was restricted to his closest family. Advance or same-day applications to visit are required and free English tours are available at 10 am and 2 pm. You can even see the *tatami*-covered bedroom in which the emperor slept on a *futon*.

To be allowed in, you have to get there 20 minutes before the time you've booked for and show your passport at the north gate.

How to get there: Take the Karasuma Line from Kyoto Station to Imadegawa Station. The journey takes about 15 minutes.

Recommended time for the visit: It takes about a morning to tour around the whole Imperial Palace compound. The guided tour will take an hour.

Like many other Japanese historical buildings, the Imperial Palace structures have been rebuilt several times. The current version dates from 1855. Walking around the palace and all its different buildings will make you feel like you are traveling back to the past.

EASTERN KYOTO

GINKAKU-JI (1 ON THE MAP)

Ginkaku-ji, the Temple of the Silver Pavilion, is a lovely Zen temple with scenic moss and sand gardens and is more serene than the Golden Pavilion across town. The original temple was built at the end of the fifteenth century by Shogun Ashikaga Yoshimasa, who wanted to emulate the construction of the Golden Pavilion which had been dreamt up by his grandfather. He planned to cover it in silver instead of gold. Due to a lack of money, it was never covered in silver, but the name stuck despite the temple having absolutely no silver on it.

The most beautiful thing about the temple are the gardens, especially the sand garden. What's strange and unique about the sand garden at Ginkaku-ji is the fact that there is an enormous pile of sand that is said to symbolize the shape of Mount Fuji. Others say that the sand represents the sea and that the mountain of sand is a volcanic island.

Dry gardens like the sand garden at Ginkaku-ji are ideal places for a moment of relaxation during your trip.

Ginkaku-ji tends to be full of tourists as it is included in many guidebooks as an essential place to visit, but it doesn't hold a candle up to the Golden Pavilion. It might even disappoint you. If you go to Ginkaku-ji, take advantage of your trip to also go along the Philosopher's Walk up to Nanzen-ji Temple.

How to get there: Take bus number 5, 17, 102, 203, or 204 up to Ginkakuji-michi, or 32 and 100 up to Ginkakuji-mae.

Recommended time for the visit: One hour is enough.

THE PHILOSOPHER'S WALK
(2 ON THE MAP)

When Kyoto became Japan's capital in the eighteenth century, one of the city's biggest problems was the heat in the summer. As the city is located in a valley surrounded by hills in the summer there is a kind of cauldron effect; the air hardly moves and it's very hot. To solve the heat problem, many canals and streams were built throughout the city to help create a cool ambience, if only thanks to the sound of water. The Philosopher's Walk is one of the many streets in Kyoto with a stream running alongside it, but this one in particular became well known because the famous philosopher Nishida Kitaro liked to walk along it every day and said it helped him find inspiration.

The walk stretches for nearly 1 mile (2 km) next to a stream shaded by hundreds of cherry trees. It's lovely during the flowering season, though a little overwhelming because of the crowds.

During the rest of the year, it's a peaceful walk. The most interesting thing you can do there is to go visit the multiple temples nearby. The most important ones are at the beginning and the end—Ginkaku-ji and Nanzen-ji. Halfway along is one of the smallest temples (Honen-in), where you can find the tombs of several former professors of the University of Kyoto, among them Nishida Kitaro, the philosopher the walk is named after. On Nishida's grave is written his philosophy of life summed up in a single phrase: "You are you, I am me, and I'm going to live just the way I believe I should."

Brain scientist Ken Mogi says that he likes to visit the Philosopher's Walk when he travels to Kyoto, but during those walks he never has any great ideas. At first, he felt a little frustrated because he hoped that walking along the Philosopher's Walk would be a great source of inspiration, just as it was more than 60 years ago for Nishida Kitaro.

After several walks, Ken Mogi began to reflect and realized that the Philosopher's Walk was too beautiful and interesting for him to think of new ideas. It turns out that the Philosopher's Walk was the path that Nishida Kitaro walked along every day to go home from work, so for him it was a routine and "boring" journey in which his mind was free to be inspired by creative ideas. Ken Mogi realized he had more ideas during the boring train journey to his laboratory in Tokyo than during the time he spent on his visits to the Philosopher's Walk. "How can it be that I have more ideas walking in the mediocre streets of Tokyo than among the beauty of the cherry trees in the Philosopher's Walk?" Ken Mogi wondered with resignation, and he concluded: "The brain must leave itself free; it must rest from processing information in order to be able to initiate creative processes. It is the lack of stimuli, more than their abundance, which is one of the prerequisites for creating and maturing new ideas." (Quotes from http://www.qualia-manifesto.com)

HOW TO GET TO EASTERN KYOTO
BY BUS 5 FROM KYOTO STATION

MAP
1. *Ginkaku-ji*
2. *Philosopher's Walk*
3. *Nanzen-ji*
4. *Kiyomizu-dera*

The Philosopher's Walk is particulary beautiful during the sakura season, although it may also be overwhelming crowded.

GOEMON

At the main gate of Nanzen-ji, look out for the statue of Goemon, the Japanese Robin Hood. Legend has it that the troops at the command of Toyotomi Hideyoshi, one of the most important feudal lords of the seventeenth century, killed Goemon's wife and he decided to take revenge for her death by trying to kill Toyotomi.

Goemon came into Toyotomi's bedroom one night while he was sleeping. But when he was about to kill him, he tripped over a small bell that woke Toyotomi and alerted the guards. Goemon ran away and hid in the gate of the Nanzen-ji Temple until they caught him.

He was sentenced to be boiled alive in a cauldron along with his son. Goemon was brave enough and strong enough to hold his son up out of the boiling water for as long as he could. Some versions of the legend say that his son survived and was pardoned by those present when they saw Goemon's superhuman effort to save him.

Goemon was sentenced to be boiled alive along with his son.

So don't expect to have many ideas walking along the Philosopher's Walk in Kyoto, because your mind will surely be busier observing its surroundings than having ideas. Just as Nishida Kitaro walked down the same path every day, each of us has our own Philosopher's Walk. It is the journey we travel along almost every day. That is our time for inspiration and creativity.

> "On summer nights you can see lots of fireflies around the Philosopher's Walk stream."

How to get there: First go to the Ginkaku-ji Temple or to the Nanzen-ji Temple (see pages 169–170).
Recommended time for the visit: You can do the whole walk from Nanzen-ji up to Ginkaku-ji in about 20 minutes. If the cherry trees are in bloom, or if you stop to see temples along the way, it will take you an hour or even longer.

NANZEN-JI (3 ON THE MAP)

Nanzen-ji Temple is one of Kyoto's most beautiful and impressive temples. It is the headquarters of the Rinzai Zen sect and its principal temple, where the leader of the cult has lived for centuries. The Rinzai Zen emphasize the use of *koan* (puzzles and questions) to take the practitioners to a higher mental state, to a deeper understanding of the nature of the world.

It is a lovely and very famous temple where the remains of the emperor Kameyama are buried, but it is not as famous as Kiyomizu-dera, which is in the same eastern mountains. The fabulous thing about Nanzen-ji is that there tends to be far fewer people than at Kiyomizu-dera and you can enjoy it much more, in peace and quiet.

In Nanzen-ji there are a number of *karesansui* (dry gravel gardens), which are not as big as the one at the Ryoan-ji Temple but are maybe even more original and varied. There is also a collection of very well-conserved paintings on *fusuma* sliding panels.

What I like the most about Nanzen-ji is not the main temple but the retreats, paths and subtemples around it where you can get off the beaten track, find fewer and fewer people, and forget that

NANZEN-JI

Nanzen-ji is one of the temples that Scarlett Johansson visited in the movie *Lost in Translation*.

Nanzen-ji's main gate is spectacular but head for the paths and subtemples around it for a serene escape from the crowds.

you are in a touristy place. If you stroll along the temple's hidden corners, you will find a small traditional Japanese garden crossed by a stream. There are also some curious remains from an aqueduct built at the end of the nineteenth century. Two of the most interesting subtemples are the Nanzen-in, just behind the aqueduct remains, and the Konchi-in, which you find walking toward the southeast.

How to get there: Take bus number 5 from Kyoto Station to Eikan-mae Station. With the Kyoto subway, go up to Keage Station on the Tozai Line. When you get there, it is 10-minute walk to the entrance.

Recommended time for the visit: A couple of hours is enough to see Nanzen-ji, but ideally you should combine it with a stroll along the mountainside seeing other small temples and strolling along the Philosopher's Walk until you get to the Ginkakuji Temple. All this can take up a long, enjoyable afternoon.

Sunsets from the large veranda at Kiyomizu-dera Temple are always stunning, especially when paired with the fall foliage.

KIYOMIZU-DERA (4 ON THE MAP)

This sprawling hillside temple is Japan's most important Buddhist temple. It is also one of the oldest wooden structures in the world; the last reconstruction was in 1633. Before arriving at the temple, there is a street full of small shops, which are ideal for buying souvenirs. Take advantage of this because there are few places in Japan where you may buy tourist gifts or postcards.

The temple's main building stands out on the hillside, rising up above the forest, supported on enormous wooden pillars. Legend has it that, in the past, people believed that those who threw themselves from the porch of the main hall and survived the jump would be granted one wish. Apparently, many people jumped during the Edo period and most of them survived the 46 ft (14 m) jump.

Upon crossing the main hall, there is a small *torii* gate next to some rather steep stairs. This is the entrance to a temple of love. One of the temple games consists of walking from one love stone to another with your eyes closed while you think about the person you love. If you manage to get to the stone without opening your eyes that means that everything will be all right with your current love or with the love you are searching for.

Apart from the views from the veranda, another point of interest is the Otowa fountain and waterfall at the exit to the temple. Three gushes of water emerge from it. Drinking from the first one will give you wisdom; drinking from the second one will bring you good health; and drinking from the third one will grant you longevity. You may drink from all three but some locals say that doing so is considered an act of greed that can bring misfortune.

How to get there: Take bus 100 or 206 from Kyoto Station to Kiyomizu-michi or Gojo-zaka Station. From there, go up the souvenir shop street to the temple entrance.

Recommended time for the visit: Two hours is enough to see the whole complex. But if you stop to have a cup of tea or get caught up in the souvenir street at the entrance, reckon on around three or four hours.

NORTH KYOTO

KIBUNE (KIFUNE) (1 ON THE MAP)

The northern part of Kyoto largely consists of steep, densely forested mountains, excellent for hiking and appreciating nature. Both the Kifune Temple and Kurama Temple lie on its slopes. Legend has it that the mother of Emperor Jinmu, the founder of Japan, boarded a *kifune* 貴船 (literally, "noble and valuable boat") in the Bay of Osaka and journeyed along different rivers until she came to the mountains in the north of Kyoto where she decided to stop and set up one of her places of residence.

The "noble and valuable" *kifune* boat that Emperor Jinmu's mother traveled in gave its name to today's River Kifune and to the Shintoist temple Kifune, the place where she decided to finish her boat journey.

What I like the most about the Kifune Temple is the fact that it is immersed in the forest. Strolling along the paths, enjoying nature as you go from one building to another is an experience that makes you forget you are in the Kyoto metropolis.

The temple's main pavilion is dedicated to the god of water. The farmers used to carry out rituals in it to ask for rain. Another of the pavilions, called Yui-no-yashiro, is dedicated to the god of marriage. Visitors write their wishes concerning love on a small piece of paper that has to be left tied to a stick or the branch of a temple tree.

You can combine the visit to Kifune with a look at the Kurama Temple, which is on the other side of the valley and may be reached on foot. Kurama temple is also a short cable car ride up the mountain from Kibuneguchi Station.

How to get there: From Gion-shijo (in the Gion neighborhood) take the Keihan Line to Demachiyanagi Station. Change to the Eizan Dentetsu Line and go as far as Kibuneguchi Station. It takes about 45 minutes to get there.

Recommended time for the visit: Two hours.

The Kibune area in the north is less visited by tourists than the rest of Kyoto.

The landscaped gardens of Shugakuin are gorgeous works of art.

The Golden Pavilion is considered one of the essential places to visit in Japan.

SHUGAKUIN IMPERIAL VILLA (2 ON THE MAP)

The Shugakuin Imperial Villa is a collection of teahouses and gardens in the northeast of Kyoto. Walking around the grounds, going through forest areas, landscaped gardens, and listening to the murmur of the streams that connect the different lakes will make you feel you are in the Japan of centuries ago. The garden belongs to the Imperial Court and can only be visited by booking in advance by calling 075-211-1215 from Japan) or +81075-211-1215 (they speak English) from abroad or booking online at http://sankan.kunaicho.go.jp/english/guide/shugakuin.html.

How to get there: From Gion-Shijo Station take the Keihan Line to Demachiyanagi Station. Change to the Eizan Line and alight at Shugakuin Station. It takes 23 minutes.

Recommended time for the visit: Two hours.

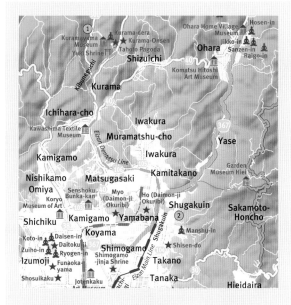

HOW TO GET TO NORTHERN KYOTO BY THE KEIHAN LINE FROM GION-SHIJO

MAP

1. Kibune Temple
2. Shugakuin Imperial Villa

WEST KYOTO

KINKAKU-JI (1 ON THE MAP)

This is one of the most beautiful temples in Japan, built for the first time over 600 years ago and rebuilt for the last time in 1955. Yukio Mishima's novel, *The Golden Pavilion*, tells the story of the tragic fire at the temple in 1950. If you want to get the maximum enjoyment out of your visit to the Golden Pavilion, read Yukio Mishima's novel first.

The first impression I had on seeing the pavilion is that it looks like a sort of fragile giant model placed next to an idyllic pond, something similar to what I felt when I visited Matsumoto Castle. The other thing that grabbed my attention was its reflection. If it's a calm sunny day, the pond turns into a kind of hypnotic mirror. In fact, it is called the "mirror pond." According to the hero of Yukio Mishima's novel, the reflection of the pavilion in the water is more beautiful than the actual building itself.

In the "mirror pond" there are several small islands, stones, and lotus flower zones that appear to have been positioned at random. But, in fact, it turns out that the "mirror pond" was designed to represent the history of creation according to Buddhist tradition. The lotus flower represents the rise of the truth in this earthly world and the islands represent continents separating the sea into nine oceans.

As well as the pond and the Golden Pavilion, if you push on into the grounds you will find other smaller temples and a teahouse where there are not usually many people and you can enjoy some peaceful time out.

How to get there: Bus 101 or 205, which you take from Kyoto Station to the Kinkaku-ji-machi stop. Or bus 50 up to Kinkaku-ji-mae.

Recommended time for the visit: A morning. You can combine it with the visit to Ryoan-ji, which you can walk to in about 15 minutes.

RYOAN-JI (2 ON THE MAP)

Ryoan-ji is a Zen temple in Kyoto famous for the beauty of its dry garden, which they say bestows peace and tranquillity on those who contemplate it.

In the dry garden there are a total of 15 stones arranged in three large groups in such a way that you can only see all the stones from one particular point. The ensemble makes your eyes notice the group on the extreme left first and gradually

(Above) *The bamboo forest is the most photographed thing in the Arashiyama and Sagano zone.*
(Left) *The Ryoan-ji dry garden is the perfect place to relax.*

switch their focus to the shorter stones in the center, and finally the bulkier group on the extreme right. Try to find the point from which you can see all 15 stones; it's not easy!

The great mystery about this small garden is that nobody knows its meaning, nor the reason it evokes such peace and tranquillity for the visitor. Who designed it, why, and which procedure they followed is unknown.

Among the traditional interpretations there is one that says the stones form the shape of a tiger crossing a river. Others say they are Chinese mountains emerging from a sea of clouds. But, in fact, all these interpretations are misguided as Zen emphasizes emptiness, nothingness.

"What makes the Ryoan-ji garden so special?"

"The spaces between the rocks" —Alan Booth.

In 2002, some scientists from the University of Kyoto used computers to look for shapes using the layout of the garden's empty zones instead of that of the stones. The result was that they found a tree pattern hidden in the empty zones, in the garden's gravel areas. They say this is why observing the garden is so pleasant; our subconscious captures the tree pattern without us noticing.

It would appear that mathematics affords us some clues to the garden's beauty. What's interesting is that the monk who

designed the position of the stones over 500 years ago didn't have a computer and probably knew nothing of math. But he came to the conclusion that it was the ideal layout. Scientists speculate that, through Zen meditation, the mind can find patterns in the subconscious (and take them to the zone of consciousness) that otherwise would not be discovered.

How to get there: Catch bus 205 or 101 from Kyoto Station.

Recommended time for the visit: A morning. You can combine it with the visit to Kinkaku-ji on the same morning and walk there.

ARASHIYAMA SAGANO (3 ON THE MAP)

We crossed the bamboo forest listening to the wind whistling between thousands of reeds tens of meters tall; we drank tea in a house that belonged to a great Japanese film actor of the early twentieth century; we got lost on temple steps that perched ever more closely to the mountainside; we took shelter in a souvenir shop when it started to rain hard; and we crossed the Tenryu-ji Temple where the most beautiful thing is the garden and the pool, both hidden behind the main building.

How to get there: The best way to get to the zone is with the JR Sagano Line from Kyoto Station to Saga Arashiyama Station. It takes 15 minutes.

Recommended time for the visit: Four hours.

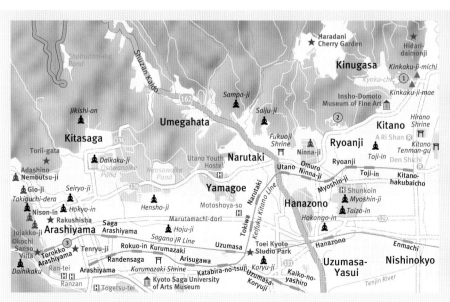

HOW TO GET TO WEST KYOTO
BY BUSES 205 OR 101 AND THE JR SAGANO LINE RESPECTIVELY

MAP
1. Kinkaku-ji
2. Ryoan-ji
3. Arashiyama Sagano

SOUTHERN KYOTO

FUSHIMI INARI TAISHA (1 ON THE MAP)

More than a third of the Shintoist temples of Japan are dedicated to the god Inari. Out of all of them, the Fushimi Inari Taisha is the most important. The messengers of Inari are the *kitsune*
foxes, which are represented by stone statues. There are normally two statues together, one female and one male, symbolizing the femininity and masculinity of Inari, who is believed to be an androgynous god.

Apart from the *kitsune* statues, one of Fushimi Inari Taisha's attractions is the great quantity of *torii* gates it has. No other temple in the world has as many and they come in all shapes and sizes. They form passageways penetrating into the
woods and making up the skeleton of the temple, which merges with the hill that is also called Inari.

How to get there: From Inari Station on the JR Nara Line, which you can take at Kyoto Station. You can also walk from Kyoto Station in about 10 minutes heading southeast.

Recommended time for the visit: A morning or even an entire afternoon. If you want to visit the whole thing, the walk becomes quite long. As you go along the *torii* gate passageway, you

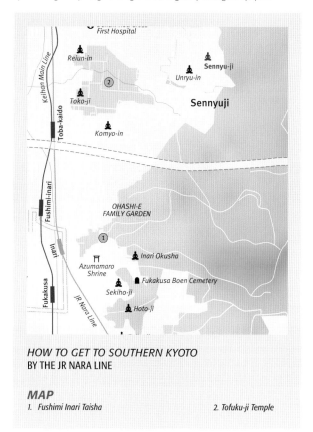

**HOW TO GET TO SOUTHERN KYOTO
BY THE JR NARA LINE**

MAP

1. *Fushimi Inari Taisha*
2. *Tofuku-ji Temple*

(Above) *One of the multiple torii passageways that make up the temple labyrinth. In spring and summer, it is common to see people dressed in traditional yukata.*
(Above left) *A statue of a kitsune with a scroll in its mouth. The most common version tends to have a key in its mouth, representing the key to the rice barn. Inari is the god of rice, agriculture, and fertility.*

climb up Mount Inari and the paths start forking. Eventually, it becomes quite monotonous seeing gate after gate, but the panoramic views from the top are worth it, especially at sundown.

TOFUKU-JI TEMPLE (2 ON THE MAP)

Tofuku-ji is a large Zen temple in southeastern Kyoto that is particularly famous for its spectacular autumn colors. The temple was founded in 1236 at the behest of the powerful Fujiwara clan. Its name is a combination of the names of two great temples in Nara that were also associated with the Fujiwara, Todai-ji Temple and Kofuku-ji Temple. Tofuku-ji has historically been one of the principal Zen temples in Kyoto, and is a head temple of one of the schools of the Rinzai sect of Zen Buddhism.

How to get there: From Kyoto Station, with the Nara line. It takes two minutes to reach Tofuku-ji Station.

Recommended time for the visit: Two to three hours to get a feel of the place. If you want to see everything, it might take a whole day.

A dry garden at Tofuku-ji comprising rock groupings set in raked sand.

CHAPTER 14
TRAVELING AROUND JAPAN

People are often afraid of traveling to such a distant and different country as Japan. But, contrary to expectations, traveling around Japan is much easier than traveling around Europe. The public transport system is the most advanced in the world, and everything is usually perfectly organized, so it's very difficult to get lost. The only big problem you'll encounter is language, but there will always be some Japanese person ready to help you, even if it's in sign language.

In the 1980s and 1990s, traveling to Japan was much more complicated than it is today. Then, the different standards of living, the cost of airfares, and having to depend on travel agencies instead of using the Internet made this dream trip difficult to undertake. Now, with a couple of travel guides and an Internet connection, you can organize a wonderful trip for yourself in no time at all. This chapter, like the previous one, is not intended as a guide but as a travel supplement, offering general advice from my personal experience.

> "Generally speaking, traveling around Japan is easier than traveling around Europe. Everything is usually perfectly organized, so it's very difficult to get lost."

GENERAL ADVICE FOR TRAVELERS

1. DON'T WORRY

People ask me tons of questions that reveal an excess of worry. "Do they sell milk in Japan?," "Is eating in restaurants very expensive?," "Do they sell bread?," "Where can I leave my baggage if I want to go out for a walk?" Rule number one is that in Japan they have everything. It's the country with the most 24-hour stores in the world, where you can buy bread and milk at any time. The fixed price menus in restaurants are cheaper than you're used to, and as for luggage, there are thousands of lockers in every train station. These are just a few examples, but for every problem you have in Japan there will be a solution. It is first and foremost a country where they know how to make things useful in order to solve problems, and where living is easy, the inconvenience of language aside.

2. CHOOSE THE RIGHT TIME TO GO

Japan is a country characterized by its distinct seasons. It may sound self-evident, but in summer they have summery weather, in fall they have fall weather, in winter wintry weather, and in spring it's spring weather. If you come in August, it will be extremely hot, and if you come in winter, it will be really cold. Ideally, you would come in spring or fall, although summer and winter also have their charm. I recommend coming between March 1 and April 20 or between May 10 and June 1. The last week in April and the first in May are not good, because they usually coincide with the famous Japanese Golden Week and all the hotels and tourist destinations are packed with people. From mid-June to mid-July is also a bad time to come because it's the rainy season. In fall, October and November are two good months, although you may have a typhoon or a rainy week. If you don't mind the cold or the heat, February and August are two months when rain is extremely unlikely. In short, don't come during the rainy season (June, July) or the Japanese holiday season (Golden Week and New Year).

3. BUYING A PLANE TICKET

Buy your ticket between two and three months before your intended travel date. Buying your ticket several months ahead is a good idea because many hotels are booked up well in advance. Airfares may cost from $800 to $1,300 depending on the season. The airlines offering the cheapest flights from the United States are United Airlines, Delta Airlines, Singapore Airlines, Continental Airlines, and All Nippon Airways. Ideally, your visit to Japan should last at least 10–12 days.

4. JAPAN RAIL PASS

One of the most expensive things in Japan is transport. To offset this, the Japanese government offers a season ticket called the Japan Rail Pass, which allows you to use any JR train for one, two, or three weeks, whatever suits you best. The Japan Rail Pass can only be bought outside Japan, so if you're interested ask at your local travel agency. If you do travel to Japan, be sure to buy it. Just one train trip from Tokyo to Kyoto will make it worthwhile. When you reach Japan, head to the JR office to swap your exchange order for the JR pass.

An advertisement for a capsule hotel called Siesta.

Mount Fuji is one of Japan's most familiar symbols. The Japanese consider it the most beautiful mountain in the world.

5. ACCOMMODATIONS

A few years ago, it was quite complicated to find hotels in Japan due to the distance and the language barrier. Nowadays, thanks to the Internet, it couldn't be easier or more efficient. In most hotels you can make a reservation with an English interface or merely by sending an email in simple English. The main types of hotels I would recommend to a traveler are:

Ryokan: These are traditional Japanese-style hotels where you sleep on a *futon* laid out on *tatami* mats and take your bath in an *ofuro* (see page 50). Their prices range from 10,000 to 20,000 yen per person.

Youth hostel: These are the equivalent of American youth hostels and are usually the cheapest option for accommodation in Japan. In Kyoto you can find places from 2,000 yen per night but in Tokyo it's normal to find prices ranging from 7,000 to 8,000 yen per night per person.

Business hotel: This is the option chosen by the Japanese when they travel within the country for business. They are inexpensive, conventional hotels with good service and usually located near big train stations. They usually cost between 8,000 and 15,000 per night per person.

Search the Internet using the keywords "Ryokan Kyoto" or "Youth hostel Tokyo" to find the place most convenient for you.

Japanese bullet trains are the most punctual in the world.

If you are adventurous, you can also try a capsule hotel or a love hotel one day. Capsule hotels are very inexpensive and in them you have a sort of enclosed bunk bed where you sleep. As for love hotels, you must go with a partner to be allowed in, and they are usually designed with motifs that stimulate sexual activity.

Adventurous options: love hotels (8,000–20,000 yen); capsule hotels (2,000–4,000 yen); or manga coffee shops (1,000–5,000 yen).

Very important: Make your reservation at least two months ahead or hotels might be booked up.

Recommended Web site for booking accommodations: http://www.jnto.go.jp/a-search/search/search_form.php

> "Since in Japan the electric power system is different, I advise taking only devices with INPUT: 100V–240V."

6. ELECTRICAL POWER

Sockets in Japan are different and the electric power system is at 110V/50Hz. It's quite similar to the United States, so you shouldn't have any trouble with your electrical devices. However, if you don't live in the United States, my advice is to read carefully the small print on the electrical transformer for the device you want to take with you. If the transformer says INPUT:100V–240V (from 100V to 240V), it may be a usable choice for Japan, but if it says INPUT: 220V, you can use it only with a converter that will cost from $25 to $60 depending on the amperage. I'd advise taking only devices with INPUT:100V–240V.

Today, it's quite common for most laptops and battery chargers for cameras to have this kind of universal transformer but mobile phones, for instance, don't have them.

As for the form of the plug, I'd suggest going to the first electronics store you find when you arrive in Japan and buying an adapter. It will cost you from 200 to 500 yen depending on the place. To buy it, simply show the sales clerk your American plug and he will help you find what you need. Once you have your plug adapter, you can recharge your laptop and camera with no trouble at all.

7. MOBILE PHONES AND INTERNET

It might seem like a contradiction being one of the most techno-logically advanced countries in the world but it is not trivial if you want to stay connected at all times as a tourist. If you want to make sure to have a connection at any time, I recommend renting a phone or a pocket WIFI router at the airport. If you don't want to spend the money renting, these are some places where there are free WIFI spots:

• Near any Family Mart and 7-Eleven conveniences store (Need to register the first time).
• At any Starbucks (Need to register the first time)
• Haneda, Narita and Osaka Airports and lately in some train lines and stations.

In order to access hundreds of thousands of hotspots around Japan, download and register with Japan Connected—Free WIFI, Free WIFI Passport or Travel Japan WIFI.

8. JAPANESE MANNERS

Japanese people are extremely polite and culturally very strict with respect to polite interaction in daily life. You should learn at least how to say *arigato* (thank you), *sumimasen* (excuse me), *konnichiwa* (hello), and *onegai shimasu* (please) to use in stores, hotels, and restaurants.

9. SHOPPING IN JAPAN

When it comes to shopping, there is a very important point you should bear in mind.

Not all electronic devices are cheaper in Japan than in the United States or Europe. This is contrary to a myth that is a vestige of the 1990s, when it was true. With globalization, today computers or memory cards for cameras are cheaper in the United States. One of the only things still worth buying in Japan is cameras, with price differences ranging from $250 to $370 depending on the model. Don't forget that you can visit Akihabara to buy electronic goods and Asakusa to buy traditional Japanese souvenirs.

Take care when you buy something. Make sure that it has an international warranty; the manual is in English and not just in Japanese; it has an adapter; and the device will work in the United States or Europe. A last piece of advice. If you show your passport, at most stores you won't get charged VAT, which is 5 percent in Japan.

10. CALCULATING EXPENSES

Accommodations and trains aside, you can calculate between 3,000 and 8,000 yen per person per day. If you are on a low budget, you can eat decently for 600–1,000 yen. If you tend more toward the gourmet side, calculate 1,000 yen for lunch and 3,000–7,000 yen for dinner. Admission to temples and museums usually costs between 300 and 1,000 yen. The expense in drinks is virtually insignificant, since water and tea are usually free in all restaurants, and soft drinks are cheaper than in the United States and Europe. Other expenses will depend on the gifts you buy.

11. CREDIT CARDS AND MONEY

Generally, you're better off changing money when you arrive in Japan, either at Narita or Kansai Airports. The exchange rate is almost always better here than outside the country, and commis-sions are low. Of course, you also have the option of exchanging money at your local bank before coming here.

It is getting easier to move around with just a credit card in Japan but bear in mind that there will be many places where it will not be accepted. Convenience stores and department stores will accept card payments but, for example, local restaurants at lunchtime will not.

In order to withdraw money, my advice is to use Seven Bank and Japan Post Bank ATMs (fees may apply). Seven Bank ATMs are found inside almost any 7-Eleven convenience stores. Japan Post Bank ATMs are located inside Japan Post offices all over the country. Other types of ATMs will generally not work with foreign credit cards.

12. PLANNING YOUR TRIP

Once you have your ticket and you know how many days you'll be spending in Japan, the time has come to plan your journey. Let me make a few suggestions, which depend on the number of days you have.

• 7 days: If you have just a week, I would split it between Tokyo and Kyoto, allowing more days for one city or the other depending on whether you are more interested in seeing Kyoto's traditional Japan or Tokyo's cosmopolitan Japan. In Tokyo, I would visit Shinjuku, Shibuya, Harajuku, Asakusa, Roppongi, and Odaiba. In Kyoto, I would visit Ryoan-ji, the Golden Pavilion, and Kiyomizu-dera.
• 10 or 12 days: Besides Tokyo and Kyoto—visiting all the places mentioned above—I would add Nara to the journey, where you'll spend an unforgettable day visiting temples and seeing deer. Spending more days in Tokyo, I would also include a day trip to Nikko, which is two hours away by train from Shinjuku Station or Ueno Station. Another possibility would be to make a reservation for one night at a *ryokan* in Nikko. While in Tokyo, I would also visit Kamakura and Yoko-hama, both day trips.
• 15 days: I would do everything mentioned above, plus one or two days in Hakone, which is close to Tokyo, or I would go to Hiroshima to walk around the city, and I would visit Miya-jima. On my way to Hiroshima, I would stop by the Okayama gardens. In Kyoto, I would visit more temples and castles, and I would spend one or two days in Osaka.
• 20 days: I would go to Kyushu, Shikoku, Okinawa, Tohoku, Matsumoto, Takayama, and Hokkaido, beautiful places all far from the capital city and for which you need 5–6 hours to travel from Tokyo.

13. HOW TO GET AROUND BY TRAIN

During your trip around Japan, you will almost always travel by train. If the train is of the JR lines, just show your JR Pass on entering. If it is a private railway or subway, you have to buy a ticket at the entrance. To buy a ticket, you must deposit the exact amount of the fare from your station of departure to the station of your destination. If you can't work it out from the maps that are usually placed above the vending machines, ask the clerk in the booth by the entrance and he will tell you how much you need to pay.

If you don't want to be thinking about buying tickets all the time, the best solution is to acquire a PASMO or SUICA. Both are rechargeable smart cards that can be used with almost all

Some stations are huge but there are signs everywhere and it's difficult to get lost if you pay attention.

The circular Yamanote Line in Tokyo is one of the easiest to use.

trains and even bus systems all over the country. Both types of cards are interchangeable and can be bought on arrival at the airport or at any train station. It costs 2,000 yen, which is divided into 1,500 yen that can be used for train rides and 500 yen as a deposit. You can recover the 500 yen deposit by returning the card at the end of the trip.

Something else you need to bear in mind and be alert to at all time is the type of train you get on. The same line usually accommodates several types of trains depending on their speed and their number of stops. First, see whether all trains stop at the station you wish to go to. If they do, it means it's an important station and you are better off using an express train. If you are going to a lesser-known station, express trains might not stop

there and you will have to use local or semi-express trains. There are many categories and types depending on the company controlling the line, so make sure you are well informed before getting on the train.

Web page to organize train routes:
http://www.jorudan.co.jp/english/norikae/

Note on the Web page: input the station of departure in one box and the station of arrival in the other box, and the Web page will give you the different routes you can follow.

"Japan has the best railroad network in the world."

"Traveling on trains, you will be able to visit almost any place in the country in comfort."

Japan

250 km
100 miles

N

Asahikawa
Hokkaido
Sapporo
Hakodate
Aomori
Akita
Morioka
Shinjo
Yamagata
Sendai
Niigata
Fukushima
Nikko
Toyama
Nagano
Utsunomiya
Kanazawa
Matsumoto
Kawagoe
Takayama
Kofu
Fukui
TOKYO
Tottori
Nagoya
Hakone
Yokohama
Matsue
Kyoto
Kamakura
Himeji
Nara
Shizuoka
Hiroshima
Okayama
Hamamatsu
Miyajima
Takamatsu
Kobe
Osaka
Yamaguchi
Matsuyama
Wakayama
Kitakyushu
Shikoku
Fukuoka
Saga
Kochi
Oita
Kyushu
Nagasaki
Kumamoto
Kagoshima
Miyasaki

Honshu

ESSENTIAL PLACES TO VISIT IN JAPAN

These are just some of the many places that I've fallen in love with on my travels around Japan. Chapter 12 contains a good guide for visiting Tokyo, but even though practically one-third of the population lives in the capital city and its surroundings, it doesn't mean the rest of the country is inferior in any way. In fact, Tokyo may be a huge city that impresses with its dimensions and variety, but if you want to see the real traditional Japan you must also leave the big cities and explore.

KAMAKURA

Kamakura is a small town on the coast near Yokohama, famous for its beaches and temples. The most important temple houses one of the biggest Buddhas in Japan. Near the temple of the Great Buddha, there is another temple devoted to Kannon Hase, which is noteworthy for the beauty of its gardens, especially in springtime when they are magnificent. Moreover, from the Hase-dera there is a spectacular view of the Kamakura coastline.

Facing the sea, the Kamakura Great Buddha is an overwhelming sight.

How to get there: *By the Shonan-Shinjuku Line from Shinjuku (Tokyo) to Kamakura Station, where you take the Enoden Line to Enoden Station. To reach the Buddha and the temple devoted to Kannon Hase, it's a 5-minute walk from the station.* **Recommended time for the visit**: *One day.*

MATSUMOTO CASTLE

In Matsumoto is one of the most beautiful castles in Japan. It's a five-story building built entirely of wood. Besides the castle, there is little else to see, but if you like skiing, Matsumoto is near the mountains of Nagano, where the Winter Olympic Games were held in 1998. **How to get there**: *From Shinjuku by the Azusa train.* **Recommended time for the visit**: *One day.*

Matsumoto Castle is considered one of the most beautiful castles in Japan.

OSAKA'S DOTONBORI DISTRICT

Osaka is the third most populated metropolis in Japan, after Tokyo and Yokohama. More than its points of interest, what I most enjoy about Osaka is walking in its downtown streets, which are lively at practically any time of day and one of the busiest shopping and restaurant zones in the city. The most famous place in the area is the Glico sweets company neon panel, which is next to the Dotonbori-bashi Bridge. It is said that Ridley Scott used the futuristic atmosphere of Dotonbori as the basis for the design of some of the scenes from his science fiction movies like *Blade Runner* or *Black Rain*.

How to get there: *Subway for 15 minutes from Shin-Osaka Station to Namba Station.*
Recommended time for the visit:
Go in the late afternoon, have dinner there, and enjoy the night scene.

The neon Glico runner sign is one of the most famous places and one of the locals' favorite meeting points.

TODAI-JI AND NARA

At the start of the eighth century Japan experienced a period of instability: earthquakes, epidemics and wars between clans. Emperor Shomu decided to initiate a temple building plan all around the country in the hope that Buddha would help to establish harmony in his territories. Todai-ji Temple in Nara was the most important one dedicated to Buddha to be built. Today it is still the biggest wooden building in the world.

The original temple was finished in 751. It is calculated that more than two million people from all over the country took part in its construction and more than 10,000 Japanese attended its inauguration, dedicated to Emperor Shomu. Since then, the temple has been destroyed by earthquakes and fires several times; the last reconstruction was in 1709. Some parts of the 49-ft (15-m)-high bronze Buddha it houses have been restored several times.

How to get there: *From Nara's Kintetsu Station, you get to the temple area in scarcely 5 minutes. From Nara's JR station it's a 25-minute walk.*
Recommended time for the visit: *The visit to Todai-ji and several of the temples of the "Historic Monuments of Ancient Nara" site can take up a day.*

Todai-ji is the main temple of the Historic Monuments of Ancient Nara site, now a UNESCO World Heritage Site.

MIYAJIMA

Miyajima (宮島), also known as Itsukushima (厳島), is a small island near Hiroshima known for its beautiful scenery, where Shinto and Buddhist temples integrate with nature.

The entire island is considered holy ground. In fact, the very name indicates this– Miyajima (Miya宮 = sacred temple, jima = 島 island). The whole island is considered to be a Shinto temple. It is the most sacred

When the tide is low you can walk all the way to the torii.

island in Japan and many gods live on it. Some monks even consider the entire island to be a god. Births, deaths, cutting down trees, or killing animals are not permitted. As a result, there are thousands of monkeys and deer living freely on Miyajima. Deer, according to the Shinto tradition, are messengers of the gods.

The island's most famous temple is the Shinto Itsukushima, a World Heritage Site. It is considered one of the most beautiful places in Japan and indeed in the world. It was built more than 1,500 years ago and has been rebuilt several times. The most famous thing about the temple is an enormous *torii* gate, which you can get to, on foot, at low tide and whose reflection can be seen in the sea at high tide.

In the past, people were not allowed to set foot on the island, which explains why the Itskushima temple is built above the sea water level on a small beach as if it were a pier. People would get to the island in a small boat, passing through the *torii* gate to purify themselves before entering holy ground. **How to get there**: *By ferry, from Hiroshima Park it takes 55 minutes and costs 1,900 yen. By train, from Hiroshima Station on the JR Sanyo Line to Miyajimaguchi Station. It takes about 25 minutes. Then you will have to get on a ferry that will take you to Miyajima. With the JR Pass, the ferry is free.* **Recommended time for the visit**: *One or two days. Any time of the day is good but I would recommend sunset.*

HIROSHIMA PEACE MEMORIAL

Hiroshima became world famous after being destroyed by the first atomic bomb dropped on a populated area. Today, the Peace Memorial Park, built as a symbol of peace, occupies an area in the center of Hiroshima. In this park, the Peace Memorial Museum tells the story of the atomic bomb and its consequences. The main tourist site is the Genbaku Dome, one of the only buildings to remain standing in the city center after the explosion. **How to get there**: *From Hiroshima Station take tram line number 2 or 6 to Genbaku Domu Mae Station.* **Recommended time for the visit**: *One day.*

The Hiroshima Peace Memorial serves as a memorial to the people who were killed by the nuclear bomb at the end of World War II.

ISE SANCTUARY AND MEOTO IWA ("THE MARRIED ROCKS")

The Ise Sanctuary Ise (Ise Jingu) is a group of over 100 temples which make up one of the most sacred places in the Shinto religion. Ise is dedicated to Amaterasu, the Sun Goddess. Tradition has it that the emperor of Japan is a direct descendent of hers. The Ise sanctuary is divided into two complexes: the Geku (Outer Sanctuary) and the Naiku (Inner Sanctuary). The former is near Ise-shi Station and the latter is a few kilometers away. The best thing to do is spend a night in Ise in some hotel or *ryokan* close to the station downtown.

That way, the Naiku is within walking distance. One of the most interesting ways of getting to the Geku is to rent a bicycle. There's a rental shop next to the station and another at the

The two rocks are connected by a rope said to act as the separation between the spiritual and earthy realms.

entrance to the Naiku. You can also go by bus from the station or by taxi. The most sacred area is the Naiku, where the Sacred Mirror (Yata no Kagami), believed to be the body of Amaterasu, is conserved, along with the Sacred Pillar (Shin no Mihashira), which is buried just beneath the mirror.

During a visit to Ise you learn a lot about the architectural origins of Shintoism. The Ise temples are designed following a style called *shinmeitsukuri*, whose building techniques have been handed down over the centuries from one generation to the next so as to be as faithful as possible to the original. Ise is rebuilt every 20 years (see page 87).

Some 9 miles (15 km) from Ise are the Married Rocks, known in Japanese as Meoto Iwa (夫婦岩), whose characters mean husband, wife and rock, respectively. They are two rocks in the sea linked by a great s*himenawa* rope (see page 23) and represent the union of the creator god Izanagi and the goddess Izanami.

Meoto Iwa is visited by thousands of tourists every year and they say that it brings good luck in affairs of the heart. **How to get there**: *From Kyoto Station with the Kintetsu-Kyoto Line it's a 177 minute journey to Ise-shi Station. The city of Ise is to the east of Nara. You can also get there from Nagoya with the Kintetsu Limited Express heading towards Ise-shi. It takes 81 minutes from Nagoya.* **Recommended time for the visit**: *Ideally two days but you can also see the most important stuff in just one day.*

MY PERSONAL EXPERIENCE

We cycled up to the torii gate, which invited us into the sacred territories of the Amaterasu Goddess via the Uji Bridge leading to the inner sanctuary of Ise. We walked through the woods as the trees gazed upon us, cooled off next to the River God, and strolled among the artificial wooden structures whose gravel-covered columns emerge right out of the ground, rising up before us and blending into their natural surroundings. At the end of our walk, we were able to glimpse Amaterasu's home, when the Wind God allowed us to, its breath caressing the white sheet that protects Kotai Jingu, the most sacred place in Japan.

KANAZAWA

Kanazawa is one of the most beautiful cities on the coast of the Inland Sea of Japan. It was one of the most important cultural centers in Japan during the Edo Period, and not having been a military objective in World War II is very well preserved. It is quite a popular tourist destination but not as busy as other places like Kyoto or Hiroshima because you can't get there by bullet train.

The city spreads out around Kanazawa-jo Castle, one of the most imposing castles in the country and the third most important after the castles of Himeji and Matsumoto. It was built by the Maeda clan at the end of the Sengoku period (~1580) and is one of the largest castles in Japan in terms of usable space. Next to the castle is the Kenrokuen Garden. It is one of the three most important/beautiful/famous gardens in Japan (日本三名園) selected by the Japanese government. The other two are Korakuen in Okayama and Kairakuen in Mito.

The name of the garden, Kenrokuen (兼六園), may be literally translated as "garden of six characteristics" and refers to the six attributes that are considered important in the design of a garden: serenity/isolation, old atmosphere/respect for ancestors, beautiful views from almost any position, refreshing (having water flows), attention to detail, and spaciousness.

In each season of the year there is something in particular that stands out in the garden. In winter, what most grabs your attention about the park are the rope and bamboo cane arrangements called *yukitsuri* (雪つり), which help prevent the

Kenrokuen's most distinctive feature in winter are the Yukitsuri, which help the tree branches maintain their shape.

tree branches from suffering and maintain their silhouette when it snows. In spring, it's the splendor of the *sakura* flowering. In summer, it's the flowers and the cicadas singing. And in autumn, it's the reddish color schemes of the park's maple trees.

Apart from the castle and gardens, the city is full of tourist attractions: a contemporary art museum, *geisha* neighborhoods, temples, and various museums, some of which are notable for the province's traditional ceramics.

How to get there: *from Tokyo Station it takes 148 minutes to reach Kanazawa using the bullet train.* **Recommended time for the visit**: *One or two days.*

Ashi Lake, in Hakone, is one of the most beautiful in the country.

HAKONE

Hakone is the area near Mount Fuji and has one of the most beautiful lakes in the country, Ashi Lake. Walking around the temples and woods near the lake is a real pleasure and, if the weather is good, you'll always have Mount Fuji in the background. I recommend cruising Ashi Lake on a boat and visiting the Hakone Shrine, which is approached by water. You can devote another day to the volcanic area of Mount Sounzan, where you'll see boiling sulfurous water issuing from the mountain.

How to get there: *From Shinjuku (Tokyo) by the Odakyu Line. It takes an hour and a half to reach Hakone-Yumoto Station. From there you may have to take a bus, depending on the hotel where you're staying.* **Recommended time for the visit**: *Two days.*

NIKKO

Nikko is a small town north of Tokyo where many temples are nestled among the lush woods in its mountains. Most of them were built by the famous Tokugawa shoguns in the Edo Period (1603–1868). In fact, even the grave of the first Tokugawa, Ieyasu, is there.

How to get there: *From Asakusa Station in Tokyo, get on the Kina Line train to Shimo-Imachi and then change to a small local train to its terminal, Tobu-Nikko. There is also a direct train from Shinjuku Station.* **Recommended time for the visit**: *One day.*

Shinkyobashi in Nikko is considered to be one of the three most beautiful bridges in Japan, especially in fall. What to see at Shinkyobashi Bridge? The simple elegance contrasting with the wildness of the river canyon, the green hills, and the rushing waters.

MY SECRET PLACES

This section is called My Secret Places but it could also be called Unknown Places or Special Places. Here we will look at some places that are not usually highlighted in travel guides but are charming and may appeal to you depending on your tastes.

SHIGUREDEN MUSEUM, ARASHIYAMA

The *karuta* is a sort of Japanese playing card that tests players' knowledge of traditional *waka* poems, popularized by the entertainment company Nintendo 100 years ago (see page 136). In the museum, check out the room with an interactive floor designed by the company. **How to get there**: *On the Sanin Line from Kyoto, stop at Pagano Arashiyama. In the station there are directions for the museum. It's a 15-minute walk from the station.* **Recommended time for the visit**: *Two hours.*

RAMEN MUSEUM, YOKOHAMA

Ramen is one of the favorite dishes of the Japanese. It consists of a noodle soup seasoned with many ingredients. The soup and the texture vary depending on the region in Japan. At the Ramen Museum in Yokohama, you can taste different types of *ramen*, study the history of this dish, which originated in China, and immerse yourself in a replica of a Japanese village set in the 1930s. **How to get there**: *From Shibuya on the Tokyu-toyoko Line to Kikuna. Change to the Yokohama Line and go to Shin-Yokohama. At the station, ask directions for the Ramen Museum.* **Recommended time for the visit**: *Three hours.*

KAWAGOE, SAITAMA

Kawagoe is a small town in Saitama, north of Tokyo, that preserves an area with very old stone houses that have survived fire and time. Kawagoe exudes a certain atemporal spirit, and the natives call it Ko-Edo—little Edo—because, it is said, when you walk along its streets you feel transported back to the Edo Period. If you want to discover what ancient Japanese cities looked like, don't skip this town. Foreigners don't come here very often but it's well known among local tourists. **How to get there**: *From Ikebukuro Station on Tokyo's Yamanote Line take the Tobu-Tojo Line to Kawagoe. By express train it takes little more than 30 minutes.* **Recommended time for the visit**: *One day.*

Travel back to the Edo Period in Kawagoe and visit Kitain Temple, part of the original Edo Castle.

SANKEI PARK, YOKOHAMA

Built by a silk merchant in 1906, Sankei Park contains several temples and traditional houses from the Edo Period. The government moved them there from other places piece by piece, also repairing the damage suffered during World War II.

How to get there: *Take number 8 or 125 bus from Yokohama Station. Stop at Sankeien-mae Station.* **Recommended time for the visit**: *Two hours.*

Sankei Park is very quiet and you can enjoy traditional Japanese landscapes.

PARK HYATT, TOKYO

This is the hotel where most of the scenes in the movie *Lost in Translation* were filmed. Inside the hotel are several cafés and restaurants with panoramic views of Tokyo and Mount Fuji. **How to get there**: *Walk from Shinjuku Station West Exit. Head southwest until you see the three towers of the hotel.* **Recommended time for the visit**: *Sunset or after.*

Park Hyatt's three connected buildings are impressive, especially at night.

KABUKI-CHO, YAKITORI STREET

Kabuki-cho at night is a vital part of Shinjuku (see page 154), with lots of nightclubs, hostess bars, *pachinko* parlors, karaoke clubs, etc. Its streets make for fascinating viewing as thousands of Japanese enjoy the night their way.

How to get there: *Take the Shinjuku Station East Exit (Tokyo) if you come by the JR lines or Exit B13 if you come by subway. Once there, ask directions for Kabuki-cho.* **Recommended time for the visit**: *From 7 pm to 5 am.*

The Kabuki-cho area is among Tokyo's liveliest areas for nightlife.

NOKOGIRIYAMA, CHIBA

I discovered Nokogiriyama after seven years in Japan. You can go there from Tokyo and come back the same day. It's a beautiful place. How could I have overlooked it for so long?

Nokogiriyama is a mountainous zone near the Chiba coast featuring the Nihon-ji Temple, where one of the biggest Buddhas in Japan is housed. The Buddha statue is a representation of Yakushi Nyorai and is 102 ft (31 m) tall, more than twice the height of the Todai-ji Buddha in Nara.

It was finished in 1783 after three years of work by 28 Buddhist monks. The Buddha statue represents "the universe enclosed within a lotus flower" and was built as a symbol of world peace and tranquillity. **How to get there**: *An hour and a half by train from Tokyo Station to Hamakanaya Station (by Sazanami fast train). You can also go by boat from Kurihama Station in Kanagawa.* **Recommended time for the visit**: *One day, starting at around six in the morning.*

MY PERSONAL EXPERIENCE

We left by train at 7 a.m. from Shinagawa Station in Tokyo heading for Kurihama. From Kurihama Station we walked to the port and at around nine thirty we boarded the Kanaya Maru boat, which took us to the other side of the bay. At around 10 a.m. we got to the port of a small village called Kanaya (金谷: the valley of money). Our gut feeling took us to a Chinese restaurant, located two minutes from the port, where we recharged our batteries.

With our bellies full, we headed towards the Nokogiriyama mountain. We walked for a while along the shoulder of a road that skirts the sea, trying to find the start of a trail that would take us to the summit, but we ended up getting lost. It's not a touristy place and it's badly signposted.

Once we'd found the way, the climb was quite easy, with well marked trails and even stairs in some areas. We crossed the woods walking at a brisk pace for an hour until we found ourselves standing in front of some enormous, mysterious

stone walls. The walls seemed both natural and artificial and the trees protected us from the light rain that was falling, sometimes more like mist than rain. It would have made a perfect scene for an episode of the television series "Lost."

It turns out it was a quarry during the Edo Period (up to about 150 years ago), which explains the mysterious shape of the cliffs. We tried to go a little further forward but we came to a dead end. We were surrounded by stone walls and forest.

We had to go back along the same trail until we came to the last fork we'd passed. We plunged in along another trail that allowed us to pass through a narrow crevice to the other side of the walls. Crossing this crevice we found ourselves in the presence of the image of an enormous Buddha engraved on one of the walls. We were the only ones there—silence, tranquillity, the timeless gaze of the Buddha, a magical air that made us feel like we were Indiana Jones exploring the area for the first time.

MOUNT TAKAO

Mount Takao, to the west of Tokyo, is an ideal destination for a day trip if you are staying at a hotel in the center. It's barely 1,800 ft (549 m) tall, so it's not tiring to climb. It's full of really beautiful temples ensconced in the lush vegetation, and if the weather is clear the view from the top is wonderful.

From there you can even see Mount Fuji. There is one inconvenient thing, though. Legend says that if you climb Mount Takao with your partner, your love is very likely to soon vanish. **How to get there**: *From Shinjuku on the Chuo Line to Takao. By express train it takes 44 minutes.* **Recommended time for the visit**: *One day.*

Temple statuettes on Mount Takao.

"Legend says that if you climb Mount Takao with your partner, your love might soon vanish."

OKUTAMA

Okutama is a mountainous area to the west of Tokyo. If you're staying in Tokyo, it's a perfect place for a relaxing trip. Okutama is Tokyo's biggest lake, which provides most of the drinking water used in the city. One of the most famous spots there is the "floating bridge" (*ukibashi*), a bridge made of buoys and decking that extends right across the lake. Near the station are several *onsen* (hot springs), where you can enjoy a bath before returning to Tokyo.

How to get there: *By express train on the Chuo Line, leaving from Shinjuku to Tachikawa or Ome. In Tachikawa or Ome, you must change lines to the Ome Line and go to Okutama. From Okutama Station, there are several buses that go to the lake. Be careful as from 5 pm on hardly any buses make the return trip.* **Recommended time for the visit**: *One day.*

TEZUKA MANGA MUSEUM, TAKARAZUKA

Devoted to the life and works of the father of *manga*, the Tezuka Museum will transport you to the magical universe of one of Japan's most important artists and show you how the canons of modern *manga* were developed. **How to get there**: *From Kyoto on the Todaido-san-yo Line, change lines at Amasagasaki (Hyogo) and travel on the Fukushiyama Line to Takarazuka. From the station, follow directions to the museum.* **Recommended time for the visit**: *Three hours.*

For any Tezuka fan, the museum devoted to him should not be overlooked.

INTERNATIONAL MANGA MUSEUM, KYOTO

Situated in the very heart of Kyoto, it houses over 200,000 *manga* volumes and has several rooms with permanent exhibitions covering the most interesting aspects of the history of this art form. Entrance costs 800 yen and it opens from 10 am to 5.30 pm.

How to get there: *From the Karasuma Oike subway station in Kyoto. Take Exit 2 and walk north for one minute.* **Recommended time for the visit:** *Two hours.*

TOEI KYOTO STUDIO PARK

Toei Kyoto Studio Park, or Toei Uzumasa Eigamura, is both a theme park and a film set for traditional Japanese movies. It has several streets with houses that recreate the atmosphere of the Japan of the Edo Period. There are many attractions and activities in which visitors may dress up as *samurai* or *geisha* to have their photo taken. There is a lot of information about activities and opening hours on this website in English: http://www.toei-eigamura.com/info/ **How to get there**: *A 5-minute walk from Uzumasa Station, which you can get to with the Keifuku Arashiyama Line.* **Recommended time for the visit**: *Two hours.*

JIMBOCHO, TOKYO

This is a Tokyo neighborhood full of second-hand bookstores. Even if you don't understand Japanese, if you like books you'll have a blast sniffing around bookshops full of volumes from tens or even hundreds of years ago, manuscripts, parchments, magazines from the war period, *ukiyo-e* engravings, drafts of famous authors' novels, photos developed by famous authors, etc. **How to get there**: *Get off at the Jimbocho Station on the Hanzomon subway line.* **Recommended time for the visit**: *You can get a feel for the place within an hour, although you're likely to spend countless hours here if books are really your thing.*

ENOSHIMA, YOKOHAMA

It is a small fishing island near Yokohama with amazing views of the Pacific Ocean and Mount Fuji. Visit the island on a sunny day and you'll be rewarded with some fantastic views. **How to get there**: *From Shinjuku on the Odakyu Line to Katase-Enoshima.* **Recommended time for the visit**: *One day.*

The view from Enoshima is spectacular.

A visit to the Okayama garden will make you want a Japanese garden at home.

KORAKUEN GARDEN, OKAYAMA

In Okayama, there is a garden called Korakuen, considered one of the most beautiful in Japan. Apart from the garden, though, there is hardly anything else of interest, so ideally you would spend a morning in Okayama's Korakuen garden and then travel on to Hiroshima to spend the afternoon and night. **How to get there**: *From Kyoto by Shinkansen to Okayama Station. It takes about one hour.* **Recommended time for the visit**: *Half a day.*

GHIBLI MUSEUM, MITAKA

This is the museum of the most famous animation company in Japan, which created *Spirited Away* and *My Neighbor Totoro*. The museum building itself is interesting and full of exhibits displaying some of the techniques used by Studio Ghibli to create their movies. One highlight is a reproduction of the desk of Hayao Miyazaki, the most respected artist and director at Ghibli and creator of most of their movies.

How to get there: *Take the Chuo Line from Shinjuku in Tokyo to Mitaka. From Mitaka follow directions to catch a bus that will take you to the entrance of the museum.* **Recommended time for the visit**: *Half a day.*

If you are an anime fan, you have to visit the Ghibli Museum.

KOYASAN, WAKAYAMA

Koyasan is the name of a group of mountains in the prefecture of Wakayama. Between these mountains is a valley where we find the small town called Koya in which are gathered more than 120 temples and a university dedicated to the study of oriental religions.

What most impressed me about my visit was the stroll along the Okunouin cemetery trails, protected by a hillside forest, which end at a mausoleum dedicated to Kukai. It is Japan's biggest cemetery and has been visited several times by the Dalai Lama.

Monk at Koyasan.

Kukai is considered to be the founder of the Shingon Buddhist sect, one of the most important in Japan. As well as establishing Buddhism, Shingon was also a poet and some historians credit him with the invention of the Japanese language's *hiragana* written syllables system.

How to get there: *From the Namba Station in Osaka, take the Nankai Electric Railway Line as far as Gokuraku-bashi. Ride the cable car up to Koyasan Station.* **Recommended time for the visit**: *Ideally, for the visit to be worthwhile you should spend a night in the village of Koya in one of the temples. Many of them are fitted out to accommodate pilgrims and tourists. English website to reserve temple lodging: http://eng.shukubo.net/*

MY PERSONAL EXPERIENCE

During our stay in Koyasan we came across a likeable monk who was talking unhurriedly on the phone. When he hung up, he came over to us and proudly began telling us stories about his temple.

"Do you see that grave in the corner?" said the monk.

"Yes, it's a dog's grave, isn't it?" we replied.

"He was called Gon, he lived with us for nearly 20 years until he died in 2002. We called him Gon because when he was a puppy he would become really happy when he heard the sound of the gong in the morning."

"It looks like the statue of the dog Hachiko in Shibuya, but it's smaller," I said under my breath while I carried on taking photos.

He raised his voice a little and said: "Our dog Gon really was a truly faithful dog, unlike Hachiko. Gon accompanied pilgrims around the mountains every day as far as the Daimon Gate in Koyasan. He acted as a guide, walking with strangers along a stretch of over 20 km every day and would come back alone just before twilight. He was a faithful, obedient, dedicated, hardworking and intelligent dog. Whereas Hachiko was a lazy, stupid, useless dog and all he did was wait in Shibuya for years and years. Moreover, what Richard Gere's "Hachiko" movie doesn't explain is that the dog Hachiko wouldn't stop crapping at the entrance to Shibuya Station. People didn't love Hachiko. In fact, they used to complain about having to put up with a flea-bitten dog crapping near where the train stopped and having to dodge his turds every day."

Yes, he said the word "turd" several times on finishing his explanation and everybody, including the monk, began to laugh.

"Do you see? Our dog Gon is cooler than Hachiko! Don't let the Tokyo people fool you."

NAOSHIMA ART ISLAND

Naoshima is an island located in the Seto Inland Sea between Shikoku and Honshu. Originally a fishing area, for the last 10 years it has been changing into a place chosen by many artists to present their works. There are several museums, exhibition spaces, and open-air sculptures. The island's most impressive museum is the Chichu Art Museum, designed by the architect Tadao Ando. For information on the museums and accommodation: http://www.benesse-artsite.jp/en/naoshima/ **How to get there**: *From Uno Station a ferry leaves for Naoshima 13 times a day. To get to Uno Station, take the JR Line (which is also called Uno) from Okayama (Shinkansen) Station.* **Recommended time for the visit**: *One or two days.*

The famous Yellow Pumpkin by Japanese artist Yayui Kusuma.

SUGAMO, TOKYO

Sugamo is one of the liveliest, and at the same time least-known districts of Tokyo. The reason it's not very well known is that this is the area where retirees go to shop. The main street, Jizo-dori, lies next to the station and is packed with stores selling food and traditional pots and pans. A walk around Sugamo will transport you to the Japan of the 1960s. You can feel tradition on every corner.

How to get there: *On the Yamanote Line. It's one of the northern stations.* **Recommended time for the visit**: *One morning.*

Sugamo is one of the most traditional districts in Tokyo.

ありがとう
BASIC JAPANESE FOR TRAVELERS

This vocabulary doesn't pretend to teach you Japanese but offers a list of phrases that are as simple as possible so you can make yourself understood. They may come in handy or they may just help you look like a foreigner making an effort to be polite, which counts for a lot.

KONNICHIWA = HELLO = こんにちは

ARIGATO = THANK YOU = ありがとう

SUMIMASEN = I'M SORRY, EXCUSE ME = すみません

ONEGAI SHIMASU = PLEASE = お願いします

HAI / IIE = YES / NO (they hardly use it) = はい / いいえ

GOMEN NASAI = I'M SORRY = ごめんなさい

JA MATA = GOODBYE = じゃまた

EIGO WA WAKARIMASU KA = CAN YOU SPEAK ENGLISH? = 英語は分かりますか

WAKARIMASEN = I DON'T UNDERSTAND = 分かりません

KORE = THIS = これ Very useful when you are pointing at something on the menu in a restaurant

EIGO MENYU WA ARIMASU KA = DO YOU HAVE AN ENGLISH MENU? = 英語メニューはありあますか

IRANAI = I DON'T WANT THAT, I DON'T NEED THAT = いらない

MIZU = WATER = 水

BIIRU = BEER = ビール

HITOTSU = ONE = 一つ

FUTATSU = TWO = 二つ

BIIRU O FUTATSU = TWO BEERS = ビールを二つ

MIZU O KUDASAI = WATER, PLEASE = 水を下さい

IKURA DESU KA = HOW MUCH IS IT? = いくらですか

WATASHI NO NAMAE WA _____ DESU = MY NAME IS _____ = 私の名前は　です

YOROSHIKU ONEGAI SHIMASU = PLEASED TO MEET YOU = 宜しくお願いします

OYASUMI NASAI = GOOD NIGHT = お休みなさい

OHAYO GOZAIMASU = GOOD MORNING = おはようございます

TOIRE WA DOKO DESU KA = WHERE IS THE TOILET? = トイレはどこですか

EKI WA DOKO DESU KA = WHERE IS THE TRAIN STATION? = 駅はどこですか

MICHI NI MAYOIMASHITA, TASUKETE KUDASAI = I'M LOST, PLEASE HELP ME = 道に迷いました、助けてください。Then show your map and point to your destination, saying *KOCHIRA NI IKITAI* (I want to go to this place). If you know the name of the place you want to go to, say the name of the place followed by *NI IKITAI*.

KOKUSAI HOSHO GA TSUTEIMASU KA = DOES IT HAVE AN INTERNATIONAL WARRANTY? = 国際保証がついてますか

ONIKU GA HAITEMASU KA = DO YOU HAVE MEAT? = お肉が入ってますか

OSAKANA GA HAITEMASU KA = DO YOU HAVE FISH? = お魚が入ってますか

YASAI GA HAITEMASU KA = DO YOU HAVE VEGETABLES? = 野菜が入ってますか

INDEX

EPILOGUE

Here ends our "trip" around Japan and its culture. I put *trip* in quotation marks because, if you really want to know a place, you have to go there. Our virtual trip isn't enough. If you've never been to these parts, go! I'm sure it will be an unforgettable experience.

But I hope this book has helped you form a general idea about life, the people, and some places here. There are thousands of subjects that have failed to get a mention.However, you know you can keep reading me every day on: www.ageekinjapan.com.

I'm not an expert on Japanese culture or an expert writer, so I'm sorry if there are any inaccuracies or mistakes, or if I become tiresome in any chapter. Send your comments and corrections to: kirainetlibro@gmail.com.

Many thanks to everybody for reading me.

—*Hector,* www.ageekinjapan.com

PHOTO CREDITS

Text and All Photography: Hector Garcia Puigcerver (kirainetlibro@gmail.com) Except the following: 33, archer: Kollotzek/Wallrafen; p141, all photographs Ignacio Izquierdo; diverse photographs, Xavi Comas, Opalworks Shutterstock.com: 16 ID 42086977 © Sergii Rudiuk; 86 ID 402721456 © Wayne0216; 87 middle ID 312119783 © af8images; 166 ID 147264293, 174 top left ID 237865357 and 184 bottom right ID 286414493 © Sean Pavone; 167 bottom ID 548555419 © Juri Pozzi; 169 top left ID 193454189 © Travel Stock; 170 ID 211073710 © Tooykrub; 171 bottom ID 397732636 © Narongsak Nagadhana; 172 top ID 482069071 © martinho Smart; 172 bottom ID 796873126 © mTaira; 173 top right ID 509272975 © seaonweb; 175 top right ID 530051005 © Phattana Stock; 179 top ID 418695343 © Sakarin Sawasdinaka; 182 bottom right ID 244958689 © Luciano Mortula—LGM; 183 right ID 213914254 © Sean Pavone; 184 top ID 519551473 © Nattee Chalerm-tiragool; 184 bottom left; ID 523324399 © Satao; 184 bottom right ID 286414493 © Sean Pavone; 185 middle ID 290113463 © DymFilms; 187 middle left ID 380220877 © Puripat Lertpunyaroj iStock.com: 32 bottom right ID 541006624 © Kavuto; 87 left ID 61192826 © fotoVoyager; 87 right ID 26184482 © aluxum; 167 top right ID 486896689 and 169 top right ID 34637998 © SeanPavonePhoto; 169 bottom right ID 478653155 © coward_lion; 175 bottom ID 629495126 © magicflute002; 185 bottom left ID 813651980 © nirad 123rf.com: 183 top left ID 55126210 © Kia Cheng Boon; 165 top ID 55480749 © pat138241 Dreamstime.com: 167 top left ID 20017426 © Pichung; 169 bottom right ID 70374006 © Denys Mistyukevych; 185 top ID 25466005 © Mrpeak; 187 below left ID 49429689 © Hai Huy Ton That Photolibrary.jp: 173 top left ID 3257994 © ふくいのりすけ Commonswikimedia.org: 103 fourth col. bottom top Minister for Foreign Affairs of Japan Fumio Kishida and comedian Daimao Kosaka posing for photos (picture cropped) © mofa.go.jp; middle Sony PlayStation 4 with DualShock controllers © Evan Amos; 142 Ken Kutaragi at the Game Developers Choice Awards 2014 © Official GDC Wikipedia.org: 103 fourth col. bottom Your Name poster © CoMix Wave Films, uploaded by Film Fan Flickr.com: Cover middle, ID 3636862418 © themonnie; bottom left ID 32854561006 © ruich_whx; 133 top and 137 middle ID 23968644197 © 政煌郭; 140 bottom ID 29600645 © Tasayu Tasnaphun; 141 top right ID 6169563331 © uzaigaijin; 141 bottom right ID 6547710359 © Jung-nam Nam

"BOOKS TO SPAN
THE EAST AND WEST"

Tuttle Publishing was founded in 1832 in the small New England town of Rutland, Vermont [USA]. Our core values remain as strong today as they were then—to publish best-in-class books which bring people together one page at a time. In 1948, we established a publishing outpost in Japan—and Tuttle is now a leader in publishing English-language books about the arts, languages and cultures of Asia. The world has become a much smaller place today and Asia's economic and cultural influence has grown. Yet the need for meaningful dialogue and information about this diverse region has never been greater. Over the past seven decades, Tuttle has published thousands of books on subjects ranging from martial arts and paper crafts to language learning and literature—and our talented authors, illustrators, designers and photographers have won many prestigious awards. We welcome you to explore the wealth of information available on Asia at **www.tuttlepublishing.com**.

Published by Tuttle Publishing, an imprint of Periplus Editions (HK) Ltd.

www.tuttlepublishing.com

Copyright©2019 by Héctor García

First published in the Spanish language under the title *Un Geek en Japón* by Norma Editorial

ISBN 978-4-8053-1391-6
ISBN 978-4-8053-1917-8 (for sale in Japan only)
(First edition ISBN 978-4-8053-1129-5; Library of Congress Control Number: 2018942081)

DISTRIBUTED BY

North America, Latin America & Europe
Tuttle Publishing
364 Innovation Drive
North Clarendon, VT 05759-9436 U.S.A.
Tel: 1 (802) 773-8930
Fax: 1 (802) 773-6993
info@tuttlepublishing.com
www.tuttlepublishing.com

Japan
Tuttle Publishing
Yaekari Building 3rd Floor
5-4-12 Osaki Shinagawa-ku
Tokyo 141 0032
Tel: (81) 3 5437-0171
Fax: (81) 3 5437-0755
sales@tuttle.co.jp
www.tuttle.co.jp

Asia Pacific
Berkeley Books Pte. Ltd.
3 Kallang Sector #04-01
Singapore 349278
Tel: (65) 6741 2178
Fax: (65) 6741 2179
inquiries@periplus.com.sg
www.tuttlepublishing.com

First English-language edition
Revised and Expanded 2019

27 26 25 24
11 10 9 8 7 6 5

Printed in China   2406EP